Beware of False Religions
&
Pagan Traditions
Part 3

Other Books by Apostle Hèlèné Fulton

Witchcraft in the Church

Only a Born-Again will make it into Heaven. Are you ready?

Beware of False Religions & Pagan Traditions Part 1

Beware of False Religions & Pagan Traditions Part 2

The Complete Deliverance Manual

Get Sanctified in 365 days. The Ultimate Devotional for men and women.

Did you sell your soul to the devil? There's a way out!

Beware of Pagan Healing & Exercises!

Beware of False Religions & Pagan Traditions
Part 3

Hélèné Fulton

Light the World Publishers
2014

Copyright © 2014 by Hélèné Fulton

All rights reserved. This book or any portion thereof may not be reproduced or used in any manner whatsoever without the express written permission of the publisher.

First Printing: 2014

ISBN 978-0-620-60892-3

Light the World Publishers

www.lighttheworldpublishers.com

For any help or orders e-mail our office:
admin@lighttheworldpublishers.com

Ordering Information:
Special discounts are available on quantity purchases by corporations, associations, educators, and others. For details, contact the publisher at the above listed e-mail address.

U.S. trade bookstores and wholesalers:

Please contact Light the World Publishers on e-mail address below.
admin@lighttheworldpublishers.com

Dedication

For all the unconditional love, guidance and teachings, all glory goes to:

God the Father
God the Son
God the Holy Spirit

To my loving husband Robert. Thank you for all the love and support. You truly have a servants heart and a love for God.

A special thanks to all my spiritual children & spiritual brothers and sisters who not only assisted with writing this book but who prays for me daily.

Tanja Davey – Thank you for allowing the Holy Spirit to guide you in the design of the cover for this book. You are a true daughter of the King of kings.

Contents

Acknowledgements vii

Foreword ix

Preface x

Introduction xvii

Chapter 1: Islamic Muslim 3

Chapter 2: Satanism 58

Chapter 3: Yin and Yang 166

Chapter 4: Pieter L White   "People of Jesurene" 187

Chapter 5: Scientology 197

Chapter 6: Episcopal Church 214

Chapter 7: Anglican Church 221

Chapter 8: Islam 224

Chapter 9: New Age 269

Appendix 1   Religions: The Occult Connection - 1 298

Appendix 2   Religions: The Occult Connection - 2 321

Notes 337

References 339

Glossary 341

Acknowledgements

I would like to thank my Spiritual brothers & sisters and spiritual children who wrote some of the Chapters in this book.

Without your dedication and hard work it would not have been possible to get this book written and published in such a short time.

By helping to write this book, you are helping to inform the world about the false teachings out there and our prayer is that those people and the people that they are teaching a false doctrine will be saved.

Foreword

My people are destroyed for lack of knowledge: because thou hast rejected knowledge, I will also reject thee, that thou shalt be no priest to me: seeing thou hast forgotten the law of thy God, I will also forget thy children.

Hosea 4:6

4 Now the Spirit speaketh expressly, that in the latter times some shall depart from the faith, giving heed to seducing spirits, and doctrines of devils

1 Timothy 4:1

Even today it still shocks me when I listen to a Television channel or hear a preacher teach God's children the wrong doctrine. Every time I think I have heard it all just to be shocked even more.

God gave me the two scriptures above to make me understand why some are teaching false doctrines and why some people will keep listening to these false teachings.

When God gave me the title of this book I had no idea that this book will be in a 3 part series because of the amount of False Religions there are in the world.

Why this book? To tell the people the truth according to God's word the Holy Bible.

If you have a problem with this book take it up with our Father in Heaven and read His Word from the King James Bible. I can only pray that your eyes will be opened then.

Preface

There are only two roads; one leads to heaven and one leads to hell. This is a spiritual fact, without change or compromise; there is no middle road and no chance to "sit on the fence".

"Wide is the gate and broad is the way that leads to destruction, and there are many who go in by it."

Matthew 7:13

[19] "I call heaven and earth as witnesses today against you, that I have set before you life and death, blessing and cursing; therefore choose life, that both you and your descendants may live"

Deuteronomy 30:19

There are numerous false religions operating in the world today, falsely broadcasting themselves as truth or as God's truth for that matter. These religions may, on the contrary, be the foundation of lifelong poverty, family breakdown, mental derangement, physical illness or varying manifestations of bizarre behaviour in the lives of people.

In a world where the motto is that "all roads lead to Rome" and suggests that everyone serves the same god, this book not only exposes these lies but also seeks to convey the truth to the many deceived individuals. These individuals have either turned their back on the true God completely or, by their actions, have allowed some of these pagan and false religious practises to creep into there every day lives. By clinging to these pagan traditions, we inadvertently give Satan a foothold in our lives.

In these books these false religions have been measured up against the word, wisdom and knowledge of God. The word of God says that His word is like fire and is a hammer that breaks rocks into pieces.

"Is not My word like a fire?" says the Lord, "And like a hammer that breaks the rock in pieces?
Jeremiah 23:29

The false religions have been measured up and are left wanting.

"Casting down arguments and every high thing that exalts itself against the knowledge of God, bringing every thought into captivity to the obedience of Christ,"
2 Corinthians 10:5

Hell was not made for humans, but for the devil and the demons. God never intended for humans to go to hell. By humans denying and turning their backs on the precious blood of His only begotten Son (who gave His life freely), they will find themselves ending up in this place of burning fire, where there is no ease to their pain.

"There shall be weeping and gnashing of teeth, when ye shall see Abraham, and Isaac, and Jacob, and all the prophets, in the kingdom of God, and you yourselves thrust out".
Luke 13:28

God has no interest in leaving anyone out. His heart is for all to be saved. God is "not willing that any should perish but that all should come to repentance."

[9] "The Lord is not slack concerning His promise, as some count slackness, but is longsuffering toward us, not willing that any should perish but that all should come to repentance."

2 Peter: 3:9

The last days are nearing and God is preparing His bride. He is bringing to light the lies that has been believed for so many years.

When the light of God shines on darkness, darkness has to flee and the enemy has no more power or place to hide. He can only operate in darkness and where he cannot be seen.

"He shall be driven from light into darkness, and chased out of the world".

John 18:18

Knowledge is power and the intention of this book is not to condemn, but rather equip believers and bring those who are in darkness into the light, so that everyone may come to know the truth….as it is the truth that sets one free.

"Yea, though I walk through the valley of the shadow of death, I will fear no evil; For You are with me; Your rod and Your staff, they comfort me"

Psalm 23:4

[31] "So Jesus said to the Jews who had believed him, "If you abide in my word, you are truly my disciples, [32] and you will know the truth, and the truth will set you free."

Scott Davey

John 8:31-32

Introduction

What it means to be Born Again

The New Birth
3 There was a man of the Pharisees named Nicodemus, a ruler of the Jews. 2 This man came to Jesus by night and said to Him, "Rabbi, we know that You are a teacher come from God; for no one can do these signs that You do unless God is with him." ³ Jesus answered and said to him, **"Most assuredly, I say to you, unless one is born again, he cannot see the kingdom of God."** ⁴ Nicodemus said to Him, "How can a man be born when he is old? Can he enter a second time into his mother's womb and be born?" ⁵ Jesus answered, **"Most assuredly, I say to you, unless one is born of water and the Spirit, he cannot enter the kingdom of God.** ⁶ That which is born of the flesh is flesh, and that which is born of the Spirit is spirit. ⁷ Do not marvel that I said to you, 'You must be born again.' ⁸ The wind blows where it wishes, and you hear the sound of it, but cannot tell where it comes from and where it goes. So is everyone who is born of the Spirit." ⁹ Nicodemus answered and said to Him, "How can these things be?" ¹⁰ Jesus answered and said to him, "Are you the teacher of Israel, and do not know these things? ¹¹ Most assuredly, I say to you, We speak what We know and testify what We have seen, and you do not receive Our witness. ¹² If I have told you earthly things and you do not believe, how will you believe if I tell you heavenly things? ¹³ No one has ascended to heaven but He who came down from heaven, *that is,* the Son of Man who is in heaven. ¹⁴ And as Moses lifted up the serpent in the wilderness, even so must the Son of Man be lifted up, ¹⁵ that whoever believes in Him should not perish but have eternal life. ¹⁶ **For God so loved the world that He gave His only begotten Son, that whoever believes in Him should not perish but have everlasting life.**

¹⁷ For God did not send His Son into the world to condemn the world, but that the world through Him might be saved.
¹⁸ "He who believes in Him is not condemned; but he who does not believe is condemned already, because he has not believed in the name of the only begotten Son of God. ¹⁹ And this is the condemnation, **that the light has come into the world, and men loved darkness rather than light, because their deeds were evil.** ²⁰ For everyone practicing evil hates the light and does not come to the light, lest his deeds should be exposed. ²¹ But he who does the truth comes to the light, that his deeds may be clearly seen, that they have been done in God."

John 3:1-21

Nicodemus was a theological professor and a member in parliament, he paid his tithe from all his income, he fasted two days a week, he prayed two hours a day. But look at what Jesus is asking Nicodemus in verse 10. *"Are you the teacher of Israel, and do not know these things?*

Even in today's modern world with millions of preachers about 95% of them are not born again and probably does not even know what it means. This is scary as they are the teachers of the gospel.

It is very easy to say that I believe the Bible. It is very easy to say I know the Bible. It is even easier to say I'm a Christian but are you really a Christian? Are you 100% sure that you will enter the kingdom of God (Heaven) when your physical body dies.
You might be a very good person doing wonderful deeds for your fellow man but have you really been born again!

Are you a new person in Jesus Christ?

Are you willing to deny yourself and give yourself completely over to Jesus Christ? Are you willing to let Jesus Christ control your life?

Jesus did not say you ought to be born again He said **you have to be** born again if you want to enter the kingdom of God.

What Jesus was saying is that it is easy to say I'm a Christian but it is different matter to really know Jesus Christ.

You cannot just do the things to show people you're a Christian; you need to know Jesus Christ Himself. Jesus said this because he knows your heart. Yes Jesus Christ knows every person's heart. He knows you say you love Him but He knows that your heart belongs to business or pleasure or even to Satan.

All the sins you're doing each day comes from within. It starts from the heart and once it reaches the mind you're already making plans to fulfill that desire. That is why God said guard your heart in His word (the Bible).

[23] Keep thy heart with all diligence; for out of it are the issues of life.

Proverbs 4:23 (KJ)

There's a lot of good people supporting the under privilege, but some people are doing it to be seen by others. God looks at what's inside your heart. Even if man lived in paradise, he'll still have an evil heart. You can only change this if you give your heart to God to control completely.

Never please people please God.
Born again means to be "born from above."
Nicodemus had a real need. He was hungry to change and he needed a change of his heart - a spiritual transformation.
New birth, being born again, is an act of God whereby eternal life is imparted to the person who believes indicates that "born again" also carries the idea "to become children of God" through trust in the name of Jesus Christ.

[17] Therefore, if anyone *is* in Christ, *he is* a new creation; old things have passed away; behold, all things have become new.
2 Corinthians 5:17

[5] not by works of righteousness which we have done, but according to His mercy He saved us, through the washing of regeneration and renewing of the Holy Spirit,
Titus 3:5

[3] Blessed *be* the God and Father of our Lord Jesus Christ, who according to His abundant mercy has begotten us again to a living hope through the resurrection of Jesus Christ from the dead
1 Peter 1:3

[29] If you know that He is righteous, you know that everyone who practices righteousness is born of Him.
1 John 2:29

[9] Whoever has been born of God does not sin, for His seed remains in him; and he cannot sin, because he has been born of God.
1 John 3:9

⁷ Beloved, let us love one another, for love is of God; and everyone who loves is born of God and knows God.

1 John 4:7

5 Whoever believes that Jesus is the Christ is born of God, and everyone who loves Him who begot also loves him who is begotten of Him. ² By this we know that we love the children of God, when we love God and keep His commandments. ³ For this is the love of God, that we keep His commandments. And His commandments are not burdensome. ⁴ For **whatever is born of God overcomes the world. And this is the victory that has overcome the world—our faith.**

1 John 5:1-4

¹⁸ We know that whoever is born of God does not sin; but he who has been born of God keeps himself, and the wicked one does not touch him.

1 John 5:18

¹² But as many as received Him, to them He gave the right to become children of God, to those who believe in His name: ¹³ who were born, not of blood, nor of the will of the flesh, nor of the will of man, but of God.

John 1:12-13

Why do you need to be born again?

2 And you *He made alive,* who were dead in trespasses and sins,

Ephesians 2:1

To the Romans in Romans 3:23, the Apostle wrote, *for all have sinned and fall short of the glory of God,* So, a person needs to be born again in order to have their sins forgiven and have a relationship with God.

[23] for all have sinned and fall short of the glory of God

Romans 3:23

How does that come to be?

[8] For by grace you have been saved through faith, and that not of yourselves; *it is* the gift of God, [9] not of works, lest anyone should boast.

Ephesians 2:8-9

When a person is "saved," he/she has been born again, spiritually renewed, and is now a child of God by right of new birth. Trusting in Jesus Christ, the One who paid the penalty of sin when He died on the cross, is what it means to be "born again" spiritually.

[17] Therefore, if anyone *is* in Christ, *he is* a new creation; old things have passed away; behold, all things have become new.

2 Corinthians 5:17

If you have never trusted in the Lord Jesus Christ as your Savior, how can you hear the Holy Spirit as He speaks to you? How will you hear the Holy Spirit when He warns you of danger?

Do you have what it takes to be a born again Christian?

Do you want a personal relationship with Jesus?

Don't say the prayer just you want "fire protection".

Become born again because you want to with all your heart.

Will you pray the prayer of repentance and become a new creation in Jesus Christ today?

[12] But as many as received Him, to them He gave the right to become children of God, to those who believe in His name: [13] who were born, not of blood, nor of the will of the flesh, nor of the will of man, but of God.

John 1:12-13

If you are tired of living a life without meaning in a materialistic world that lacks compassion and love, a world that has chosen mammon as it's god and that will sacrifice anything and anybody to achieve its ultimate goal: "financial freedom", then please consider the alternative.

Jesus Christ is waiting for you every single day to open up your heart to Him and to invite Him into your life. If you prayed this prayer with a sincere and a true heart - then you can be assured that the Lord has prepared a place for you in heaven.

Once you are ready to take the next step the following prayer will be your ticket to Eternity:

The Prayer that will change Your Eternal Destiny

"Father, I thank You that Jesus died for me. I confess I have broken Your laws. Forgive my sins. I receive the pardon right now. Lord Jesus, come into my life. Give me a new heart with new desires. And by Your Spirit, give me the power to live a life that is pleasing to You. Father please fill me with the Holy Spirit. Thank you for forgiving me as You have promised. Thank You for the gift of eternal Life."

Congratulations and welcome to the family of God. No matter what you've done in your life, you've received a full pardon in God's eyes. That's how easy it is for you.
But it was not free - it cost God the life of His beloved Son, Jesus Christ in your place. Just thank Him for loving you so much.

Write this date in your Bible as this is the date the new you were born.

Why do we get Baptized

The English word "Baptism" comes from the Greek word "Baptizo", which means to, dip under, immerse, and whelm that is, to cover wholly with fluid. So this cannot include sprinkling a few drops of water on a baby's forehead.
You need to get baptised because Jesus was baptised and He **left an example for us to follow** in His steps.

John Baptizes Jesus
[13] Then Jesus came from Galilee to John at the Jordan to be baptized by him. [14] And John *tried to* prevent Him, saying, "I need to be baptized by You, and are You coming to me?"
[15] But Jesus answered and said to him, "Permit *it to be so* now, for thus it is fitting for us to fulfill all righteousness." Then he allowed Him.
[16] When He had been baptized, Jesus came up immediately from the water; and behold, the heavens were opened to Him, and He saw the Spirit of God descending like a dove and alighting upon Him. [17] And suddenly a voice *came* from heaven, saying, "This is My beloved Son, in whom I am well pleased."
Matthew 3:13-17

Jesus was baptised to "fulfil" or "complete" all righteousness by being **obedient** to His Father's (God) will. He was not baptised because He was a forgiven sinner, for He had no sin. He was always righteous. If Jesus was not baptised, He would have disobeyed His Father's will and would no longer have been righteous.

Obedience pleases God and brings the blessing of God.

[21] For He made Him who knew no sin *to be* sin for us, that we might become the righteousness of God in Him.

2 Corinthians 5:21

Christians are also righteous and so like Christ are baptised to fulfil or complete all righteousness, by an act of obedience.

It is a commandment of God in scripture and children of God desire to obey God.

[15] And He said to them, "Go into all the world and preach the gospel to every creature. [16] He who believes and is baptized will be saved; but he who does not believe will be condemned.

Mark 16:15-16

Do you love God? Look what the Bible tells us.

[15] "If you love Me, keep My commandments.

John 14:15

Are there any special conditions you need to fulfil before you can be baptised?

[35] Then Philip opened his mouth, and beginning at this Scripture, preached Jesus to him. [36] Now as they went down the

road, they came to some water. And the eunuch said, "See, *here is* water. What hinders me from being baptized?"

³⁷ Then Philip said, "If you believe with all your heart, you may." And he answered and said, "I believe that Jesus Christ is the Son of God."

³⁸ So he commanded the chariot to stand still. And both Philip and the eunuch went down into the water, and he baptized him.

³⁹ Now when they came up out of the water, the Spirit of the Lord caught Philip away, so that the eunuch saw him no more; and he went on his way rejoicing.

Acts 8:35-39

When the Ethiopian eunuch asked the evangelist Phillip: "What hinders me from being baptized?" "

The Evangelist answered and said: "If you believe with all your heart, you may."

And he answered and said, "I believe that Jesus Christ is the Son of God."

⁹ that if you confess with your mouth the Lord Jesus and believe in your heart that God has raised Him from the dead, you will be saved.

Romans 10:9

Once you are saved, you are ready for baptism. There is no special spiritual level you have to reach to prepare yourself for baptism. When you are saved you are re-born with God's righteousness and there is nothing else you can do to prepare yourself for baptism.

Water baptism is a symbolic burial, by which the new born again Christian publicly declares they have died, and are now beginning a new life, in Christ.

Water baptism outwardly demonstrates what has happened inwardly. Water baptism helps you to grasp the reality of the spiritual truth that the old "you" has died.

Water baptism is only as important as the person being baptized believes it to be. Water baptism is their confession, and a public commitment.

You die to the old you when you accept Jesus Christ as your Lord and Savior. So some people see baptism as a burial to that old self. When they come out from under the water they come out as a new person.
But unless the person really believes they died, there is no need for a burial.

It is not something you do to impress God or your pastor, but something to impress on our mind what happened to us inwardly. Water baptism is for your benefit not God's.

³⁸ Then Peter said to them, "Repent, and let every one of you be baptized in the name of Jesus Christ for the remission of sins; and you shall receive the gift of the Holy Spirit.

Acts 2:38

Peter is not giving a new way for water baptism but is instructing these disciples in the authority of the name of Jesus Christ that since they have repented and been forgiven of their sins, they must now obey God and get baptised.

⁴¹ Then those who gladly received his word were baptized; and that day about three thousand souls were added *to them.*
Acts 2:41

Some Christians have struggled to receive the infilling of the Holy Spirit, because in their hearts they have determined to disobey God and not get baptised by immersion.

⁴⁷ "Can anyone forbid water, that these should not be baptized who have received the Holy Spirit just as we *have?*" ⁴⁸ And he commanded them to be baptized in the name of the Lord. Then they asked him to stay a few days.
Acts 10:47-48

Peter used his authority in the name of Jesus Christ to order them to be baptised and was not giving new instructions for water baptism.

We baptize people through our authority in Jesus Christ in the name of the Father and the Son and the Holy Spirit.

Why was Jesus baptized in water? He was, and is, our pattern. And, in a sense, He was, at that point, dying to His past life.

He was beginning His public ministry.

Jesus was declaring that He was dead to any selfishness and existed solely to do the will of Father God.

Must you be baptized to be saved? No. Once you have accepted Jesus Christ as your Lord and Saviour, you are saved.

⁴³ And Jesus said to him, "Assuredly, I say to you, today you will be with Me in Paradise."

Luke 23:43

Jesus told this criminal that he will be with Him. This man was not baptized.

³⁸ He who believes in Me, as the Scripture has said, out of his heart will flow rivers of living water." ³⁹ But this He spoke concerning the Spirit, whom those believing in Him would receive; for the Holy Spirit was not yet *given,* because Jesus was not yet glorified.

John 7:38-39

¹⁷ And these signs will follow those who believe: In My name they will cast out demons; they will speak with new tongues

Mark 16:17

The household of Cornelius became believers, received the Holy Spirit, and began speaking in tongues, *before* being baptized in water.

According to Jesus receiving the Holy Spirit happens *only* to those who are believers, and they are therefore saved.
So, these believers were born again and ready for Heaven, before they were baptized in water.
If any of you want to be baptized and you are staying in Gauteng feel free to contact us on the e-mail provided in the front of this book.

The Doctrine of Christ

⁹ Whosoever transgresseth, and abideth not in the doctrine of Christ, hath not God. He that abideth in the doctrine of Christ, he hath both the Father and the Son.

2 John 1:9

There is nothing more important to Christianity than the fundamentals of the Bible - the Doctrine of Christ.

A "doctrine" is simply a teaching. Doctrines are composed of words. Thus words are critically important. The great theological battles and debates of our generation are being fought over the meaning of words, whether it is the word "repentance" or the word "inspired," the spiritual battle is raging.

God deliver us from deeper-life theologians who can quote the Bible, dissect it and expound upon it, but they never share the gospel with their neighbors and let the world die and go to Hell.

We aim to encourage everyone to be a soul-winner.

³⁰ The fruit of the righteous is a tree of life; and he that winneth souls is wise.

Proverbs 11:30

This is one Scripture that you won't hear often from the "intelligence" crowd.

Granted, it is "God that giveth the increase"

⁷ So then neither is he that planteth any thing, neither he that watereth; but God that giveth the increase.

1 Corinthians 3:7

Our part is to preach the gospel, sharing the good news of Jesus Christ Who died, was buried and rose again three days later for our sins.

15 Moreover, brethren, I declare unto you the gospel which I preached unto you, which also ye have received, and wherein ye stand;
² By which also ye are saved, if ye keep in memory what I preached unto you, unless ye have believed in vain.
³ For I delivered unto you first of all that which I also received, how that Christ died for our sins according to the scriptures;
⁴ And that he was buried, and that he rose again the third day according to the scriptures:

1 Corinthians 15:1-4

Thus, it is critically important that we never stop ringing the bell of the fundamental doctrines of the Christian faith, including the deity of Jesus, the virgin birth of Christ and His bodily, literal, resurrection from the dead. In an age when psychology is replacing Bible-preaching in our churches, and entertainment is replacing the power of God, the Doctrine of Christ cannot be stressed enough.

What is the Doctrine of Christ? It is THE TRUTH about Jesus Christ, as taught in the Word of God. The Doctrine of Christ includes, but is not limited to (as taught in the King James Bible):

➢ The Godhead, often called the "Trinity" one God

> ⁴ Hear, O Israel: The LORD our God is one LORD
> **Deuteronomy 6:4**

Composed of the 3 literal Persons of God the Father, God the Son, and God the Holy Spirit.

¹⁹ Go ye therefore, and teach all nations, baptizing them in the name of the Father, and of the Son, and of the Holy Ghost:
²⁰ Teaching them to observe all things whatsoever I have commanded you: and, lo, I am with you always, even unto the end of the world. Amen.

Matthew 28:19-20

⁷ Go to, let us go down, and there confound their language, that they may not understand one another's speech.

Genesis 11:7

⁹ For in him dwelleth all the fulness of the Godhead bodily.

Colossians 2:9

¹⁶ And Jesus, when he was baptized, went up straightway out of the water: and, lo, the heavens were opened unto him, and he saw the Spirit of God descending like a dove, and lighting upon him:
¹⁷ And lo a voice from heaven, saying, This is my beloved Son, in whom I am well pleased.

Matthew 3:16-17

➢ The Godhead became FLESH in Jesus Christ

1 In the beginning was the Word, and the Word was with God, and the Word was God.
² The same was in the beginning with God.
³ All things were made by him; and without him was not any thing made that was made.

John 1:1-3

¹⁴ And the Word was made flesh, and dwelt among us, (and we beheld his glory, the glory as of the only begotten of the Father,) full of grace and truth.

John 1:14

¹⁶ And without controversy great is the mystery of godliness: God was manifest in the flesh, justified in the Spirit, seen of angels, preached unto the Gentiles, believed on in the world, received up into glory.

1 Timothy 3:16

⁹ For in him dwelleth all the fulness of the Godhead bodily.

Colossians 2:9

- ### Jesus is the only BEGOTTEN Son of God

¹⁶ For God so loved the world, that he gave his only begotten Son, that whosoever believeth in him should not perish, but have everlasting life.

John 3:16

- ### Jesus is God Almighty

1 In the beginning was the Word, and the Word was with God, and the Word was God.
² The same was in the beginning with God.
³ All things were made by him; and without him was not any thing made that was made.

John 1:1-3

¹⁴ And the Word was made flesh, and dwelt among us, (and we beheld his glory, the glory as of the only begotten of the Father,) full of grace and truth.

John 1:14

¹⁶ And without controversy great is the mystery of godliness: God was manifest in the flesh, justified in the Spirit, seen of angels, preached unto the Gentiles, believed on in the world, received up into glory.

1 Timothy 3:16

⁹ For in him dwelleth all the fulness of the Godhead bodily.
Colossians 2:9

⁸ I am Alpha and Omega, the beginning and the ending, saith the Lord, which is, and which was, and which is to come, the Almighty.

Revelation 1:8

➢ Christ's death, burial and bodily resurrection

15 Moreover, brethren, I declare unto you the gospel which I preached unto you, which also ye have received, and wherein ye stand;
² By which also ye are saved, if ye keep in memory what I preached unto you, unless ye have believed in vain.
³ For I delivered unto you first of all that which I also received, how that Christ died for our sins according to the scriptures;
⁴ And that he was buried, and that he rose again the third day according to the scriptures

1 Corinthians 15:1-4

➢ Jesus' sinless life and perfection

²¹ For he hath made him to be sin for us, who knew no sin; that we might be made the righteousness of God in him.

2 Corinthians 5:21

²¹ For even hereunto were ye called: because Christ also suffered for us, leaving us an example, that ye should follow his steps:
²² Who did no sin, neither was guile found in his mouth

1 Peter 2:21-22

¹⁵ For we have not an high priest which cannot be touched with the feeling of our infirmities; but was in all points tempted like as we are, yet without sin.

Hebrews 4:15

> ## Jesus' literal, physical, blood sacrifice for our sins

¹⁸ Forasmuch as ye know that ye were not redeemed with corruptible things, as silver and gold, from your vain conversation received by tradition from your fathers;
¹⁹ But with the precious blood of Christ, as of a lamb without blemish and without spot

1 Peter 1:18-19

¹² Neither by the blood of goats and calves, but by his own blood he entered in once into the holy place, having obtained eternal redemption for us.

Hebrews 9:12

²² And almost all things are by the law purged with blood; and without shedding of blood is no remission.
²³ It was therefore necessary that the patterns of things in the heavens should be purified with these; but the heavenly things themselves with better sacrifices than these.
²⁴ For Christ is not entered into the holy places made with hands, which are the figures of the true; but into heaven itself, now to appear in the presence of God for us:

Hebrews 9:22-24

> ## Jesus Christ's virgin birth
> ¹⁴ Therefore the Lord himself shall give you a sign; Behold, a virgin shall conceive, and bear a son, and shall call his name Immanuel.

Isaiah 7:14

²³ Behold, a virgin shall be with child, and shall bring forth a son, and they shall call his name Emmanuel, which being interpreted is, God with us.

Matthew 1:23

- ➤ Jesus' bodily ascension into Heaven

¹¹ Which also said, Ye men of Galilee, why stand ye gazing up into heaven? this same Jesus, which is taken up from you into heaven, shall so come in like manner as ye have seen him go into heaven.

Acts 1:11

- ➤ Jesus' bodily return at the Second Coming

¹¹ Which also said, Ye men of Galilee, why stand ye gazing up into heaven? this same Jesus, which is taken up from you into heaven, shall so come in like manner as ye have seen him go into heaven.

Acts 1:11

⁷ Behold, he cometh with clouds; and every eye shall see him, and they also which pierced him: and all kindreds of the earth shall wail because of him. Even so, Amen.

Revelation 1:7

These are all fundamental doctrines of the Bible-believing, Christian faith.
Please understand that I didn't know any of these doctrines when I got saved as a young girl. All I knew was that I was a sinner and Jesus was the Savior. That's all I knew for years to come, until I gradually learned the Doctrine of Christ. You don't need to know all this to be saved; but if a person is taught these doctrines from the Bible, and they still deny them, then something is wrong. A saved person will not deny the

Virgin Birth of Jesus if they've been taught so from the Scriptures.

I was saved at age 9. I had never heard of these doctrines, except that Jesus was the only Savior in Whom I needed to trust for salvation, to be forgiven of my sins. But years later when I was first taught these doctrines, I immediately knew they were true and accepted them as facts, because I was already saved and had the Holy Spirit dwelling within. I NEVER denied any of these Biblical fundamentals as a Christian, because the Bible teacher who first taught them to me used the Scriptures to prove them. A true believer will accept Biblical teachings; not strongly deny them.

If you would have asked me if Jesus was God when I got saved, I wouldn't have known, because I hadn't been taught that yet from the Bible. But when someone showed me in the Bible that Jesus was God, I got excited and wanted to learn all I could about my Savior. The Holy Spirit bears witness in my heart and said, that's true, Jesus is God almighty! I knew it was true because I saw it in the Word of God and the Holy Spirit said, that is correct.

I once spoke with a Catholic man about the deity of Jesus Christ. He immediately told me that he did not believe that Jesus was God. I quoted him some Scriptures as evidence of the deity of Christ; but he didn't care, he still maintained that Jesus could not possibly be God. I knew right there that he was as unsaved as the Devil. So you see, if you are truly saved, then you will receive THE TRUTH.

²⁷ My sheep hear my voice, and I know them, and they follow me:

John 10:27

The King James Bible translators were very honest and scholarly in their work, even putting words in italics that they added to clarify the meaning in the original languages of Hebrew and Greek. In John 8:24, the masculine pronoun "he" is in italics, which means the literal translation is...

²⁴ I said therefore unto you, that ye shall die in your sins: for if ye believe not that **I am** he, ye shall die in your sins.

John 8:24

If you still want absolute solid proof of Christ's claim of deity, then read:

⁵⁷ Then said the Jews unto him, Thou art not yet fifty years old, and hast thou seen Abraham?
⁵⁸ Jesus said unto them, Verily, verily, I say unto you, Before Abraham was, **I am**.

John 8:57-58

¹⁴ And God said unto Moses, **I AM THAT I AM**: and he said, Thus shalt thou say unto the children of Israel, I AM hath sent me unto you.

Exodus 3:14

Here again we see that Jesus professed to be the "I AM" of Exodus 3:14. Jesus is almighty God!!!

Any Religion that deny Jesus Christ is a False Religion!

<Author Name>

<Book Title>

[1]Chapter 1: Islamic Muslim

What is Islam? What Do Muslims Believe?

Muslims strongly criticize Christians and say that Jesus is not the Son of God, yet they take personal offense at any criticism of Islam. They have tracts and apologetics against Christianity, but they don't want anybody exposing their silliness and wickedness. Why? Because in Arab countries any criticism of Muhammad or the Quran is viewed as a criminal offense punishable by death. There was jihad called for by Khadafy and Saddam Hussein during the Gulf War simply because the soldiers were perceived as Christians. Did you know that Christians are considered infidels according to the Islamic religion?

Mosques are popping up all over the world and people are flocking to Islam. Why are people so stupid that they will forsake Jesus and go halfway around the world just to try to find another way to get into heaven. Just like other false religions, Islam has many faces. Islam in other countries is much different from Islam in the Middle East. You hear, "they are hard-working people" I do not doubt this. But their holy book says something different. Either you convert to Islam or die! Their native lands say something different. No Islamic country is a democracy.

I'm going to let the Quran (Yusef Ali's translation (1)) and its prophet, Muhammad, speak for themselves.

---

[1] In this Chapter we used the King James Bible for all Scripture

Hélèné Fulton

Muslims worship a culture and a man named Muhammad

Islam, in all actuality, is the deification of Muhammad's seventh century Arabian culture. They must dress the way Muhammad and his women did, eat what they ate, speak like he did, make his political views their own, and pray the way he did. They must accept that everything that Muhammad did, taught, and believed is the word of Allah (who is NOT the God of the Bible). The whole religion is based on the lifestyle and fables of one man. This is important to remember - Islam is 7th century Arabia imposed on people living in the 20th century. This will become increasingly evident as we continue.

Muslim scholar Dr. Ali Dashti, a former Foreign Minister of Iran, explains in his book 23 Years: A Study of the Prophetic Career of Mohammad that Islam must be understood in terms of its essential identification with seventh-century Arab culture (Morely, p. 21).

This idea of a culture being "divine" might be a bit difficult for us Westerners to understand but it is foundational to Islam. "Christianity" is "supracultural" in that it allows people to live, dress, and eat in accordance with the culture in which they are living (Morely, 21). If Islam did that, there would be no Islam, it is ALL about culture. Eat this 'cause Muhammad did, don't eat that 'cause Muhammad didn't, pray toward Mecca which is the culture you worship, don't pray with your back to your back to Mecca 'cause you disrespect your god, your culture. All of this insignificant, temporal stuff done by a heathen named Muhammad has been elevated to divine law.

A Muslim must pray 5 times a day towards Mecca which is in Arabia thus he is reminded that he must be obedient to Arabia, a country, a culture.

Throwing stones at the Devil

A Muslim is required, despite cost or hardship, to go on a pilgrimage to the Kabah (an edifice which at one time held over 350 idols one of whom was Allah) in Mecca at least once in his lifetime. Poor third-world Muslims skimp and save for their ENTIRE lifetime in order to fulfill this "pillar" of Islam so that they will be eligible for paradise. What do they do when they get to Mecca? Run around throwing stones at the devil, of course!

Must adopt Muhammad's political views

There was no concept of personal freedom in Muhammad's seventh century Arabia, so no Islamic country today is a democracy. They are all run by dictators as in the days of Muhammad.

Why Muslims are so violent

Sure, in other courtries, they've tried to "Christianize" their beliefs and many of us gullibly believe that Muslims are peace-loving people but history, Muhammad, terrorism, and Jihad tell a different story, my friend. It is written in their law that Muslims must kill those that don't convert. Their leader, Muhammad made his fortune plundering and killing. Don't think it happens today? Looking at Algeria. Look at worldwide terrorism. Look at Khadafy, the Shaw of Iran, Saddam Hussein, Arafat's Palestine, etc. The word "assassin" came from a secret sect of Moslems who killed people while supposedly high on hashish. Violence and Islam are good friends.

Why does it seem like they are always fighting and terrorizing people? Why is Islam so militant and overbearing? If we make a simple analysis of the foundation of this religion, the answers will become very apparent. It all begins and ends with a man named Mohammad. The Hadith (another "holy" book of Islam) says that Jihad, or holy war, is the second best thing to believing in Allah and his apostle (Muhammad).

Allah's apostle was asked, "What is the best deed?" He replied, "To believe in Allah and his Apostle." The questioner then asked, "What is the next?" He replied, "To participate in Jihad in Allah's cause." (Hadith vol. 1, no. 25).

The Hadith also says that Murderous Muslims could take the property of people they killed during a Jihad (there are different types of Jihad). In addition to killing infidels like Christians and Jews, Muslims are also commanded to kill anyone who leaves Islam (Hadith vol. 4, no. 260).

The Quran requires violence. Sura 9:5 says,

Fight and slay the pagans wherever ye find them, and seize them, beleaguer them, and lie in wait for them in every strategem of war.

Sura 5:33 records what is done to infidels who resist Islam:

Their punishment is...execution, or crucifixion, or the cutting off of hands and feet from the opposite sides, or exile from the land.

Muhammad also burned out eyes with hot irons (Hadith vol. 1, no. 234) and deprived people of water until they died (vol. 8, no. 796).

In Islamic countries you can be incarcerated and tortured without due process - this was all part of 7th century Arabia. The dictator could do whatever he wanted to. I read an article in the Washington Post about Saddam Hussein's son. They said that he was a terror. One night he raped a woman and when she complained, he killed her. He did stuff like that all the time and one night he got shot up getting out of his car and was paralyzed.

The following is an article from [2]The Frontline Fellowship that does extensive missionary work in the Sudan, a country where crazy Muslims are killing, plundering, and destroying in the name of jihad. You can order their video "Sudan: The Hidden Holocaust" from their website.

Jihad - Islamic Holy War

The relentless and often vicious persecution by Muslims against Christians is seldom recognised or understood. Many assume that the concept of Jihad,

---

[2] http://www.frontline.org.za/

or holy war, espoused by Muslim leaders like the Aytollah Khomeini and demonstrated in terror bombings are aberrations not truly representative of Islam:

"We shall export our revolution, to the whole world. Until the cry 'Allah Akbar' resounds over the whole world. There will be struggle. There will be Jihad . . . Islam is the religion of militant individuals . . . Islam will be victorious in all the countries of the world, and Islam and the teachings of the Quran will prevail all over the world . . . This is the duty that all Muslims must fulfil . . ."

These were the often repeated public pronouncements of the Ayatollah Khomeini after the revolution in Iran in 1979 (*"The Blood of the Moon"*, by George Grant).

Nor was the Ayatollah alone in such militant threats. Abdul Aziz Ibn Saud declared: *"We shall never call for or accept a negotiated peace. We shall only accept war - Jihad - the holy war. We resolve to drench the lands of Palestine and Arabia with the blood of the infidels or to accept martyrdom for the glory of Allah".*

The President of Sudan, Lt. Gen. Al Bashir, has often spoken of Jihad. At the 40th anniversary of Sudan's independence, Al Bashir celebrated the spirit of Jihad which was engulfing the people of Sudan. The head of Sudan's ruling party, the National Islamic Front (NIF), Dr. Al Turabi, has often declared his goal of an Islamic empire controlling (initially) the horn of Africa (Eritrea, Ethiopia, Somalia, Kenya, Uganda and Sudan). This he calls the Grand Islamic Project.

Hélèné Fulton

At a two week conference of Muslim leaders from 80 countries, hosted by Muammar Gaddafi in Tripoli, Libya (October 1995), strategies to transform Africa into an Islamic continent were discussed. Participants openly admitted that their goals were to make Arabic the primary language of the continent and Islam the official religion. One SA member of parliament, Farouk Cassim declared: *"It will probably be the biggest revolution to sweep Africa."* Head of the Islamic Propagation Centre International (IPCI), Yousuf Deedat, announced afterwards that South Africa was high on the agenda of the Islamic offensive: *"We are going to turn South Africa into a Muslim state. We have the money to do it,"* (Sunday Times 22/10/95). At present less than 2 percent of South Africans are Muslims.

What few Westerners understand, however, is that those Muslim leaders who call for the overthrow of all governments and the establishment of an Islamic superstate controlling all aspects of life for every person on earth are not extremists on the fringe of Islam. Actually, *Jihad*, the subjugation and forcible conversion of all people to Islam and world domination are central tenants of Islam. *Jihad* is ranked by many Muslims as **the sixth pillar of Islam**.

Jihad was so important to the founder of Islam, Muhammad, that he declared it to be **the second most important deed in Islam.**

"Allah's apostle was asked, 'What is the best deed?' He replied, 'To believe in Allah and his Apostle.' The questioner then asked, 'What is the next (in goodness)?' He replied, 'To participate in Jihad

(religious fighting) in Allah's cause.'" – The Hadith, Al Bukhari, Vol. 1 no 25.

Muslims, in fact, divide the world into two sectors: *Dar-al-Islam* (the House of Islam) and *Dar-al-Harb* (The House of War). The only countries considered to be at peace are those where Islamic law (the *Sharia*) is enforced.

Islam in Arabic means submission, surrender or subjugation. A *Muslim* is one who submits. The Arabic word for peace is *Salam*. *Islam* is the active form of *Salam*. Muslims see themselves as a *"peace making force"* using argument, intrigue, commerce, threats, terrorism, warfare and every other means possible to secure Islam as the only religion worldwide.

Muslims are not permitted to make peace with a non-Muslim country until its inhabitants surrender to Islam. They can agree to a cease fire for a period of time – but never to peace with non-Muslims.

The Quran teaches that Muslims are superior to others: *"Ye (Muslims) are the best of peoples evolved for mankind . . ."* Surah 3:110.

Muslims are forbidden to befriend Jews or Christians: *"O ye who believe! Take not the Jews and the Christians for your friends and protectors. They are but friends and protectors to each other. And he amongst you that turns to them (for friendship) is one of them . . ."* Surah 5:54.

Islam instructs its adherents to fight until their opponents submit. Christians and Jews may be spared if they pay "Jizya" – a penalty tax – with willing submission: *"Fight those who believe not in God nor the last day . . . Nor acknowledge the religion of truth, (even if they are) of the people of the Book, until they pay Jizya (tribute taxes) with willing submission, and feel themselves subdued"* Surah 9:29.

"Fight and slay the pagans wherever ye find them and seize them, beleaguer them, and lie in wait (ambush) for them in every strategem (of war) . . ." Surah 9:5 (also 2:193).

For those who resist Islam – execution or mutilation is decreed: *"The punishment of those who wage war against Allah and His apostle, and strive with might and main for mischief through the land is: execution or crucifixion, or the cutting off of the hands and feet from opposite sides or exile from the land . . ."* Surah 5:36.

The **Hadith**, which is a record of the words and deeds of Muhammad, is also viewed by Muslims as inspired. Next to the Quran, it is the most important source of Islamic Law. It's teachings are regarded as binding on all Muslims.

The Hadith teaches that apostasy is punishable by death: *"Whoever changes his Islamic religion, kill him."* Vol. 9:57.

A Muslim may not be punished for killing a non-Muslim: *"No Muslim should be killed for killing a kafir (infidel)."* Vol 9:50

Those who die in holy war are guaranteed to go to Heaven. *"The person who participates in Jihad (Holy *battles) in Allah's cause and nothing compels him to do so except belief in Allah and His apostle, will be recompensed by Allah either with a reward or booty (if he survives) or will be admitted to paradise (if he is killed)."* Vol 1:35

It may be hard for Christians to understand the concept of such a militant religion, but the primary aim of Islam is not spiritual but political. The ultimate purpose of Islam is the establishment by force of a worldwide Islamic state where Sharia law is enforced on all.

To achieve this is the goal of Jihad. Islamic scholars identify a multitude of forms that Jihad can take:

1. There is the Jihad of Words. Muhammad was a brilliant and gifted orator silencing his enemies in a war of words. In Arab culture it was customary for feuding tribes to select a poet to mock and provoke the opposing forces with spontaneous verses of cursing. These linguistic warriors engaged in verbal combat seeking to inspire their own side with a sense of superiority and strength whilst undermining the morale of the enemy. This war of words, which Muslim leaders today such as Gaddaffi, Saddam Hussein and Yassar Arafat still engage in, is actually a war of nerves.

2. There is the **Jihad of Deception**. When Muslims are small in number they can follow the example of Muhammad's 83 followers who fled from persecution in Mecca to Abyssinia (present day Ethiopia). There the Christian *Negus* (king) offered them refuge. When the Meccans demanded their

return as slaves, the Muslim exiles declared that Islam was merely a variation of Christianity. The Muslims selectively recited those passages of the Quran that agree with the Bible such as the virgin birth and miracles of Jesus and His ascension to Heaven and ultimate return. They remained silent on the unbridgeable differences (such as the denial of the Trinity and the atonement) between the Quran and the Bible. As a result the Christian Abyssinians protected the Muslims from the Meccans.

In this way, when it was most vulnerable, Islam grew and developed in a Christian environment. (If we only demonstrate our Christian love without proclaiming the truth of the Gospel we could strengthen anti-Christian forces).

Muhammad compromised with the Meccan merchants during a particularly intense time of persecution. Formerly he had fearlessly condemned polytheism. Then, under pressure, he accepted the Meccan belief that Allah had a wife, *Al-lat*, and two daughters, *Al Uzzo* and *Manat* (Surah 53:20-23). Later Muhammad repudiated these so called *Satanic Verses* and claimed that all previous prophets had been tempted by demonic influence.

3. There is **the Jihad of the Sword**. After fleeing to Medina (the *Hijra*) in AD622, Muhammad started to summon his followers to attack and plunder the caravans of Mecca. His followers initially resisted these calls until Muhammad presented a series of *"revelations"* commanding *Jihad* (holy war) and

permitting looting (*"Whoever has killed an enemy and has proof of that, will possess his spoils"* – The Hadith, Vol. 4 no. 370). Where the booty was not large enough, Muhammad held captives as hostages until their families paid a high ransom for their release. Hostage taking has continued to be a common practise in Islam to this day. Those who participate in *Jihad* are granted a blanket absolution (Surah 8:17) and guaranteed to go straight to Paradise (Heaven) if killed.

4. There is the **Jihad of Taxation and Financial Reward**. Those who refuse to submit to Islam are forced to pay a special tax for non- Muslims (*Jizya*). Those who convert to Islam are often offered financial rewards or scholarships.

5. There is the **Jihad of Slavery**. Those Muslims who engage in *Jihad* not only can seize property, extort ransoms and demand taxes, but also capture slaves. The only places in the world today where slavery is still practised are in some Muslim countries. In Sudan, the Islamic government uses slavery as an incentive to encourage Arab Northerners to attack the Christian Blacks in the South, and as a weapon of terror to destabilize non-Muslims. According to the *Sharia Law*, Muslims are allowed to enslave, own and sell human beings.

6. There is the **Jihad of the Sharia Law**. Non-Muslims are degraded to a lower class status and are denied equal access to the law because their testimony is not valid against a Muslim. This even applies to murder *("No Muslim should be killed for*

killing an infidel"). The death penalty is applied to anyone who renounces Islam and converts to another religion.

When the wealthy Bedouins of Arabia professed faith in Allah to escape attack, Muhammad did not accept their confession. (*"The desert Arabs say 'We believe'. Say, 'Ye have no faith; but ye (only) say 'We have submitted.'"* Surah 49:14) Islam does not place much value on personal faith, but demands surrender to the political rule of the *Sharia*.

It is significant that the calendar of Islam does not begin with the birth of Muhammad, nor the onset of his supposed *"revelation"*, nor the assembling of the first Muslim community, nor the flight of Muslim refugees to Abyssinia. The 12 years of persecution in Mecca were not considered the start of their new religion. The Muslim calendar only begins when Islam became a political state in Medina.

7. There is the **Jihad of Polygamy**. The devastating defeat of the Muslim forces by the Meccans in the battle of Uhud (AD625) led to what could be considered one of Islam's greatest victories. So many of his men were killed that Muhammad permitted his men to take up to 4 wives (Surah 4:3, 4). With the advent of Western medicine, infant mortality has plummeted. And the Muslim birthrate has skyrocketed. Muslims are increasing in number twice as fast as other religions. This is due to birth control and abortion in Western lands and polygamy in Muslim lands. Muslims are not increasing much by missionary outreaches, but by

having many children. Polygamy (rather than persuasion) has become one of Islam's most effective weapons for Holy War, providing Islam with a disproportionate numerical advantage.

There is the **Jihad of the Spirits**. According to the Quran, Muslims are not only men and women but also spirits who fight for the spread of Islam (Surah 46:29-33 and 72:1-15). Also a Muslim is to fight on Muhammad's behalf both in his life and after his death (Hadith Vol. 1 chapter 43).

Clearly Islam is a religion of force which denies basic freedom. No Muslim even has the freedom to change or leave his religion. The huge block of over 1 billion Muslims presents **the greatest political and military threat to the Western world and the greatest missionary challenge (editor's note: I do not agree with this, the Great Whore is the greatest enemy of the gospel of Christ) to the Christian Church**.

Muslim states are the most severe persecutors of Christians, and Muslim terrorist groups are the most vicious hijackers, kidnappers, bombers and assassins. As the recent East African bombings remind us, Islam is a challenge that we cannot ignore.

How we chose to respond, in prayer, publications, proclamation, projects and persistent vigilance will determine much of the course of history in the coming 21st century.

Peter Hammond

Islam and women

Hélèné Fulton

Muhammad wrote in the Sura 4:3 that it is unlawful to have more than four wives, but he had more than four. Muslim scholar Ali Dashti lists 22 women in Muhammad's life, including 16 wives. He also stole his adopted son's wife Zaynab and made her his own. One wife, Aesha, was only eight or nine years old when he took her to bed.

Female Muslims must be covered head to foot like Muhammad's women who needed it in the desert sun and sand.

Women are treated bad in Islam. Let's look at the Quran, Sura 4:34:

Men are the managers of the affairs of women...Those you fear may be rebellious - admonish; banish them to their couches and **beat them**.

Muslim women can be kept prisioners in their own homes and denied the right to go outside the house if the husband orders. They can't even vote in some countries. In Iran they must carry written permission from their husbands to go outside the house. In Saudi Arabia, they are prohibited from driving a car. When some women in Saudia Arabia drove cars in the fall of 1990, they were castigated from every direction and admonished not to talk to Western reporters. One woman said, "The issue is not driving. It is that here in Saudi Arabia, I exist as a person from the bellybutton to the knees."

I've heard some foolish people say that the Bible degrades women. What a lie that is! God made us male and female with distinct responsibilities. I perceive that the lawless and rebellious are the ones who think that having children and rearing them is demeaning. I perceive that the prideful and arrogant are the ones that think they have something to prove to men and the world at large. What a pitiful existence trying to be just the opposite of what God says. That is all it is. What freedom we women have in Christ. I used to think being a Christian was about bondage, but that was a lie from the devil. It is ultimate freedom (and I'm a woman too)!

[28] There is neither Jew nor Greek, there is neither slave nor free, there is neither male nor female; for you are all one in Christ Jesus.

Galatians 3:28

The Quran has NO earthly sources

According to the Islam religion, the teachings of Muhammad and the Quran came STRAIGHT FROM HEAVEN and cannot have any earthly source. Yet Western scholarship easily shows that ALL of Islam is based on the customs and fables of pre-Islamic Arabia and misinterpretation of the Bible by Muhammad.

Even the word, "Islam" wasn't new with Muhammad. It originally meant, *defiance of death, heroism, to die in battle.*

Today, it is supposed to mean *submission.*

Now given all the terrorism from the Middle East and fighting between the Shiite and Sunnis which definition better fits Islam? "to die in battle" or "submission"? The Quran commands Muslims to convert everyone to

Islam or else kill them. "Islam" existed before Muhammad came on the scene so there is an earthly source.

Also, the Quran is not written in a heavenly language, it is written the Quraish dialect (Hadith vol. 6, no. 507) which was Muhammad's tribe. On top of that it is easily translated. It didn't fall out of heaven as they claim. Neither is it non-translatable as Muslims are taught that it is.

Let's move on. Even the word "Allah" was not invented by Muhammad. It was already well known. Allah is a purely Arabic word al = the and ilah = god. It is not taken from the Hebrew or Greek word for God. It is not even the Arabic word for God. It is the name of a peculiar deity - Allah, the moon god. See the section on Allah. The Encyclopedia of Islam says:

The Arabs, BEFORE the time of Mohammed, accepted and worshipped, after a fashion, a supreme god called Allah. (ed. Houtsma)

Allah was known to the PRE-Islamic Arabs; he was one of the Meccan deities. (ed. Gibb)

Allah...appears in PRE-Islamic poetry...By frequency of usage, al-ilah was contracted to allah, frequently attested to in pre-Islamic poetry. (ed. Lewis)

[3]This article from NYTimes.com

---

[3] http://www.nytimes.com/2002/03/02/arts/02ISLA.html?ex=1016124256&ei=1&en=d59d0758bbf378c7

Hélèné Fulton

Radical New Views of Islam and the Origins of the Koran

March 2, 2002 - By ALEXANDER STILLE

To Muslims the Koran is the very word of God, who spoke through the Angel Gabriel to Muhammad: "This book is not to be doubted," the Koran declares unequivocally at its beginning. Scholars and writers in Islamic countries who have ignored that warning have sometimes found themselves the target of death threats and violence, sending a chill through universities around the world.

Yet despite the fear, a handful of experts have been quietly investigating the origins of the Koran, offering radically new theories about the text's meaning and the rise of Islam.

Christoph Luxenberg, a scholar of ancient Semitic languages in Germany, argues that the Koran has been misread and mistranslated for centuries. His work, based on the earliest copies of the Koran, maintains that parts of Islam's holy book are derived from pre-existing Christian Aramaic texts that were misinterpreted by later Islamic scholars who prepared the editions of the Koran commonly read today.

So, for example, the virgins who are supposedly awaiting good Islamic martyrs as their reward in paradise are in reality "white raisins" of crystal clarity rather than fair maidens.

Christoph Luxenberg, however, is a pseudonym, and his scholarly tome ""The Syro-Aramaic Reading of the

*Koran" had trouble finding a publisher, although it is considered a major new work by several leading scholars in the field.
Verlag Das Arabische Buch in Berlin ultimately published the book.*

The caution is not surprising. Salman Rushdie's "Satanic Verses" received a fatwa because it appeared to mock Muhammad. The Egyptian novelist Naguib Mahfouz was stabbed because one of his books was thought to be irreligious. And when the Arab scholar Suliman Bashear argued that Islam developed as a religion gradually rather than emerging fully formed from the mouth of the Prophet, he was injured after being thrown from a second- story window by his students at the University of Nablus in the West Bank. Even many broad-minded liberal Muslims become upset when the historical veracity and authenticity of the Koran is questioned.

The reverberations have affected non-Muslim scholars in Western countries. "Between fear and political correctness, it's not possible to say anything other than sugary nonsense about Islam," said one scholar at an American university who asked not to be named, referring to the threatened violence as well as the widespread reluctance on United States college campuses to criticize other cultures.

While scriptural interpretation may seem like a remote and innocuous activity, close textual study of Jewish and Christian scripture played no small role in loosening the Church's domination on the intellectual and cultural life of Europe, and paving the way for unfettered secular thought. "The Muslims have the benefit of hindsight of the European experience, and they know very well that once you start questioning the holy scriptures, you don't know where it will stop," the scholar explained.

The touchiness about questioning the Koran predates the latest rise of Islamic militancy. As long ago as 1977, John Wansbrough of the School of Oriental and African Studies in London wrote that subjecting the Koran to "analysis by the instruments and techniques of biblical criticism is virtually unknown."

Mr. Wansbrough insisted that the text of the Koran appeared to be a composite of different voices or texts compiled over dozens if not hundreds of years. After all, scholars agree that there is no evidence of the Koran until 691 - 59 years after Muhammad's death - when the Dome of the Rock mosque in Jerusalem was built, carrying several Koranic inscriptions.

These inscriptions differ to some degree from the version of the Koran that has been handed down through the centuries, suggesting, scholars say, that the Koran may have still been evolving in the last decade of the seventh century. Moreover, much of what we know as Islam - the lives and sayings of the Prophet - is based on texts from between 130 and 300 years after Muhammad's death.

In 1977 two other scholars from the School for Oriental and African Studies at London University - Patricia Crone (a professor of history at the Institute for Advanced Study in Princeton) and Michael Cook (a professor of Near Eastern history at Princeton University) - suggested a radically new approach in their book "Hagarism: The Making of the Islamic World."

Since there are no Arabic chronicles from the first century of Islam, the two looked at several non-Muslim, seventh-century accounts that suggested Muhammad was perceived not as the founder of a new religion but as a preacher in the Old Testament tradition, hailing the coming of a Messiah. Many of the early documents refer to the followers of Muhammad as "hagarenes," and the "tribe of Ishmael," in other words as descendants of Hagar, the servant girl that the Jewish patriarch Abraham used to father his son Ishmael.

In its earliest form, Ms. Crone and Mr. Cook argued, the followers of Muhammad may have seen themselves as retaking their place in the Holy Land alongside their Jewish cousins. (And many Jews appear to have welcomed the Arabs as liberators when they entered Jerusalem in 638.)

The idea that Jewish messianism animated the early followers of the Prophet is not widely accepted in the field, but "Hagarism" is credited with opening up the field. "Crone and Cook came up with some very interesting revisionist ideas," says Fred M. Donner of the University of Chicago and author of the recent book "Narratives of Islamic Origins: The Beginnings of Islamic Historical Writing." "I think in trying to reconstruct what happened, they went off the deep end, but they were asking the right questions."

The revisionist school of early Islam has quietly picked up momentum in the last few years as historians began to apply rational standards of proof to this material.

Mr. Cook and Ms. Crone have revised some of their early hypotheses while sticking to others. "We were certainly wrong about quite a lot of things," Ms. Crone said. "But I stick to the basic point we made: that Islamic history did not arise as the classic tradition says it does."

Ms. Crone insists that the Koran and the Islamic tradition present a fundamental paradox. The Koran is a text soaked in monotheistic thinking, filled with stories and references to Abraham, Isaac, Joseph and Jesus, and yet the official history insists that Muhammad, an illiterate camel merchant, received the revelation in Mecca, a remote, sparsely populated part of Arabia, far from the centers of monotheistic thought, in an environment of idol-worshiping Arab Bedouins. Unless one accepts the idea of the angel Gabriel, Ms. Crone says, historians must somehow explain how all these monotheistic stories and ideas found their way into the Koran.

"There are only two possibilities," Ms. Crone said. "Either there had to be substantial numbers of Jews and Christians in Mecca or the Koran had to have been composed somewhere else."

Indeed, many scholars who are not revisionists agree that Islam must be placed back into the wider historical context of the religions of the Middle East rather than seeing it as the spontaneous product of the pristine Arabian desert.

Hélèné Fulton

"I think there is increasing acceptance, even on the part of many Muslims, that Islam emerged out of the wider monotheistic soup of the Middle East," says Roy Mottahedeh, a professor of Islamic history at Harvard University.

Scholars like Mr. Luxenberg and Gerd- R. Puin, who teaches at Saarland University in Germany, have returned to the earliest known copies of the Koran in order to grasp what it says about the document's origins and composition. Mr. Luxenberg explains these copies are written without vowels and diacritical dots that modern Arabic uses to make it clear what letter is intended. In the eighth and ninth centuries, more than a century after the death of Muhammad, Islami commentators added diacritical marks to clear up the ambiguities of the text, giving precise meanings to passages based on what they considered to be their proper context. Mr. Luxenberg's radical theory is that many of the text's difficulties can be clarified when it is seen as closely related to Aramaic, the language group of most Middle Eastern Jews and Christians at the time.

For example, the famous passage about the virgins is based on the word hur, which is an adjective in the feminine plural meaning simply "white." Islamic tradition insists the term hur stands for "houri," which means virgin, but Mr. Luxenberg insists that this is a forced misreading of the text. In both ancient Aramaic and in at least one respected dictionary of early Arabic, hur means "white raisin."

Mr. Luxenberg has traced the passages dealing with paradise to a Christian text called Hymns of Paradise by a fourth-century author. Mr. Luxenberg said the word paradise was derived from the Aramaic word for garden and all the descriptions of paradise described it as a garden of flowing waters, abundant fruits and white raisins, a prized delicacy in the ancient Near East. In this context, white raisins, mentioned often as hur, Mr. Luxenberg said, makes more sense than a reward of sexual favors.

In many cases, the differences can be quite significant.
Mr. Puin points out that in the early archaic copies of the Koran, it is impossible to distinguish between the words "to fight" and "to kill." In many cases, he said, Islamic exegetes added diacritical marks that yielded the harsher meaning, perhaps reflecting a period in which the Islamic Empire was often at war.

A return to the earliest Koran, Mr. Puin and others suggest, might lead to a more tolerant brand of Islam, as well as one that is more conscious of its close ties to both Judaism and Christianity.

"It is serious and exciting work," Ms. Crone said of Mr. Luxenberg's work. Jane McAuliffe, a professor of Islamic studies at Georgetown University, has asked Mr. Luxenberg to contribute an essay to the Encyclopedia of the Koran, which she is editing.

Mr. Puin would love to see a "critical edition" of the Koran produced, one based on recent philological work, but, he says, "the word critical is misunderstood in the Islamic world - it is seen as criticizing or attacking the text."

Some Muslim authors have begun to publish skeptical, revisionist work on the Koran as well. Several new volumes of revisionist scholarship, "The Origins of the Koran," and "The Quest for the Historical Muhammad," have been edited by a former Muslim who writes under the pen name Ibn Warraq. Mr. Warraq, who heads a group called the Institute for the Secularization of Islamic Society, makes no bones about having a political agenda. "Biblical scholarship has made people less dogmatic, more open," he said, "and I hope that happens to Muslim society as well."

But many Muslims find the tone and claims of revisionism offensive. "I think the broader implications of some of the revisionist scholarship is to say that the Koran is not an authentic book, that it was fabricated 150 years later," says Ebrahim Moosa, a professor of religious studies at Duke University, as well as a Muslim cleric whose liberal theological leanings earned him the animosity of fundamentalists in South Africa, which he left after his house was firebombed.

Andrew Rippin, an Islamicist at the University of Victoria in British Columbia, Canada, says that freedom of speech in the Islamic world is more likely to evolve from within the Islamic interpretative tradition than from outside attacks on it. Approaches to the Koran that are now branded as heretical - interpreting the text metaphorically rather than literally - were widely practiced in mainstream Islam a thousand years ago.

"When I teach the history of the interpretation it is eye-opening to students the amount of independent thought and diversity of interpretation that existed in

the early centuries of Islam," Mr. Rippin says. "It was only in more recent centuries that there was a need for limiting interpretation."

"Allah" does not mean "God" in Arabic

The Encyclopedia of Religion and Ethics says this:

The origin of this (Allah) goes back to PRE-Muslim times. **Allah is NOT a common name meaning "God" (or a "god"),** and the Muslim must use another word or form if he wishes to indicate any other than **his own peculiar deity**.

Allah was a pre-existing god. He was well known to Muhammad's Quraysh tribe. Scholars quickly point out that **Allah was one of the names used for the MOON god who was married to the sun goddess**. Together they produced three goddesses who were called "the daughters of Allah. Their names were Al-Lat, Al-Uzza and Manat. These were considered high gods - at the top of the plethora of Arabian deities. Muhammad's father's literal Arabic name was Abd-**Allah**. His uncle's name was Obied-**Allah**. His family was devoted to the moon god for at least two generations before Muhammad. The Arabian pagans prayed towards Mecca because that is where their idols/gods were sitting. Since Allah was one of the idols in the Kabah it only made sense to turn toward their god and pray. Praying toward Mecca continues to this day.

Allah is clearly not the God of the Bible. He is an Arabian idol that sat in the Kabah with a bunch of other idols. The pagans prayed in the direction of

Mecca because that is where their gods (including Allah) resided heaped on top of each other in the Kabah. This is not news to educated Muslims, they generally understand this point. Allah is the moon god, that's probably why there is the crescent moon and star on the Muslim flag.

In conclusion, the Quran took Allah from the existing Arabic paganism and superimposed it on top of the God of the Bible. A dumb idol that can neither hear, nor speak, nor think.

"Well," you might say, "what about Arabic Bibles that say, 'Allah' for the word God?"
"Well," I would say, "the missionaries got intimidated by Arabs to use Allah instead of the Arabic word of God." I also might say, "Many missionaries are turning to dynamic equivalency which means that they do not translate word for word but rather look for similar ideas to convey meaning. The King James is the only Bible that does word for word translation - that's called formal equivalency."

Allah vs. God

The Quran	The Bible
Allah is unknowable	God is knowable
Allah is nonpersonal	God is personal
Allah is not a spirit	God is a Spirit
Allah is not a Father, nor Jesus the Son of God	God is one existing in three persons, not three gods, but one God
Allah can do anything with no limitations	God cannot go against His immutable nature e.g. God cannot lie
Allah is capricious	God is trustworthy

Allah has no feelings towards man	God loves man
Allah doesn't personally enter human history	God came in the flesh to bring about man's salvation.
Allah provides no saviour or intecessor. You're on your own. No concept of grace	God provided a Saviour through His manifold grace

It is clear to see that the God of the Bible is NOT the god of the Quran, Allah.

About Muhammad

Muhammad is the "prophet" of Islam. At age 40 he claimed that he was a prophet and apostle (he took these terms from the Bible. They had no history in Arabian religion). The Quran gives **four conflicting accounts** of how he was called to be a prophet - (1) In Suras 53:2-18 and 81:19-24, Allah personally appeared. (2) In Suras 16:102 and 26:192-194 he was called by "the Holy Spirit". (3) In Sura 15:8 the angels announced his prophetic ministry; and , (4) The angel Gabriel told him of his ministry and hands him the Quran.

Who were Muhammad's first supposed converts? Genies! Yes, Muhammad supposedly preached to and converted genies in Suras 46:29-35; 72:1-28. How convenient that there was no one around to confirm his prophethood.

Muhammad killed and plundered many people. During the Nakhla Raid, he sent some of his thugs to loot a caravan killing one man and enslaving others. This was his first battle. Do you wonder why so many terrorists are Muslims? The acorn doesn't fall far from the tree.

The "prophet" Muhammad did not even foresee his own death in 632 A.D. As a result, he left no instructions for his successors. Soon there were warring sects in Islam such as the Shiites and Sunnis who fight to this day. So not only are Muslims fighting infidels like Christians and Jews, they are fighting each other!

Muhammad stole his son's wife.

Muhammad wanted his son's wife and when his son didn't want to give her up, Muhammad had a "convenient revelation" from heaven which said a father can take his adopted son's wife. Read Sura 33:36-38:

...When Zaid had accomplished what he would of her, then we gave her in marriage to you, so that there should not be any fault in the believers, touching the wives of their adopted sons, when they have accomplished what they would of them; and Allah's commandment must be performed. There is no fault in the prophet, touch what Allah had ordained for him.

Muslim view of Jesus

Islam claims that Muhammad and Jesus were both Muslims and prophets of Allah. Whoa, Nelly! They say that Allah has no son and they are right. Allah is not the omniscient, omnipresent, omnipotent God of the Bible - so they are right, Jesus is not the son of Allah.

He is the Son of God. Muslims say that the Bible is corrupt, we can't trust it - yet the Quran claims to based on the Bible. Islam says:

- Jesus is not the Son of God.
- Jesus did not die for our sins.
- Jesus was not crucified.
- Jesus was not divine as well as human.
- Jesus is not the Saviour.

These are not issues of the Bible being corrupt as the Muslims say it is. These are issues of the Quran out-and-out contradicting the Bible. These are issues of Muslims blaspheming. See Suras 4:157; 5:19, 75; 9:30.

Differences between Muhammad and Jesus

The coming of Muhammad was not foretold. Muhammad came on the scene claiming that he converted genies that nobody seen. And now a whole host of people worship this man and his fake god that is no god. Muhammad did many treacherous things including robbing and plundering for his own wealth. He also commanded his followers to kill all that would not submit to Muhammad's made-up religion.

Today in Africa and around the world, Muslims are killing anyone who will not submit to Islam.

Of late, Muslims are trying to say that Muhammad was sinless, but Muhammad admitted that he is a sinner.

"Muhammad replied..."O Allah, set me apart from my sins..." Hadith vol. 1, no. 711

Hélèné Fulton

In Sura 18:10, Allah tells Muhammad:

Say, I am but a man like yourselves.

Jesus on the other hand was CLEARLY prophesied about hundreds, THOUSANDS of years before His coming. Jesus is the express image of God and His sacrifice stands in demonstration of the love of God. Islam has nothing to point to that reveals the love of God. In fact the Quran says that there is no intercessor or Saviour. You've got to save yourself. See Sura 6:51, 70; 10:3.

Jesus rose from the dead, Muhammad did not. Jesus was the Son of God, Muhammad was not. Jesus did many miracles, Muhammad did not. Jesus was seen by over 500 people when He went up to heaven, Muhammad was put in a grave. Jesus quoted scriptures written thousands of years before His coming while Muhammad made up his own scriptures and claimed that he preached to genies as his proof of being a prophet. Muhammad even contradicted himself when he quoted his various fairy tales. Muhammad sinned against many people. Jesus sinned against no one. Not ONE of Jesus' enemies could ever truthfully say anything bad about Him. People that Muhammad tortured could certainly talk bad about him.

Muhammad is obviously inferior to Jesus, and as a result, Muslim theologians have borrowed events from the life of Jesus and attributed them to their "prophet".

Muhammad not assured of paradise

Muhammad was not sure if he was going to heaven himself:

The Prophet said, *"By Allah, though I am the Apostle of Allah, yet I do not know what Allah will do to me."* Hadith vol. 5, no. 266

Bones, palm leaves, rocks and the Quran

Though he was supposed to be a prophet, Muhammad had no clue that he was going to die when he did. He therefore died without compiling his revelations - don't be mistaken, Muhammad didn't actually write them down himself. When Muhammad would have his visions/seizures he would recite and others would either try to remember what he said or they wrote his words on rocks, palm leaves, animal bones, papyrus, wooden boards, etc. Some of the words got eaten by animals who munched on the palm leaves that they were written on. Some of the Suras were never written down - people just tried to remember what Muhammad said while he was in his trance. Oh, real reliable. Yet a Muslim will tell you that the Bible is untrustworthy!

Much confusion reigned because the memory of one person would contradict the memory of another - but the Bible is corrupt? No, the Quran and its writers were corrupt. The "revelations" of the Koran are not even laid out in chronological order. There no logical order of ideas. In fact, there is no beginning, middle, and end. The Bible tells us about the creation of the earth and mankind (Genesis) and goes all the way through human history until the end of the world and the final judgment (Revelation).

The Bible had approximately 40 authors and was written over a period of approximately 1600 years. It flows seemlessly. The Quran, on the other hand, came through one man (who didn't even write it), during his lifetime with nothing to support it. It is obvious which is superior.

The fact that the Quran claims to be the second part of the Bible shows that it is not because it directly contradicts the Bible while not fitting the literary style or structure found in the Old and New Testaments.

The Muslims claim that the Quran is perfect in Arabic and that it can't be translated. That's pretty dumb - anything can be translated. They also claim that it came directly from heaven with no earthly sources, but in doing a little research it is evident that the Quran did come from earth, more specifically, from Muhammad's pre-Islamic Arabia. The customs and culture found in the Quran fit pre-Islamic Arabia to a "T".

Muslims claim that the Quran is perfect because God preserves His word - but yet they say the Bible is corrupt. If the Quran is supposedly based on the Bible and the Bible is corrupt, why would God preserve the Quran?

Muhammad gets the Bible all wrong

Mistakes in the Quran. (it should be noted that many of the stories in the Quran come from the Jewish Talmud, the Midrash, and many apocryphal works - for

instance Nimrod threw Abraham in the fire. You'll see this in Jewish extra biblical literature.)
- Christians worship three gods: the Father, the Mother (Mary), and the Son (Jesus) (Sura 5:73-75, 116) Yusuf Ali's translation deliberately mistranslates Sura 5:73 by saying "They do blaspheme who say: God is one of three in a Trinity". The words "in a Trinity" are not in the Arabic text. The Aramaic says, "Allah is the third of three".
- Christians bow in prayer towards Jerusalem (Sura 2:144, 145)
- Wine and sex in heaven (Sura 2:25; 4:57; 11:23; 47:15). Was this not Muhammad's desire?
- It took eight days to create the earth. (Sura 41:9, 10, 12 - 4+4+2=8 days). The Bible says six days. Other Suras say six days (7:51, 10:3)
- One of the sons of Noah refused to go into the ark and was drowned in the flood (Sura 11:32-48). The Bible says all three went in.
- The ark came to rest on Mount Judi (Sura 11:44). The Bible says it came to rest on Mount Ararat.
- Abraham father's name was Azar (Sura 6:74). The Bible says it was Terah.
- Abraham lived in the valley of Mecca (Sura 14:37). The Bible says he lived in Hebron.
- Abraham went to sacrifice Ishmael (Sura 37:100-112). The Bible says it was Isaac.
- Abraham built the Kabah (Sura 2:125-127). The Bible does not say this.
  - Abraham was thrown into a fire (by Nimrod). The tale of Abraham being delivered from Nimrod's fire came from the Jewish Midrash Rabbah and was incorporated into the Quran (see Suras 21:51-71; 37:97,98). It must be also pointed out that Nimrod and Abraham did not live at the same time.

Muhammad was always mixing people together in the Quran who did not live at the same time. The Bible tells us Nimrod lived MANY CENTURIES BEFORE ABRAHAM - HE COULD NOT HAVE DONE THIS.

- Throughout the Quran - Nimrod and Abraham, Haman and Moses, Mary and Aaron, etc. were all pictured as living and working together. Moses and the flood are found together, the tower of Babel and Pharaoh, etc. like they all happened at the same time.
- Man who bought Joseph was named Aziz (Sura 12:21ff). The Bible says it was Potiphar.
- Quran messes up numerous Bible people. Goliath becomes Jalut, Saul becomes Talut, Enoch Idris, John the Baptist Yahya, Jonah Yunus, etc. Because Muhammad had no Bible to read he frequently got the names and events all wrong - but then again, he was supposed to be a prophet!
- Pharaoh's wife adopted Moses (Sura 28:8, 9). Bible says it was Pharaoh's daughter.
- Noah's flood took place in Moses day (Sura 7:136, 7:59).
- Crucifixion was used in Pharaoh's time (Sura 7:124)
- Mary gave birth to Jesus under a palm tree (Sura 19:22)
- Mary mother of Jesus is Moses' sister Miriam (Sura19:28). Muhammad was clueless.
- Made up miracles of Mary (Sura 19:23-26).
- Zacharias could not speak for only three days (Sura 19:10)
- The test of how soldiers drank water came in the days of David and Saul (Sura 2:249, 250 - actually it was years earlier with Gideon.

Other Mistakes

- Abrah's army defeated by birds dropping stones on them. History says Abrah's army withdrew after smallpox broke out.
- The Kabah was build by Adam and rebuilt by Abraham. It was built by pagans to worship a black rock that fell out of the sky. Abraham never lived in Mecca.
- Sura 20:87, 95, the Jews made the golden calf in the wilderness at the suggestion of Samaritans - there were no Samaritans at that time.
- Alexander the Great was a Muslim and worshipped Allah and lived to an old age (Sura 18:89-98). Yusuf Ali and the Concise Dictionary of Islam confirm that Zul-qarinain in the Quran is Alexander the Great.
- Alexander the Great followed the setting sun and found that it went down into the waters of a muddy spring (Sura 18:85, 86). Does that sound like a fairy tail or what?
- Contradictions are too numerous to name...

Black Muslim movement founded by a bi-racial man

Elijah Poole, son of a Baptist minister, hooked up in 1931 with Wallace D. Fard who was apparently a bi-racial man and religious teacher. Black Muslims call him "Master Fard Muhammad". Fard told his followers to dress like Arab Muslims did in the Middle East (you see Wallace D. Fard sold African clothing so of course, he sold them the clothing). Poole renounced the Christian faith and his birth name. Fard gave him the name Karriem.

Going from house to house using Watchtower materials, Fard tore down his black followers' faith in the gospel of Jesus Christ and replaced it with his own form of Islam.

The Hadith calls Muhammad was a white man, so Black Muslims serve the one they speak against. Meanwhile, the Hadith calls black people "raisin heads" (vol. 1, no. 662 and vol. 9, no. 256) and refers to them as slaves. If someone dreamed of a black woman, she was an evil omen of disease (vol. 9, nos. 162, 163). Muhammad had black slaves (vol. 6, no. 435). Yet and still Louis Farrakhan and his followers will tell us Christianity is the white man's religion. Jesus came for all regardless of color but Black Islam is specially designed just to lead Black folks to hell!

The Nation of Islam (Black Muslim movement) plays on the racism against black people by white people hence you hear them use terms like "white devils", etc. When I was in college, before I started walking with the Lord, Louis Farrakhan came to my 94% white campus. I really had had no interest in seeing him until all the white students got up in arms. As a black student, the whites treated me badly, so I went to see Farrakhan just because they didn't like the man. I am sorry to say that I agreed with a lot of what he said and I perceive a lot of other black folks are agreeing with this false prophet today and joining this blasphemy called Islam.

Now that I am walking with the Lord I know that the man, Louis Farrakhan, mixes truth and error. He hits the nail on the head in many instances of how we black folks are treated and then mixes in a healthy dose of lies like he is the messiah and has seen the "mother ship". This is not to mention all the heresy of "the real" Islam.

Black Muslim movement seen as spurious

Orthodox Islam does not want to be identified with the Black Muslim movement in America. It is seen as heretical and is not considered part of Islam.

Elsewhere on this page you will read that (1) Black people are called raisin heads in the Hadith (2) Muhammad had black slaves and (3) he warned that dreams of black women meant disease was forthcoming!

The Hadith

This is another sacred book of Islam which Muslims claim is inspired. It's supposed to tell you what to do to get paradise and sundry other stuff. You must EARN Allah's forgiveness by following a bunch of rules and rituals. This stuff is indefensible:

- One of the major sins is not to protect oneself from urine. If you pee on yourself you go to hell, yet Muhammad ordered people to drink camel's milk and urine!
- You must not face Mecca when you are defecating. You must not use your right hand to

hold or wipe yourself. You must wash your private parts after going to the bathroom.
- Satan stays in the upper part of the nose all night (vol. 4, no. 516)
- Muhammad would spit so followers could smear it on their faces.
- Bad breath, having gas, and yawning are sins when done in Muhammad's presence - I don't think Allah was offended, I think it was Muhammad.
- Muhammad was superstitious and was afraid that evil spirits might enter his body while urinating or defecating. He was also afraid of a strong wind, and kissed and adored black stone in the Kabah. Muhammad thought that placing a green palm leaf on grave of the dead would lesson their pain as they died, and said clean your private parts with an odd number of stones. Believed that Jews were transformed into rats (vol. 4, nos. 524, 569 and chap. 32) and magic.
- Muhammad supposedly had the sexual strength of 30 men.
- There are no recorded miracles of Muhammad in the Quran but when followers saw Muhammad's inferiority to Jesus they started making some up in the Hadith: Muhammad cut the moon in half with a sword, a palm tree cried like a baby because Muhammad wouldn't preach under it, Muhammad made water flow out of his fingernails so that people could drink - the Hadith contradicts itself on how many supposedly people drank it. These "miracles" go on and on.
- Islam is to be primarily spread through the sword (but then again, how else can you get people to believe these fairy tales?). The best deed is to believe in Allah and his Apostle. The next best

thing is to participate in Jihad which is religious FIGHTING (vol. 1, no. 25). Murderous Muslims could take the property of people they killed during a Jihad.
- Anyone who leaves Islam must be killed (vol. 4, no. 260).
- Christians and Jews that don't embrace Islam go to hell.
- Women are deficient in intelligence and religion.
- Majority of people in hell are women (vol. 1, nos. 28, 301; vol. 2, no. 161)
- Child looks like the parent that had "discharge first" during intercourse.
- Stars created by Allah to throw at devils as missiles.
- Spirits eat dung and bones.

Muhammad was a sinner

The Hadith makes clear that Muhammad was a sinner - NOT sinless as some Muslims now claim:

"Muhammad replied..."O Allah, set me apart from my sins..."   vol. 1, no. 711

JESUS vs. Muhammad

Mohammed was the prophet of war

Christ is the Prince of Peace

[6] For unto us a child is born, unto us a son is given: and the government shall be upon his shoulder: and his name shall be called Wonderful, Counsellor, The mighty God, The everlasting Father, The Prince of Peace.

⁷ Of the increase of his government and peace there shall be no end, upon the throne of David, and upon his kingdom, to order it, and to establish it with judgment and with justice from henceforth even for ever. The zeal of the LORD of hosts will perform this.

Isaiah 9:6-7

Mohammed's disciples killed for the faith

Christ's disciples were killed for their faith

⁷ I have fought a good fight, I have finished my course, I have kept the faith:

2 Timothy 4:7

Mohammed promoted persecution against the "infidels"

Christ forgave delivered and converted the chief persecutor

¹³ Who was before a blasphemer, and a persecutor, and injurious: but I obtained mercy, because I did it ignorantly in unbelief.
¹⁴ And the grace of our Lord was exceeding abundant with faith and love which is in Christ Jesus.
¹⁵ This is a faithful saying, and worthy of all acceptation, that Christ Jesus came into the world to save sinners; of whom I am chief.

1 Timothy 1:13-15

Mohammed was the taker of life

Christ was the giver of life

²⁷ My sheep hear my voice, and I know them, and they follow me:

[28] And I give unto them eternal life; and they shall never perish, neither shall any man pluck them out of my hand.

John 10:27-28

Mohammed and his fellow warriors murdered thousands

Christ murdered none but saved many

[48] He that rejecteth me, and receiveth not my words, hath one that judgeth him: the word that I have spoken, the same shall judge him in the last day.

John 12:48

Mohammed's method was COMPULSION

Christ's aim was voluntary CONVERSION

[19] Repent ye therefore, and be converted, that your sins may be blotted out, when the times of refreshing shall come from the presence of the Lord.

Acts 3:19

Mohammed practiced FORCE

Christ preached FAITH

[29] Jesus answered and said unto them, This is the work of God, that ye believe on him whom he hath sent.

John 6:29

[35] And Jesus said unto them, I am the bread of life: he that cometh to me shall never hunger; and he that believeth on me shall never thirst.

John 6:35

Mohammed was a WARRIOR

Christ is The DELIVERER

²⁶ And so all Israel shall be saved: as it is written, There shall come out of Sion the Deliverer, and shall turn away ungodliness from Jacob:

Rom 11:26

¹³ Who hath delivered us from the power of darkness, and hath translated us into the kingdom of his dear Son:

Col. 1:13

¹⁰ And to wait for his Son from heaven, whom he raised from the dead, even Jesus, which delivered us from the wrath to come.

1 Thessalonians 1:10

Mohammed conquered his enemies with the sword

Christ conquered his enemies with another kind of sword, the sword of the Spirit which is the Word of God

¹² For the word of God is quick, and powerful, and sharper than any twoedged sword, piercing even to the dividing asunder of soul and spirit, and of the joints and marrow, and is a discerner of the thoughts and intents of the heart.

Hebrews 4:12

³⁷ Now when they heard this, they were pricked in their heart, and said unto Peter and to the rest of the apostles, Men and brethren, what shall we do?

Acts 2:37

Mohammed said to the masses, "Convert or die!"

Christ said, "Believe and live!"

[47] Verily, verily, I say unto you, He that believeth on me hath everlasting life.
John 6:47

[11] And Jesus took the loaves; and when he had given thanks, he distributed to the disciples, and the disciples to them that were set down; and likewise of the fishes as much as they would.
John 6:11

[25] And when they had found him on the other side of the sea, they said unto him, Rabbi, when camest thou hither?
[26] Jesus answered them and said, Verily, verily, I say unto you, Ye seek me, not because ye saw the miracles, but because ye did eat of the loaves, and were filled.
John 6:25-26

Mohammed was swift to shed blood

[15] Their feet are swift to shed blood:
[16] Destruction and misery are in their ways:
[17] And the way of peace have they not known:
Romans 3:15-17

Christ shed His own blood for the salvation of many

[7] In whom we have redemption through his blood, the forgiveness of sins, according to the riches of his grace
Ephesians 1:7

Mohammed preached "Death to the infidels!"

Christ prayed "Father, forgive them, for they know not what they do"

³⁴ Then said Jesus, Father, forgive them; for they know not what they do. And they parted his raiment, and cast lots.

Luke 23:34

Mohammed declared a holy war (Jihad) against infidels

Christ achieved a holy victory on Calvary's cross

¹⁴ Blotting out the handwriting of ordinances that was against us, which was contrary to us, and took it out of the way, nailing it to his cross;
¹⁵ And having spoiled principalities and powers, he made a shew of them openly, triumphing over them in it.

Colossians 2:14-15

and His followers share in that victory

³³ These things I have spoken unto you, that in me ye might have peace. In the world ye shall have tribulation: but be of good cheer; I have overcome the world.

John 16:33

Mohammed constrained people by conquest

Christ constrained people by love

¹⁴ For the love of Christ constraineth us; because we thus judge, that if one died for all, then were all dead:

2 Corinthians 5:14

Modern terrorists derive their inspiration from Mohammed and carry out their despicable atrocities in the name of his god

Christians derive their inspiration from the One who said, "Blessed are the peacemakers"

⁹ Blessed are the peacemakers: for they shall be called the children of God.

Matthew 5:9

Modern day disciples of Mohammed respond to the terrorist attacks by cheering in the streets

Modern day disciples of Christ are deeply grieved at past atrocities carried out by those who were "Christians" in name only (the Crusades, the Spanish Inquisition, etc.).

Many Muslims are peaceful and peace-loving because they do not strictly follow the teachings of their founder

Many Christians are peaceful and peace-loving because they do strictly follow the teachings of their Founder

¹⁷ Recompense to no man evil for evil. Provide things honest in the sight of all men.
¹⁸ If it be possible, as much as lieth in you, live peaceably with all men.
¹⁹ Dearly beloved, avenge not yourselves, but rather give place unto wrath: for it is written, Vengeance is mine; I will repay, saith the Lord.
²⁰ Therefore if thine enemy hunger, feed him; if he thirst, give him drink: for in so doing thou shalt heap coals of fire on his head.
²¹ Be not overcome of evil, but overcome evil with good.

Romans 12:17-21

Mohammed said the Koran is authoritative only in Arabic, and only in his dialect

The Bible is authoritative in many languages around the world, for God knows all things and can inspire (and preserve) His Word in more than one language.

Mohammed hated music

Jesus and His disciples sang hymns, and the Apostle commanded the Lord's Church to sing.

[30] And when they had sung an hymn, they went out into the mount of Olives.
Matthew 26:30

[19] Speaking to yourselves in psalms and hymns and spiritual songs, singing and making melody in your heart to the Lord;
Ephesians 5:19

[16] Let the word of Christ dwell in you richly in all wisdom; teaching and admonishing one another in psalms and hymns and spiritual songs, singing with grace in your hearts to the Lord.
Colossians 3:16

Mohammed allowed that a Mullah, Imam, or Mufti of Islam can be a terrorist and an amoral like Osama bin Laden.

The Bible requires that a leader in the Church of the Lord Jesus Christ must be above reproach, and when this is not true, Christians demand such a fallen leader be removed from leadership.

3 This is a true saying, if a man desire the office of a bishop, he desireth a good work.

² A bishop then must be blameless, the husband of one wife, vigilant, sober, of good behaviour, given to hospitality, apt to teach;
³ Not given to wine, no striker, not greedy of filthy lucre; but patient, not a brawler, not covetous;
⁴ One that ruleth well his own house, having his children in subjection with all gravity;
⁵ (For if a man know not how to rule his own house, how shall he take care of the church of God?)
⁶ Not a novice, lest being lifted up with pride he fall into the condemnation of the devil.
⁷ Moreover he must have a good report of them which are without; lest he fall into reproach and the snare of the devil.
1 Timothy 3:1-7

¹⁹ Against an elder receive not an accusation, but before two or three witnesses.
²⁰ Them that sin rebuke before all, that others also may fear.
1 Timothy 5:19-20

Islam calls on its followers to observe Five Pillars, while all other aspects of life can be vulgar and not affect the Muslim's prospects in Paradise.

The Bible calls on the Christian to submit to the total change of his life by the Spirit of God - NO area of life and/or thought is left to the choice of the follower.

12 I beseech you therefore, brethren, by the mercies of God, that ye present your bodies a living sacrifice, holy, acceptable unto God, which is your reasonable service.
² And be not conformed to this world: but be ye transformed by the renewing of your mind, that ye may prove what is that good, and acceptable, and perfect, will of God.
Romans 12:1-2

The Muslim looks forward to eternity in Paradise where there will be virgins who are used for eternal perpetual copulation.

The Bible believing Christian looks forward to being with Jesus Christ in total sinless, holiness, and is delighted with that.

[8] We are confident, I say, and willing rather to be absent from the body, and to be present with the Lord.
2 Corinthians 5:8

Mohammed said the witness of a woman was half the value of the witness of a man; and Muhammed said a woman goes to Paradise because she satisfies her husband sexually.

The Bible teaches that a husband is to love his wife and be willing to die for her.

[25] Husbands, love your wives, even as Christ also loved the church, and gave himself for it;
Ephesians 5:25

Mohammed called upon his servants to fight

Jesus said, "My kingdom is not of this world; if My kingdom were of this world, then would My servants fight . . . but now is My kingdom not from hence"

[36] Jesus answered, My kingdom is not of this world: if my kingdom were of this world, then would my servants fight, that I should not be delivered to the Jews: but now is my kingdom not from hence.
John 18:36

Mohammed ordered death to the Jews (see A. Guillaume, The Life of Muhammad, Oxford University Press (1975), p. 369)

Christ ordered that the gospel be preached "to the Jew first"

[16] For I am not ashamed of the gospel of Christ: for it is the power of God unto salvation to every one that believeth; to the Jew first, and also to the Greek.

Romans 1:16

The Koran says, "Fight in the cause of Allah" (Qu'ran 2.244)

The Bible says, "we wrestle not against flesh and blood" and "the weapons of our warfare are not carnal"

[12] For we wrestle not against flesh and blood, but against principalities, against powers, against the rulers of the darkness of this world, against spiritual wickedness in high places.

Ephesians 6:12

[2] Honour thy father and mother; which is the first commandment with promise;

Ephesians 6:2

[4] (For the weapons of our warfare are not carnal, but mighty through God to the pulling down of strong holds;)

Corinthians 10:4

The Koran says, "Fight and slay the Pagans wherever ye find them" (Qu'ran 9.5)

Hélèné Fulton

Christ said, "Preach the gospel to every creature"

¹⁵ And he said unto them, Go ye into all the world, and preach the gospel to every creature.

Mark 16:15

The Koran says, "I will inspire terror into the hearts of unbelievers" (Qu'ran 8.12)

God inspires His terror into the hearts of believers

¹³ Sanctify the LORD of hosts himself; and let him be your fear, and let him be your dread.

Isaiah 8:13

The Koran (Qu'ran) is a terrorist manual which condones fighting, conflict, terror, slaughter, and genocide against those who do not accept Islam

The Bible is a missionary manual to spread the gospel of peace to all in the world

¹⁵ And how shall they preach, except they be sent? as it is written, How beautiful are the feet of them that preach the gospel of peace, and bring glad tidings of good things!

Romans 10:15

Mohammed's Mission was to conquer the world for Allah

Christ's mission was to conquer sin's power and penalty by substitutionary atonement

²¹ For he hath made him to be sin for us, who knew no sin; that we might be made the righteousness of God in him.

2 Corinthians 5:21

¹⁸ For Christ also hath once suffered for sins, the just for the unjust, that he might bring us to God, being put to death in the flesh, but quickened by the Spirit:

1 Peter 3:18

Mohammed considered Christ a good prophet

Christ pronounced Mohammed to be a false prophet

¹⁰ The thief cometh not, but for to steal, and to kill, and to destroy: I am come that they might have life, and that they might have it more abundantly.

John 10:10

¹¹ And many false prophets shall rise, and shall deceive many.

Matthew 24:11

Mohammed claimed that there was but one God, Allah

Christ claimed that He was God

³⁰ I and my Father are one.
³¹ Then the Jews took up stones again to stone him.

John 10:30-31

⁵⁸ Jesus said unto them, Verily, verily, I say unto you, Before Abraham was, I am.
⁵⁹ Then took they up stones to cast at him: but Jesus hid himself, and went out of the temple, going through the midst of them, and so passed by.

John 8:58-59

¹⁸ Therefore the Jews sought the more to kill him, because he not only had broken the sabbath, but said also that God was his Father, making himself equal with God.

John 5:18

⁹ Jesus saith unto him, Have I been so long time with you, and yet hast thou not known me, Philip? he that hath seen me hath seen the Father; and how sayest thou then, Show us the Father?
John 14:9

Islam is geocentric, that is, the whole universe is centered on the Kaaba in the Grand Mosque in Mecca in Arabia, and all Muslims pray facing that direction

Jesus Christ is the center of all Christian worship and fellowship, for He is "in the midst" where his saints meet anywhere on earth.

²⁰ For where two or three are gathered together in my name, there am I in the midst of them.
Matthew 18:20

²² Ye worship ye know not what: we know what we worship: for salvation is of the Jews.
²³ But the hour cometh, and now is, when the true worshippers shall worship the Father in spirit and in truth: for the Father seeketh such to worship him.
John 4:22-23

Mohammed's Tomb: OCCUPIED!

Christ's tomb: EMPTY!

Islam must be received, or you can be killed for rejecting it.

The Faith offered by Jesus Christ is for "whosoever will" to receive, and all men are permitted to reject it.

[17] And the Spirit and the bride say, Come. And let him that heareth say, Come. And let him that is athirst come. And whosoever will, let him take the water of life freely.

Revelation 22:17

[16] For God so loved the world, that he gave his only begotten Son, that whosoever believeth in him should not perish, but have everlasting life.

John 3:16

Those who leave Islam are killed in most Islamic nations.

Those who leave the true Church of Jesus Christ are allowed to do so with no revenge.

Muhammed taught that you are allowed to live in any manner of wickedness you choose - as long as you die in a holy jihad for allah.

The LORD Jesus Christ teaches that unless you follow after peace (with ALL men), and holiness YOU WILL NEVER SEE THE LORD (for salvations' sake)

[14] Follow peace with all men, and holiness, without which no man shall see the Lord:

Hebrews 12:14

[11] Seeing then that all these things shall be dissolved, what manner of persons ought ye to be in all holy conversation and godliness,

2 Peter 3:11

Now, is a Muslim submitted to Allah and Islam because he loves Allah? NO! He dare not leave Islam, and he is loyal purely out of fear.

Hélèné Fulton

The true Bible believer is loyal to Jesus Christ purely out of love.

[18] **There is no fear in love; but perfect love casteth out fear**: because fear hath torment. He that feareth is not made perfect in love.

1 John 4:18

[19] We love him, because he first loved us.

1 John 4:19

We love him, because he first loved us.

This concept is 100% alien to Islam - There is no love in Islam - Only fear and hate.

Chapter 2: Satanism

Written By: Tanya Davey

Satan Thrown Out of Heaven

[7] "And war broke out in heaven: Michael and his angels fought with the dragon; and the dragon and his angels fought, [8] but they did not prevail, nor was a place found for them in heaven any longer. [9] So the great dragon was cast out, that serpent of old, called the Devil and Satan, who deceives the whole world; he was cast to the earth, and his angels were cast out with him.[10] Then I heard a loud voice saying in heaven, "Now salvation, and strength, and the kingdom of our God, and the power of His Christ have come, for the accuser of our brethren, who accused them before our God day and night, has been cast down. [11] And they overcame him by the blood of the Lamb and by the word of their testimony, and they did not love their lives to the death. [12] Therefore rejoice, O heavens, and you who dwell in them! Woe to the inhabitants of the earth and the sea! For the devil has come down to you, having great wrath, because he knows that he has a short time."

Revelation 12:7-12

Aleister Crowley and Anton LeVey may claim to be the founding "Fathers of modern Satanism" but exactly when and where Satanism first began can be debated at length. We can however identify satanic actions, activity and behaviour throughout history and even in the bible.

Satanism's roots and origins can be traced from different sources and philosophies throughout history. One such suspected root is the dualistic thinking of the Zoroastrian religion; a pre-Islamic religion from Iran / Persia, dating back as far as the 6th century B.C. Zoroastrian was founded by the Iranian prophet, Zarathustra. Zoroastrian is still practised in isolated areas of Iran but is more popular in India were the religion is commonly known as Parsiism.

A second historical root is Gnosticism. Gnosticism is a blend of Jewish monotheism, Babylonian astrology and Iranian dualism. Most Gnostic teachings were secret or were kept hidden (occult). Gnosticism says that the world was made by an imperfect spirit called the demiurge.

"The term occult means "hidden" or those things or teachings that is "unknown" or secret. The occult is the seeking after knowledge of unknown information, knowledge that is gained beyond the five senses. Therefore, knowledge is received by some supernatural involvement or connection." - **Satanism: The World of the Occult by Russ Wise.**

[1] "In the beginning God created the heavens and the earth."
Genesis 1:1

The world was created by God, a perfect God, as there is no darkness in Him.

[1] "In the beginning was the Word, and the Word was with God, and the Word was God. [2] He was in the beginning with God. [3]

All things were made through Him, and without Him nothing was made that was made."

1 John 1:1-3

[48] "Therefore you shall be perfect, just as your Father in heaven is perfect."

Matthew 5:48

[5] "This then is the message which we have heard of him, and declare unto you, that God is light, and in him is no darkness at all."

1 John 1:5

Another potential root, forming part of Satanists general consensus on their historical root is Sumerian from the 4th century BC with its god "Enki" or "EA".

Sumerian with its god "Enki" or "EA" was the first major attempt at a deity based religious system, and it was also the first to contain Satan.

Although they are not called Satanists, the rituals and acts performed in the bible among the Canaanites, for example, display characteristics or components of Satanic acts. People worshiped Satan under the names of "gods" like Baal and Molech. This included practices such as using children as human sacrifices, sacrificing the first-born from every marriage, animal sacrifices, prostitution and passing their children through fire. Canaanite sexual and homicidal rituals carried out on infants are used in satanic rituals.

> ²¹ And you shall not let any of your descendants pass through *the fire* to Molech, nor shall you profane the name of your God: I *am* the LORD.
>
> **Leviticus 18:21**

During the past centuries, satanic practices can be seen as far back as the 17th and 18th centuries. Rumours of Devil worship surfaced during witchcraft trials in the late 17th century, although there are no suggested organized and hierarchical satanic cults during that time. But this does not mean that they did not exist.

- Catherine dé Medici (1519-1589) was the Queen of France. She allegedly performed a Black Mass Ritual (described later) involving human sacrifice to save her sick son Phillip.
- Catherine Deshayes, also known as "La Voisin", was a French fortune teller, poisoner and an alleged sorceress. She was one of the chief public figures forming part of the "affaire des poisons / Affair of the Poisons", a major murder scandal in France which took place in 1677–1682 during the reign of King Louis XIV. Catherine Deshayes was said to have, not only participated, but also arranged Black Masses. Her clientele included the elite and even royals. Her clients prayed to the devil to fulfil their wishes. A noticeable custom that is still used in Black Mass today is a woman posing naked as an altar.
- Another is Maria de Naglowska (1883-1936) who was a Russian occultist, mystic, author and journalist who wrote and taught about sexual magical ritual practices. She established and led

an occult society known as the "Confrerie de la Flèche d'Or" (Brotherhood of the Golden Arrow) in Paris from 1932 to 1935. She referred to herself as "a satanic woman." One ritual (for which there exists a first-hand account) recalls that the ceremony included a naked Maria lying upon the altar and a male placing a cup / vessel upon her genitalia.

We can see from these accounts that there are striking resemblances or similarities that coincide with the Black Mass Rituals practised in history and those practised today.

Satanism is also connected to the Hell-Fire Club of the 18th century England, that was founded by Sir Francis Dashwood (1708-1781) and the Black Order of Germany in the 1920's and 1930's.

Ophite Cultus Satanas or Our Lady of Endor Coven was founded in Ohio by Herbert Arthur Sloane in 1948. This group was heavily influenced by Gnosticism. They worshiped Satanas, which was their name for Satan. Satan is defined in Gnostic terms as "the Serpent in the Garden of Eden who revealed the knowledge of the true god to Eve."

All of these practises were, in most part hidden from the public, but satanic practices went mainstream with the founding of The Church of Satan on April 30, 1966 by Anton LeVey.

Although some of these historical and biblical cases are not directly referred to as Satanism, it is fitting to apply the "the duck test" - If it looks like a duck, swims like a duck, and quacks like a duck, then it probably is a duck.

Traditions

A lot can be said about people's fear for witchcraft and occult-related activities but such fear cannot match the horrific images and blasphemous spirit that lends itself to Satanism. Satanists can be placed in a total different category than members of other false religions for the fact that they have made a conscious decision to worship Satan.

The very idea of worshipping Satan is the polar opposite of Christianity. Satanists see Christians as their arch nemesis. That is why it is so important for parents and law enforcement to understand the belief system, activities and symbolism of Satanism.

Satanism is a broad term referring to anyone whose worldview features a positive and approving interpretation or view of Satan. A Satanist is someone who sees Satan as a liberator, father and lord and who teaches that he is a good god. This is in complete contrast to what the Bible teaches us about who Satan really is. Satanists say that making the choice to serve Satan as god and lord of their lives, is one of the most rewarding, uplifting and fulfilling spiritual journeys they could ever take. **"The horned orders magical existence" by Brother Nero.**

Satan is a pride-filled being, initially created by God to serve God. However, like all of us, God also gave Satan a free will to choose. He chose to exercise that free will in the form of rebellion against God, causing him and a third of the angels to be cast out of heaven.

I sometimes wonder if we truly grasp the fact that Satan managed to convince a third of God's angels to rebel against Him. These angels were in heaven; they saw God each and every day; the magnificence; the almighty power that has no limits; the loving kindness that has no end but yet Satan was such a good liar and was so convincing, he managed to make a third of the angel's rebel. No wonder Satan can only be taken on through the Name and the power of Jesus, who made a mockery of Satan and his demons at the cross. Even when the archangel Michael was fighting with the devil over Moses' body all he said to the devil was "The Lord rebuke you!"

[18] "And He said to them, "I saw Satan fall like lightning from heaven."

Luke 10:17-2

[14] "I will ascend above the heights of the clouds; I will be like the Most High."

Isaiah 14:14

[9] "Yet Michael the archangel, in contending with the devil, when he disputed about the body of Moses, dared not bring against him a reviling accusation, but said, "The Lord rebuke you!"

Jude 1:9

The announcement made by Satan in Isaiah 14:14 tells us a great deal about the lies that exist at the very core of Satan and every one of his followers. He is a terrible, prideful, egotistical, self-centred, selfish being. He also succeeds in making his followers and worshippers just as prideful, egotistical, self-centred and selfish as he is. When you read about Satanism and the nature of Satanists you get a glimpse of the "heart" of Satan.

Satanism is a very brutal religion that is based on the belief that man is a naturally selfish and violent being. Rev Caesar 999's, the founder of the Church of The Antichrist 999, calls Satanists (in his version of the satanic bible), "Self Believers" and Satan the "god of self."

Satanism challenges the biblical teaching regarding man's relationship with others. They regard themselves as better than others and to them it is all about the "self" over the needs of other's. This self-indulgence contributes to the effort of empowering Satan to defeat the Creator, God, and to gain control of the world. They see God as a "spiteful, hateful monster and an attacker of human beings."

"Don't be concerned for your own good but for the good of others"

1 Corinthians 10:24

In Rev. Caesar 999's satanic bible, chapter 10, the question is asked; why shouldn't a Satanists every desire be fulfilled, why shouldn't every fantasy not come to life? They believe that their every need must and should be met!

In reality the God word talks about self-denial.

[24] "Then Jesus said to His disciples, "If anyone desires to come after Me, let him deny himself, and take up his cross, and follow Me."

Matthew 16:24

[9] "The heart is deceitful above all things, And desperately wicked; who can know it?"

Jeremiah 17:9

To Satanists, Satan is the very source of self-awareness, wisdom and freedom. He is the provider of power over oneself, others and outside situations. This power will permit them to live by whatever moral and ethical codes they wish to. Satan is the bearer and supplier of knowledge and he and his demons gives true understanding of a person's abilities and potential. Through Satan and his demons they believe they have the capability to think for themselves, develop their own intellect and to understand the universe and the world around them. Satanist believe that without all of this, they would be nothing more than mindless slaves to the Christian God. For this reason they not only respect and appreciate Satan, they worship him. Many Satanists do not call Satan by his name, and simply refer to him as "Master".

[7]"The fear of the Lord is the beginning of knowledge, but fools despise wisdom and instruction."

Proverbs 1:7

[13] "However, when He, the Spirit of truth, has come, He will guide you into all truth; for He will not speak on His own authority, but whatever He hears He will speak; and He will tell you things to come."

John 16:13

Satan is the giver of all things false, the only true wisdom and understanding comes from the Holy Spirit; we should ask Him. He will lead us in the spirit, truth and in the will of God. We are merely to ask and be willing to follow.

[2] "The Spirit of the Lord shall rest upon Him, The Spirit of wisdom and understanding, The Spirit of counsel and might, The Spirit of knowledge and of the fear of the Lord"

Isaiah 11:2-5

Spiritual / Theistic Satanists believe that their "Creator", Satan's original plan for their lives, is to take their Satanic knowledge and apply it for a "total transformation of their souls into godhead status."

Here we come across the first lie the devil caught Eve with in the Garden of Eden. The old lie of "human transformation into godheads," is still sadly used today. It worked on Eve in the garden and it still continues to work to this day. Satan has managed to fool millions of humans with the same lie for thousands of years.

[1] "Now the serpent was more cunning than any beast of the field which the Lord God had made. And he said to the woman, "Has God indeed said, 'You shall not eat of every tree of the garden'?"[2] And the woman said to the serpent, "We may eat the fruit of the trees of the garden; [3] but of the fruit of the tree which is in the midst of the garden, God has said, 'You shall not eat it, nor shall you touch it, lest you die.'"[4] Then the serpent said to the woman, "You will not surely die. [5] For God knows that in the day you eat of it your eyes will be opened, and you will be like God, knowing good and evil."[6] So when the woman saw that the tree was good for food, that it was pleasant to the eyes, and a tree desirable to make one wise, she took of its fruit and ate. She also gave to her husband with her, and he ate."

Genesis 3:1-6

Satanists are of the opinion that things Christians have traditionally considered or seen as "evil" may not be. They view God as a tyrant, and far more of an "evil" being than Satan. To them, God is the one who ordered the Israelites to slaughter all the Canaanites. In the New Testament, He is also said to punish people eternally for the sins of one "little" lifetime. In their opinion it is "good", even "heroic" and not "evil", for Satan to rebel against such a tyrant.

Let's take a look at some of the things Christians have traditionally considered "evil" and are perfectly acceptable or even encouraged by Satanists.

The Satanic Bible by Rev Caesar 999	**The Bible**
Prostitution	
"There is nothing wrong with sex and if you can	"[27]For a harlot is a deep pit, and a seductress is a

support yourself through having sex with others more power to you" "By making prostitution illegal violates their rights of religious freedom and their rights to capitalize off of their own bodies" "Prostitutes and other like them should be praised for their ingenuity, spirit and will to be free, by not buying into Christian prunist fanatical bullsh!t as it is a mental programming" Satanism's belief is that Christians have taken a prostitute, something that they see as being positive and beautiful which limks to ancient spiritual purity and "Twisted" it (the prostitute) into something negative. They believe Christianity turned a prostitute into a modern, degraded, dirty, filthy, diseased creature. It is also believed that Christians have turned words such as slut and whore into something ugly.	narrow well. 28 She also lies in wait as for a victim, and increases the unfaithful among men." **Proverbs 23:27-28** 3 " For the lips of an immoral woman drip honey, and her mouth is smoother than oil; 4 but in the end she is bitter as wormwood, Sharp as a two-edged sword. 5 Her feet go down to death, Her steps lay hold of hell." **Proverbs 5:3-5**
The Satanic Bible by Rev Caesar 999	**The Bible**
Homosexuality	

"Christians have built a social wall between them and gay people. Christians want to convert homosexuals in a diabolic tactic. Gays, lesbians and bisexuals, you are truly people of the self-god or Satan. Satan condones your sexual practices and will never teach against them"	[22] "You shall not lie with a male as with a woman. It is an abomination." **Leviticus 18:22** [13] "If a man lies with a male as he lies with a woman, both of them have committed an abomination. They shall surely be put to death. Their blood shall be upon them." **Leviticus 20:13** [26] "For this reason God gave them up to vile passions. For even their women exchanged the natural use for what is against nature. [27] Likewise also the men, leaving the natural use of the woman, burned in their lust for one another, men with men committing what is shameful, and receiving in themselves the penalty of their error which was due.[28] And even as they did not like to retain God in their knowledge, God gave them over to a debased mind, to do those things which are not fitting;" **Romans 1:26-28**
The Satanic Bible by Rev Caesar 999	**The Bible**
Drugs	
"We must legalize certain drugs, for there will always be drugs and a market to sell them to"	"God always requires our willing participation in obedience to His will, decision making, and revelation of His truth, our salvation and redemption, and even the manifestation of the gifts

	of the Holy Spirit. Satan is into mind control, not God" My Life 4 Jesus "For God hath not given us the spirit of fear; but of power, and of love, and of a **sound mind**." **2 Timothy 1:7**

Prostitution

Since Biblical times prostitution has been known as a way for woman to make money. It is probably one of the oldest professions known to man. God is not a man that utters words for no reason. He says in His word that prostitution is immoral and a sin. When He speaks it is because He is warning us about the immanent destructive danger lurking in the darkness. God forbids the involvement with prostitutes because He loves us and does not want to see us get hurt or destroyed. Getting involved, or even becoming a prostitute, is detrimental to men, women, marriages, families, and lives. There are physical, mental, emotional and spiritual aspects of sexual intercourse; it is not just a physical act where sexual tension is released. A sexual relationship can never simply be casual with no strings attached!

God says "when we commit sexual immorality, we are sinning against our own body" and this is where "ungodly soul ties" are formed. When you lie down with a prostitute or become one, each time you have sex outside of a marriage un-godly soul ties are formed; this is a spiritual principle according to
1 Corinthians 6:16.

Every time sexual intercourse takes place between two people they become one flesh and they are united in every possible way.

[16] "Or do you not know that he who is joined to a harlot is one body with her? For "the two," He says, "shall become one flesh."
1 Corinthians 6:16

"If you lie down with dogs, you get up with fleas"- Benjamin Franklin

According to 1 Thessalonians 5:23, man is made up of three parts: spirit, soul and body. Soul ties are intimate bonds made with another human being.

[23] Now may the God of peace Himself sanctify you completely; and may your whole spirit, soul, and body be preserved blameless at the coming of our Lord Jesus Christ.
1 Thessalonians 5:23

Each time you sleep with a prostitute or any person other than your marriage partner, you become joined to the person or people you have sex with. Your spirit, emotions, every aspect of your being is united with that person and un-godly soul ties are formed. Soul ties are exactly what they sound like. They are ties from one person's soul to another's.

When two people are separated after a sexual act, in the spiritual realm they have "become one flesh", parts of their souls may remain attached even after they go their separate ways. This is similar to two items being glued together and a residual portion of one of the two items inadvertently staying behind after separation. This is what prostitution and sex outside of marriage results in. Every time we partake in this we attach ourselves to all kinds of people through fornication and adultery and that is why so many of our lives are in such turmoil and we are not free to live for Jesus.

Significant emotional trauma and damage in our souls are associated with sexual immorality; this also includes the "solo" sex sins such as masturbation and pornography. Prostitution not only destroys the spirit and soul in such a way that it leads to physical and spiritual death but it also splinters personalities.

[18] "Flee sexual immorality. Every sin that a man does is outside the body, but he who commits sexual immorality sins against his own body."

1 Corinthians 6:18

God forbids involvement with prostitutes because He knows that such involvement is detrimental to both men and women. Sexual sin is a slippery slope which invariably leads to other sin. Remember, you are not doing God a favour by not sleeping around. God's instruction not to sleep around before marriage is for your own soul. God understands the implications in the spiritual world and what you may bring into your marriage when sleeping around if this is not dealt with before getting married.

Homosexuality

Hélèné Fulton

The Bible's view of homosexuality is not politically correct; the politically correct view is that if two people love each other why would they not have the right to marry? The reason is that it undermines the basis of God's created order where God made Adam, a man, and Eve, a woman, not two men or two women. The origins of homosexuality could be multiple. The belief that homosexuality may be genetic is false and unbiblical. People say "I did not choose my homosexual feelings". This may be true, but like any other thought that comes into the mind a person has the choice to act on them or to cast them down. You as a person have the choice to look at gay pornography, go to gay bars and to have sexual relationships with other men / woman. It is a person's own decisions. This therefore comes down to one thing "learned behaviour" which is sin.

[4] "For the weapons of our warfare are not carnal but mighty in God for pulling down strongholds, [5] casting down arguments and every high thing that exalts itself against the knowledge of God, bringing every thought into captivity to the obedience of Christ, [6] and being ready to punish all disobedience when your obedience is fulfilled."

2 Corinthians 10:4-6

The Bible doesn't refer to homosexuality all that often, but when it does it condemns it as sin. Unlike other sin, homosexuality carries a heavy judgment directed by God Himself on those who commit as well as support it. The judgment? Those who practice it are given over to their own desires which means that their hearts are hardened by their sins and they can no longer see the error of their way as seen in Romans 1:26-28. If they do not see their error they will not ask forgiveness. Without forgiveness they will die with their sins and face God's holy judgement.

There are now a total of sixteen countries worldwide that permit same-sex marriages; Netherlands, Belgium, Spain, Canada, South Africa, Norway, Sweden, Portugal, Iceland, Argentina, Denmark, France, Brazil, Uruguay, New Zealand and Britain. Britain has been the latest nation to do so, legalising same-sex marriages in England and Wales at midnight on 29 March 2014.

Two other countries have regional or court-directed provisions enabling same-sex couples to share in the freedom to marry; Mexico and the United States.

Andrea Williams, chief executive of Christian Concern, spoke to BBC news and said: "We can't just redefine an institution; redefine something that always has been because we say it's something that we want. This is actually very self-centred. This is not about rights; it's about seeking cultural dominance and seeking to redefine marriage for all of us."

The Archbishop of Canterbury, Justin Welby, said on Friday night "The Church of England would now drop its opposition to same-sex marriage, as Parliament had spoken." **BBC news UK 29 March 2014**.

Are we simply to delete this text from the Bible with a permanent marker because man says so? God is the ultimate being. No one is bigger, smarter, more powerful or more sovereign. So who gives man the authority to overrule the word of God and make what is called sin not a sin anymore, making the God given instruction null and void?

[25] "Because the foolishness of God is wiser than men, and the weakness of God is stronger than men."
1 Corinthians 1:25

Homosexuality is not a special practice that it is exempt from God's righteous judgment simply because man claims he / she is born that way. Every person or country that condones Homosexuality encourages people to stay trapped in sinfulness, and in this way they will reject Christ's redemptive work on the cross and without Jesus, they will have no forgiveness. Without forgiveness, they will have no salvation. Without salvation, there is only eternal damnation in hell. We don't want this for anyone. Only the power of God can set you free from the entrapments of sexual immorality.

As God intended the human body to be His holy temple, all forms of sexual immorality are detestable, rebellious acts against God. It is a powerful gateway into the demonic world. Satanists know very well that this type of sin permits possession by numerous strong demons and therefore sexual orgies and unspeakable vile sexual acts form the basis of the majority of the satanic rituals.

Satan constantly tries to violate the human body. Innocent children and animals are particularly vulnerable. Satan's plan is that the younger the child can be "damaged" the better. This is all in the effort to desecrate the human body as the temple of the Holy Spirit.

[18] "Flee sexual immorality. Every sin that a man does is outside the body, but he who commits sexual immorality sins against his own body. [19] Or do you not know that your body is the temple of the Holy Spirit who is in you, whom you have from God, and you are not your own? [20] For you were bought at a price; therefore glorify God in your body and in your spirit, which are God's."

1 Corinthians 6:18-20

Drug abuse is another serious moral problem in society today. Drugs bring about confusion and an altered state of mind. Anyone under the influence of drugs is not of a sound mind but is under the control of the drug. God says in 1Corinthians 14:33 that He is not the author of confusion. Drugs brings confusion and mind control.

Drugs and alcohol are always used by Satan to cloud and control the human mind. During drug and alcohol abuse many strong demons enters people, making it possible for the devil to use them in his service. God clearly forbids the abuse of mind-altering alcohol and drugs.

[18] "And do not be drunk with wine, in which is dissipation; but be filled with the Spirit, [19] speaking to one another in psalms and

hymns and spiritual songs, singing and making melody in your heart to the Lord"

Ephesians 5:18-19

Today a lot of modern music, movies, and TV programs glorify illegal drugs, such as marijuana. It is not even frowned upon any longer that marijuana is openly promoted at concerts, on CDs, even on clothes, indicating the acceptance of marijuana use as being socially accepted.

Many popular cultural shows and celebrities openly support drugs such as Marijuana; Danny DeVito, Susan Sarandon, Sting, Miley Cirrus and many other are pro the legalization of Marijuana.

Celebrities who have died as a result of a drug overdose

- Corey Monteith: At age 31 who played in the Glee TV series;
- Sid Vicious: The bassist for the punk rock band Sex Pistols;
- Dee Dee Ramone bassist and main songwriter of the punk rock band the Ramones;
- Kurt Cobain: The Nirvana frontman
- Peter Farndon founding member of the rock band The Pretenders
- Lenny Bruce: The standup comedian
- Jim Morrison: The Doors
- Billie Holiday: The jazz singer

- Paula Yates: The partner of INXS rocker Michael Hutchence
- Jimi Hendrix: Guitarist
- Hillel Slovak: founding member of the Red Hot Chilli Peppers
- Judy Garland: The superstar singer/actress
- Elvis Presley
- Chris Farley: comedian and actor
- John Belushi: The Animal House comedian
- Whitney Houston
- Corey Haim: The former child
- Janis Joplin: The legendary "Me and Bobby McGee" singer's manager
- Heath Ledger: actor
- Marilyn Monroe
- River Phoenix
- Dana Plato: The former "Diff'rent Strokes" child star
- Anna Nicole Smith
- Philip Seymour Hoffman: The Oscar-winning actor

In **Mary K Baxter "A Divine Revelation of the Spirit Realm"**, she relates a series of visions and revelations of the spirit world which God showed her. These particular visions are a powerful way of telling people what happens when someone gets addicted.

"A marijuana demon slipped a smooth rope around a beautiful young woman. At first the rope felt good to her. But the demon tightened the rope just a little. When she took another hit, he tightened the rope a little more. After a little while, I noticed that the smooth

tope had turned into a chain. Still, she could easily slip the chain on or off at this point. But as time passed, the chain got tighter and tighter. Finally, she could no longer take it off, and she was bound. The demon that did this to her wooed her and cajoled her, while all the time it was binding her and chaining her. Then the monster began tormenting her mercilessly." **Mary K Baxter with DR. T.L Lowery; A Divine Revelation of the Spiritual Realm pg. 156**

Every single sinner, including prostitutes, homosexuals, drug addicts and Satanists have the opportunity to receive salvation and eternal life from God, through His Son Jesus. Jesus did not die for a selected few; He died for every sinner past, present and future, to be cleansed of all their unrighteousness and be given a brand new life! Remember God does not hate the person, He hates the sin.

God even used a prostitute named Rahab in the fulfilment of His plan. As a result of her obedience, she and her family were rewarded and blessed (Joshua 2:1; 6:17-25). No person is beyond being saved by The Blood Of The Lam (Jesus Christ).

C. S. Lewis put the idea this way: "Merely to over-ride a human will (as His felt presence in any but the faintest and most mitigated degree would certainly do) would be for Him useless. He cannot ravish. He can only woo." by **Robin Schumacher the confidant Christian**

There might be certain aspects of Satanist groups that differ in some way from one another, but one of the biggest similarities (that stands out) is the hatred for mankind and a distinct dislike or distaste for anything Christian. They have a distaste for Christ, the Bible or the truth which can vary from a general dislike or distain to an absolute anger and hatred towards Christianity, Christ and God that can surpasses human hatred.

Satanists believe that Christianity is a form of mind control and that Christians are "deluded" beings because of our belief and faith in Christ, Son of God.

Firstly, God is a loving God and love means freedom of choice. He will never force Himself on anyone! The choice is yours, He will never drag a person kicking and screaming into His kingdom and He will never violate your freedom of choice. No mind control is needed in Christianity.

Secondly, Satanists claim that Christianity is mind control which is an absolute contradictions when compared to Satanism. Satanists claims to be all about "Do What Thou Wilt" and "Without Satan Satanists would be mindless slaves." But Satanism is all about the abuse of a person's will and mind control. They will search for ways to over-ride a person's will to make it ineffective.

Mind control is a known tactic used by Satanists to over-ride a person's will and to control their minds without them knowing. This happens because of the mind's ability to separate the conscious and the unconscious. It is possible to install mind-control in an unconscious mind without the person knowing or being aware of it.

Satanists use mind-control to gain absolute control over individuals or groups. Through this they become mindless, will less slaves. Through mind control Satanists create a world of illusion to protect "secrets" from the outside world and other groups; secrets such as children being tortured and human sacrifices that are carried out.

Within the satanic order individuals are not respected, only power is. Through mind control power can actually be installed into children and people. This increased power can allow the body of an individual to endure more pain and survive torture. It can even increase human capabilities such as slowing down respiration or heartbeat and enhance mental alertness.

They implement mind-control to smother a child's ability to think on their own. This is where Satanist contradicts themselves and show themselves to be liars, just like their father. They believe that through Satan and his demons they have the capability to think for themselves and develop their own intellect which is yet another contradiction to what really goes on in Satanism. They want people to be mindless slaves. Independent thinking is like a plague in the groups that employ programming. No child or person should challenge or question the group's theology.

Satanists are of the opinion that the only thing pure about Christianity is our stupidity. This is on the top of the list of Satanic Sins and the Cardinal Sin of Satanism. "It's too bad that stupidity isn't painful. Ignorance is one thing, but our society thrives increasingly on stupidity. It depends on people going along with whatever they are told. The media promotes a cultivated stupidity as a posture that is not only acceptable but laudable. Satanists must learn to see through the tricks and cannot afford to be stupid."
Anton Szandor LaVey; The Nine Satanic Sins.

They refer to Jesus, as "The Nazarene". Everything that the Bible tells us about who Jesus is and how He is described in the bible is exactly what is despised and seen as weak and is the exact opposite of what Satanist aspire to be. Satanist furthermore rejects the reality of sin. This means they will not acknowledge their need for a saviour, so no need for Jesus.

"Behold the crucifix; what does it symbolize? Pallid (feeble) incompetence hanging on a tree" The book of Satan II

In fact Satanists claims that Jesus is a fictitious character that is a result of "stolen" ideas from the Pagan legend Odin. Odin was the main Norse Viking god who was, first and foremost, a powerful wizard. He sacrificed one of his eyes in order to gain supreme knowledge and also hung himself from the World Tree, Yggdrasil, for nine nights without food or drink and with a spear in his side to gain the knowledge and power of the Runes.

But why so much hate and distrust by Satanists and the world towards Jesus? The reason; once He came down to earth they knew there was no more hiding their sins. Satanists are individuals who are deceived and ill-informed about the Christian faith and about our loving, caring, merciful God.

In the book **"Satanism a beginners guide to the religious worship of Satan Vol1"**… it is explained to a teenager what he / she needs to do in an instance where and when they get "forced" to go to church by their parents; they should "anoint" themselves and ask Satan and his demons to protect them against the Holy Spirit. He continues to say that they should turn this negative experience into an opportunity to learn as much about the "enemy" as possible.

We can see hear how blinded they are by Satan's lies and that they have demonic seals over their spiritual senses to prevent them from coming to the truth and being set free.

[3] But even if our gospel is veiled, it is veiled to those who are perishing, [4] whose minds the god of this age has blinded, who do not believe, lest the light of the gospel of the glory of Christ, who is the image of God, should shine on them.

2 Corinthians 4:3-4

"And the judgment is based on this fact: God's light came into the world, but people loved the darkness more that the light, for their actions were evil. And who does evil hates the light and refuses to go near it for fear their sins will be exposed."

John 3:19-22

Currently there are at least four categories that we can place Satanists in. These groups' beliefs and rituals vary greatly within each group and sometimes even from individual to individual.

1. **Religious Satanist or Organized Satanism**: These are Satanists belonging to organized and legal Satanic Churches. They are members of organizations or structured groups like the Church of Satan, Temple of Set etc. These organisations receive the same tax exempt status as mainstream religious institutions.

2. **Self-Styled Satanist / Independent Satanists:** They are quite different. The vast majority of Satanists are self-styled and self-directed, meaning that they put together their own system and act upon their own will. They are not connected to any satanic sect. They are rogue and solitary people who are often involved in crimes such as child molestation, rape, torture and murder. Usually these people are loners who are unable to relate to people in a normal healthy fashion and practise their faith alone. Some do practise their faith in a small group, but these groups generally have no leaders or structure to turn to for instruction and advice. Inspiration must be found through research, study and practice. This offers the Satanist a lot of freedom to have whatever eclectic practices they consider necessary. They feel they can identify with the ultimate outsider, Satan.

People who fall into this category are people like Ted Bundy, the "Night Stalker" Richard Ramirez and Clifford Snt Joseph.

At Richard Ramirez's (better known as the "Night Stalker") first court appearance, he raised his hand with a pentagram drawn on it and yelled, "Hail, Satan." He was convicted on 13 counts of murder. He left satanic symbols at the scenes of his crimes, carving a pentagram on one of his victims and on the bedroom wall of another. In Ramirez's formal statement at his death sentence hearing, he said "Legions of the night, I will be avenged. Lucifer dwells within us all."

Ramirez was one of many deceived people who believed the lies of Anton LaVey's assertion in the Satanic Bible; that Satanists could reign in hell. Ramirez believed his human sacrifices to Satan would earn him a place as a ruler in hell.

His reaction after receiving 19 death sentences… "Big deal. Death always went with the territory. See you in Disneyland."
Ramirez died at the age of 53 in a hospital of liver failure on Friday, June 7th 2013. He has been on death row awaiting execution since the trial ended in 1989.

In San Francisco, Clifford Snt Joseph, was found guilty of murdering a man during a satanic ritual. The victim's body was mutilated with a pentagram carved into his chest, sexually abused and the body drained of all its blood.

3. **"Dabbler" / Youth Subculture Satanist:** The majority in this group are teenagers and sadly the age bracket is becoming younger and younger. A couple of years ago the targeted age group were children in their teens whereas now within this group, children twelve years and younger can often be found. To Satan the younger the child the more impressionable the mind. Within this group one finds teens that feel rejected and alienated from family, disregarded by society and labelled as an outcast. The majority of these dabblers have not been appropriately socialised, making Satanism a very attractive option. Dabblers are often in extreme rebellion and have problems with authority. To them Satan becomes their "god" of rebellion. He is in essence the personification and the father of rebellion. Many of the dabblers lack a good family support system and have low self-esteem. They are in search of a feeling of belonging and self-worth; the need to be somebody. They are easy pickings for satanic recruiters. What a shame for these lives to be lost in this way.

   Generally, they lack a well-developed theology. They take most of their beliefs from information found on the internet, various books, pop culture, depictions of Satanism, and even from Christian tracts about Satanic evil (all the better to shock their parents, teachers, and pastors with), combined with an unhealthy dose of teen angst. At first dabblers will often be involved in petty crimes such as vandalism, although occasionally, they have been linked to more serious criminal activity, including property theft, assault, and the murdering of animals, including pets. Aleister Crowley killed his first animal at the age of eleven. Dabbling in Satanism opens doors for Satan and demons to enter people's lives and although some dabblers may "grow" out of Satanism by the time they reach their twenties, others become deadly disciples. They can be extremely dangerous because of their individually constructed satanic rituals.

Experts agree that, given several cases seen, dabblers can become brutal killers. One such a case was Elyse Pahler who was murdered by three teenagers.

"Fifteen year old Elyse Pahler's body was discovered near her home in Arroyo Grande, California in March 1996. She had been raped and murdered by acquaintances Jacob Delashmutt, Joseph Fiorella and Royce Casey. The perpetrators apparently returned to the corpse and had sex with it on several occasions. The body was located after Casey confessed to the crime following his conversion to Christianity. All three eventually pleaded no contest to her murder and are now imprisoned and serving 25 years to life. The trio had lured Elyse from her house with the stated intention of killing her as part of a satanic ritual. Although the crime bears many of the hallmarks of similar sexually motivated murders. In their defence, the defendants said they had needed to commit a "sacrifice to the devil" in order to give their heavy metal band, Hatred, the "craziness" to "go professional".- **Read more about this murder of Elyse Pahler From Wikipedia, the free encyclopaedia**.

"Most of what brings this stuff on is people dabbling in the occult,"- Professor Carl Raschke of University Denver - Article: "Satanic "dabbler" can become deadly disciples" by Rob Johnson. Posted June 13, 1993A

4. Traditional or Hard core Satanists (Generational Satanists)

These are Satanist that are born in to a generational line of Satanists. They are Satan's thoroughbreds or the "special forces." They are born and raised into Satanism and are also known as "hereditaries". They have grown up within the ideology of the satanic coven. Their ancestral roots are traced back to England and Europe and are connected to "old money". They are definitely not your average "Jo" on the street. You will not find them dressed in black, head shaven, body pierced and tattooed. They are the elite and in some cases even hail from aristocratic lines. They are more likely to be the pillars of the community or even present themselves as Christians.

But like a definite undercurrent they know who they are and are exactly aware of their place in Satan's plan.

It is in these multi-generational satanic families that a lot of SRA (Satanic Ritual Abuse) takes place. Whilst growing up, and because of some obscure reason of occult doctrine (such as birth order, astrology chart etc.), some children are abused in the most horrific ways and other children are brought up pampered, trained and thought to regard themselves as "gods". This can happen within the same family, where one child is abused and the sister or brother is pampered.

What is Satanic Ritual Abuse?

"Ritual abuse can be defined as emotional, physical and sexual abuse done in combination with the performance of rites that are normally part of a belief system and worship of a deity"

1.　Ritual abuse is a very different form of the abuse of a child or non-consenting adults. The abuse can be mental, physical, emotional, spiritual and / or sexual. It is an extremely sadistic form of abuse which often includes mind control, torture, murder, child pornography and prostitution. Basic human values are destroyed and the abusers in return train and indoctrinate their own distorted belief system.

2.　Its purpose is to deepen the silence of the already desperately battered individual who is often a powerless, poor, young and innocent individual. The victim's ritual abuse is about secrecy, power and total control.

3.　Often the victims are programmed to commit suicide in the event of revealing information or secrets about rituals, organizations and leaderships within the cult.

4.   Although we might not know if these different groups are connected in the physical world they will most certainly be connected in the spiritual fight.
As in many different religions there are also different denominations within Satanism. These groups are called covens, grottoes or pylons. Every organisation / denomination defines "Satanism" in different ways. Being a left hand path and an individualistic religion, especially when it comes to morals and rules, Satanists are advised by Anton LeVey through the satanic bible that Satanists should have the ability to decide for themselves what is just and what is right or wrong in life. This in itself can cause beliefs to differ greatly among Satanists. What's more is that there are very few absolutes or universals in or among Satanists and Satanism.

"The Satanist (……) should have the ability to decide what is just" Satanic Bible by Anton LaVey (1969)

Satanic groups that appeared after 1960 are widely diverse and groups vary from Atheistic Satanism all the way up to worshiping Satan as a powerful, controlling and VERY REAL DEITY in the form of Theistic Satanism. Within these groups a number of different branches or levels exist. Within these different denominations Satanism's definition is bitterly fought over but customs, rules, regulations and even styles of worship can vary greatly.

Although many of these cults are less known and publicized they none the less remain very powerful. Some groups are small while others are very large and powerful and have very influential people as part of their organization. Some of the bigger, more powerful groups / cults, are in control of the smaller groups and these controlling groups are very secretive. Someone would never know of their existence unless the specific group would want it known. Satanist could spend a life-time in a particular group without knowing that they were directly or indirectly being controlled by another organization / group or cult.

In these Cults you have various levels, allowing you to progress into higher, deeper and more powerful levels of Satanism. The deeper and more powerful the levels become, the more secretive and firmer the discipline and rules become. If any of the creeds or rules are broken, there are always consequences.

Atheistic Satanism

LaVeyan Satanism (Church of Satan)

LaVeyan Satanism is probably the most well-known branch of Satanism. LaVeyan Satanists claim to be atheists, agnostics or apatheists who are adamant that their reliance and dependence are on the "self" rather than putting their faith on any outside power. They have taken their name from the Creator of the Church of Satan and the author of one of the Satanic Bibles, Anton Szandor LaVey. They are a very "selfish" group, and have no problems being called "selfish" or even "self-centred". It is an individualistic, self-indulgenced "eye for an eye" type of Satanism. To these Satanists it's not about worshiping the devil as much as it is about worshiping oneself as the centre of one's own universe, while seeking earthly success and power. They regard Satan only as a symbol of man's inherent nature; an imaginary character that represents the reality of the "Beast in Man".

[14] "But if you have bitter envy and self-seeking in your hearts, do not boast and lie against the truth. [15] This wisdom does not descend from above, but is earthly, sensual, demonic. [16] For where envy and self-seeking exist, confusion and every evil thing are there."

James 3:14-16

LaVeyan Satanism is a "small religious group that is unrelated to any other faith, and whose members feel free to satisfy their urges responsibly, exhibit kindness to their friends, and attack their enemies."

"If you love only those who love you, why should you get credit for that? Even sinners love those who love them and if you do good to those who do good to you, why should you get credit? Even sinners do that much! Love your enemies! Do good to them."

Luke 6:32-33; 35

This is a big debate amongst Satanists themselves. (Regarding Satan as a real deity or not) In the Book **Satanism: "A Beginner's Guide to the Religious Worship of Satan Vol 1"** Brother Nero states the following: "Practicing Satanism without developing a relationship with Satan and the other Demonic Spirits is like drinking beer without the alcohol. What's the point? You get nothing out of it."

Anton LaVey deceived a lot of people by promoting a "watered down" version of Satanism to all the ignorant masses. Although LaVey proclaimed that Satan was only a representation of the forces of nature and not a real deity, he acknowledged to his most trusted inner circle in the Church of Satan exactly the opposite….

Susan Atkins: a former associate of Anton LaVey, who spent personal time with him, told Pastor Joe Schimmel in a personal interview, "Anton told me as a Satanist he does believe in the God of the Bible but he refused to worship Him and made a conscious decision to worship Satan instead." LaVey admitted that the image that he presented publicly was deceptive, declaring: "If they're at all intelligent (other true Satanist)…they'll realize that there's only so much I can say publicly…I will not advance things in print which make my position untenable….How long would the Church of Satan have lasted if I hadn't appeased and outraged in just the right combination? It required a certain amount of discretion and diplomacy to balance the outrage." **Lucifer Rising, P 133**

Michael Aquino said that Anton would at times refer to Satan as "the man downstairs". Church of Satan member Ed Webber replied to the question of LaVey believing in Satan as symbolic or literal replying: "Not at all. He was quite definitive that he did believe in the existence of Satan. This is what made the concept of a Church of Satan so fascinating."
Satanists who are denying a literal Satan is a smokescreen that demon-possessed- people use to

deceive others. Anton LaVey worshipped and lived for a very real and literal Devil.

Is anyone really surprised that the founder of the Church of Satan and self-proclaimed "Black Pope" is a deceiver and a lair? Anton LaVey deceived a lot of people who joined the Church of Satan. Or is anyone surprised that the devil, and the father of lies, disguises his religion so that people don't think they are literally serving Satan? This is how he has, and continues to; successfully deceive so many people into believing that they are simply worshipping a "symbol" rather than the literal devil or SATAN himself. He is probably laughing his head off. He relishes in such ignorance. LaVey himself was severely deceived as he stated in his Satanic Bible that he would reign with Satan in hell. To those Satanists that proclaim not serving and worshiping Satan as a true being, cannot deny they are serving, magnifying or exalting whatever is defined as Satan.

[9] So the great dragon was cast out, that serpent of old, called the Devil and Satan, who deceives the whole world; he was cast to the earth, and his angels were cast out with him.

Revelation 12:9

Revelation 12:9 tells us that Satan is the one deceiving the whole world and this is exactly what is happening every day, even within Satan's own namesake religion. The lower level Satanists do not realize the evilness and intentions among their own inner circle of Satanists; this inner circle of Satanists only views the lower level Satanists as measly puppets or pawns to be used and discarded. A lot of Satanists are deceived in this very way, especially the leaders or the inner circle of the church of Satan, who believe that when they die they will have some "honorary" position in his kingdom. Satan views every single Satanist as a disposable pawn that will be discarded the moment that they die or when his need for them comes to an end. There is no doubt this will happen. He is the ultimate user and an abuser with tons of strings attached and at the end will discard every single one of them into the pits of hell.

*In Her book A Divine Revelation of Hell" God gave Mary K. Baxter visions of hell and asked her to tell all that she saw that hell is a real place and that God is asking people to choose life. Whilst in hell during one of her visits, Jesus and Mary arrived at the cell of a witch. While she lived on earth she chose to serve Satan, selling her soul to him. Not only did she practise witchcraft, but taught it to. The Witch gained great favour with Satan knowing exactly how to use the kingdom of darkness's power to her and Satan's advantage. After the woman died she went straight to hell and asked Satan for the kingdom he had promised her. And this is what happened: "But at last, Satan had laughed and scorned her. He told her, "I deceived you and used you all those years. I will never give you my kingdom." **A Divine Revelation of Hell" Mary K. Baxter. pg. 93 paragraph 2.***

"Oh, yes, "Satan said, "you did serve me well on earth. You brought me more than 500 souls." He lied and said to her, "Your punishment will not be as bad as the

*other." **"A Divine Revelation of Hell"** - **Mary K. Baxter. pg 93 paragraph 4.***

The bible makes it clear that Hell was created as a place of torment for Satan and his angels. When this once powerful fallen angel is rendered powerless by the Almighty God, as one of the weakest beings in the universe, his followers will scorn, and ridicule him. All those who were once deceived by him will mock him.

"Better to reign in Hell, than to serve in Heaven." John Milton, Paradise Lost

Theistic Satanism

This group is also known as Traditional Satanists, Spiritual Satanists or Devil worshipers. They are lot more secretive and great emphasis is put on the spiritual aspects of Satanism. Theistic Satanists revere and worship Satan as a supernatural deity / god and openly admit doing so.

Theistic Satanism is also not just one single religion. It is a group of religions and spiritualities with a common feature of revering Satan in one way or another. Some are pantheistic, some are polytheistic, and some are Gnostic-based, among others.

Their basic belief is that there are two gods that are mirror images in all aspects and that they are in an eternal conflict to rule the world. Satanists believe that the two gods are unendingly powerful and determined.

They believe that these twin gods created the world together.

They see one god as good and one as bad and, as stated previously, the definition of what is good and what is bad depends on the opinion the person has of the god. According to this believe both gods are vehemently trying to convince humanity that he is good and the other god is evil.

The only truth about this theology is that God and Satan are completely opposite in the aspect of good against bad, and that is where it ends. There is and will always be Only One God and only He and He alone is the sole creator of heaven and earth. Evil does exist but there is no other god that is in opposition to the Almighty. No god that could ever be placed as a mirror image to the God of Abraham, Isaac and Jacob.

[6]"Thus says the Lord, the King of Israel, And his Redeemer, the Lord of hosts: 'I am the First and I am the Last; Besides Me there is no God."

Isaiah 44:6

[5]"I am the Lord, and there is no other; There is no God besides Me. I will gird you, though you have not known Me,"

Isaiah 45:5

[21]"Tell and bring forth your case; Yes, let them take counsel together. Who has declared this from ancient time? Who has told it from that time? Have not I, the Lord? And there is no

other God besides Me, A just God and a Savior; There is none besides Me.

Isaiah 45:21

Fact… Satan is a creation and not a creator, whom was defeated at the cross, PERIOD.

[13]"You were in Eden, the garden of God; Every precious stone was your covering: The sardius, topaz, and diamond, Beryl, onyx, and jasper, Sapphire, turquoise, and emerald with gold. The workmanship of your timbrels and pipes was prepared for you on the day you were created.
[14] "You were the anointed cherub who covers; I established you; You were on the holy mountain of God; You walked back and forth in the midst of fiery stones. [15] You were perfect in your ways from the day you were created, till iniquity was found in you."

Ezekiel 28:13-15

[15]"Having disarmed principalities and powers, He made a public spectacle of them, triumphing over them in it."

2 Colossians 2:15

To be a Theistic Satanist a person is required to have had a profound spiritual experience involving Satan and to regard Christian theology, or at least some aspects of it, as absurd.

Theistic Satanists believes that Satan is someone who relates to human beings. They feel that he encourages them to be true to themselves, think for themselves, to excel at whatever their talents may be and to do what they need to do in order to better their material situation. They feel that he accepts them exactly the way they are…and does not need them to change.

This is what God says about material possessions…

[19] "Do not lay up for yourselves treasures on earth, where moth and rust destroy and where thieves break in and steal; [20] but lay up for yourselves treasures in heaven, where neither moth nor rust destroys and where thieves do not break in and steal. [21] For where your treasure is, there your heart will be also.
Matthew 6:19-21

[10] "For the love of money is a root of all kinds of evil, for which some have strayed from the faith in their greediness, and pierced themselves through with many sorrows."
1 Timothy 6:10

Let us rather gather treasures up in heaven.

One of the Theistic Groups was formed by Michael Aquino, who was initially a leader in Anton LaVey's Church of Satan. He left to begin his own satanic order called the Temple of Set (another name for Satan). He took a number of LaVey's followers with him, even attracting the likes of Anton's daughter Zeena LaVey.

Michael Aquino was such a rabid, hard core Satanists he even tattooed the number "666" on his scalp and openly admitted serving Satan as a god on television.

[7] " Do not be deceived, God is not mocked; for whatever a man sows, that he will also reap. [8] For he who sows to his flesh will of

the flesh reap corruption, but he who sows to the Spirit will of the Spirit reap everlasting life."

Galatians 6:7-8

Organizations

Church of Leviathan: The Church of Leviathan was founded by Robert Fraize, and has been recognised as a Religious Organization since June 6, 2012, in the state of Massachusetts, USA. This church is a crossroads of all Occult spiritual faiths and the majority of their members are Theistic Satanists. The Church of Leviathan recognizes "the dragon" as the one true deity and their mission is to serve and teach the spiritual occult community.

[7] "And war broke out in heaven: Michael and his angels fought with the dragon; and the dragon and his angels fought, [8] but they did not prevail, nor was a place found for them(a) in heaven any longer. [9] So the great dragon was cast out, that serpent of old, called the Devil and Satan, who deceives the whole world; he was cast to the earth, and his angels were cast out with him."

Revelation 12:7-12

Church of Satanic Brotherhood: They believe that Satan is more of a concept and not a literal deity. They say they are realist and not idealists. He is seen as a life attitude representing humanity's true nature. They believe that seeking knowledge and truth is important, and that one should live for the here and now and not what might happen after death. This is a church for people who are more interested in indulgence rather than denying themselves anything. To them kindness are only for those who deserve it and that a person should not waste time and effort on those that don't deserve it. They believe strongly in the "The Nine Satanic Sins" of Anton LeVay.

[44] "But I say to you, love your enemies, bless those who curse you, do good to those who hate you, and pray for those who spitefully use you and persecute you, [45] that you may be sons of your Father in heaven; for He makes His sun rise on the evil and on the good, and sends rain on the just and on the unjust. [46] For if you love those who love you, what reward have you? Do not even the tax collectors do the same?"
Matthew 5:44-46

Cult of Cthulhu: This a legally recognized religion in the United States and was established in 2008 by High Priest Venger, who is also known as Darrick Dishaw. "Cthulhu Cult is the integration of H.P. Lovecraft's Cthulhu Mythos, Satanism, Chaos Magic, the Fourth Way, and other Left Hand Path traditions.

"It is also the fruition of my special plan: to see this world's flaws, to understand why they exist, and then finally... to overcome them"- Venger Satanis, Cult of Cthulhu Bible.

Cultus Diabolus/ Orthodox Satanism: This is a Traditional Satanic group and dedicated to the worship of Satan as their deity. It is a relatively new group and was established on October 31st 2009 by High Priest LaBolt and High Priestess Sinister. For a person to join this group, they need to be committed to Satan. The founders of this group were the "Official Florida Coven / Chapter" of the Cathedral of the Black Goat.

They dissolved their affiliation with the Cathedral of the Black Goat on July 20th 2012. The leadership of Cultus Diabolus is called "The Unholy Trinity".

First Satanic Church: The First Satanic Church was formed by Karla LaVey, Anton LaVey's daughter on October 31st 1999, and founding members of the Church of Satan. After Anton LaVey's death in 1997 the church of Satan came under new administration and its headquarters were moved to New York City. Karla LaVey, felt this was a disservice to her father's legacy and she re-formed the Satanic Church in San Francisco, California. She continues to run it in the same way her father had run the organization. The First Church of Satan follows the teaching of Aleister Crowley rather than the teachings of Anton LeVey.

Magistry of the Black Goat: This is a relatively new satanic group that claim they are advancing the faith in Satan.

Magnum Opus Coven: This group stands on the belief that Satan is an actual deity, and not just an idea. They know demons are real and that they manifest themselves in a human form. They believe in personal divinity and believe that a Satanist is a god!! They believe that the weak will always be abused by the strong and that self-help for the weak is the only remedy for this injustice; those deserving of kindness should be shown kindness. Guilt and shame have no place in the life of a Satanist, they are merely tools of the Judeo-Christian establishment. Satanic magic is real and powerful and an awesome tool to be used by the Satanist. They believe in the Nine Satanic Statements authored by Anton LaVey.

The Order of Nine Angles: This group "represent a dangerous and extreme form of Satanism". This group first attracted public attention during the 1980s and 1990s after being mentioned in books detailing fascist Satanism. Presently, the ONA is organized around clandestine cells named "traditional nexions" and around what is called "sinister tribes".

The Church of Satan: This was formed by Anton Szandor LaVey on Walpurgisnacht, April 30, 1966. LaVey proclaimed that night as the beginning of the Satanic Era or the first day of the year of Satan "anno Satanas". The Church of Satan is probably one of the most well-known satanic organisations in the world. The church encouraged its congregation to discover, use and expand all their abilities and talents without being limited by conservative ideas of decent behaviour. Church of Satan's worship is based on the belief that people need rituals, doctrine, fantasy and enchantment. They encourage free love and experimentation with drugs. They believe that this church is the symbol which best suits the nature of who people really are and to them Satan represents pride, liberty, and individualism; qualities often defined as Evil by those outside of satanic churches. Power to regulate members is in the hands of the Head of the Church. To become an active member of the church of Satan requires you to be already doing something to advocate Satanism.

The Temples of Satan / The Temple of Set: This is a left-hand path initiatory order consecrated and founded in Santa Barbara, California during the summer solstice of June 1975, by Michael A. Aquino. This group was established by certain members of the priesthood of the Church of Satan. These members left the Church of Satan because of administrative and philosophical disagreements with its founder Anton LaVey. Temple of Set claims to be the world's leading left-hand path religious organization. Newcomers take the title "Setian". In 2007 this organisation claimed to have 200 members. The belief system in general is referred to as Setianism. In theory Setianism is similar to theistic Satanism. The Temple of Set has developed in a more Crowleyan direction, basing its spiritual inspiration and belief on Set the Egyptian god of evil. Temple of Set deliberately sets out to separate themselves from The Church of Satan in several ways. One of the most significant or noticeable ways is in religion and sociology. The philosophy of the Temple of Set may be summed up as "enlightened individualism" or an enhancement and improvement of oneself by personal training, experimenting and initiation. This process is certainly different and unique for each individual. The members differ on their opinion of Satan or Set as being "real" or not, but they are not expected or required to have the same opinion. Members of the Temple of Set are mostly male, between the ages of twenty and fifty.

The Satanic Temple: This is a Theistic Satanic group that was founded in 2000 and is based in New York. This group represents a variety of Satanists that uses the literal Satan as a mythic foundation. The Satanic Temple desires to actively participate in public affairs and provide outreach to the wider public. This has manifested in several public political actions and efforts at lobbying, with a focus on the separation of Church and State. The only requirements to be a member are to support the tenets and beliefs of the organization, and to name yourself a member.

THE ORDO TEMPLI ORIENTIS (OTO): This is the best-known of the hard-core, British-based Satanist cults. The OTO is a direct off-shoot of the work of Britain's leading twentieth-century Satanist, Theosophy leader Aliester Crowley. OTO enthusiasts claim this organization is an offshoot of Templar freemasonry, and hint at very influential protection being received from among Templars very high in British freemasonry.

A persons search of feeling important and powerful plays a significant role in becoming a Satanist. They believe the occult can provide them with those "needs". Satanism and the occult is an attractive alternative belief system to Christianity because it is all about the "SELF" and feeding the flesh as opposed to Christianity where it is death to self and death to flesh. Where God shows a "red light" Satan flashes a "green light". Satanism gives permission to do whatever a person desires. People making a choice to become a Satanist wants unlimited and uncapped pleasure and live by whatever rules they please.

[19] " Now the works of the flesh are evident, which are: adultery, fornication, uncleanness, lewdness, [20] idolatry, sorcery, hatred, contentions, jealousies, outbursts of wrath, selfish ambitions, dissensions, heresies, [21] envy, murders, drunkenness, revelries, and the like; of which I tell you beforehand, just as I also told you in time past, that those who practice such things will not inherit the kingdom of God

Galatians 5:19-21

Rituals

Rituals, and the manner in which they are carried out, play a very important role in Satanism. Satanic Rituals centres on the worship and praying to Satan, firstly to please Satan and secondly to search and bargain for things such as fame, money and many other things.

Satan derives power through worship in the form of human or animal sacrificial offerings, sexual intercourse that is engaged in during the rituals along with all the human emotion that goes into these types of rituals. Rituals affects people on all levels; mentally, emotionally, physically and spiritually.

Sexual intercourse plays a big role in the satanic rituals because energy that is released during this sexual act can be used to destroy. The sexual union can also be used for initiation into the cult. Through these acts people get linked with demons and other cult members.

Through these rituals power is released to empower curses, spells and incantations. Satanists must perform the rituals to the letter and any mistake is severely punished; making them absolute slaves to their master the devil.

Satanism's purpose for sacrifices is to gain power, to transfer power and to strengthen and share in the power of Satan and his demons.

ADOLF HITLER carried out blood sacrifices to open his mind up to a high level of demonic spiritual control.

Animal sacrifices include the killings and mutilation of cats, dogs, chickens and it has even been reported that lambs were stolen from a petting zoo to be used in a ritual. Satanists do blood sacrifices to conciliate or appease demons and Satan, to get their cooperation and to give them power. It is much easier and takes less effort for Satanists to perform sacrifices than to spend time and effort in performing meticulous rituals. By performing these cruel acts of killings and murder they gain the power of more powerful demons.

In the book **"Satanism: A beginners guide to the religious worship of Satan Vol 1"**, Brother Nero justifies animal sacrifices by saying that everything lives and everything must die, and the animals used during these rituals would have inevitably been eaten by a predator anyway. "Many of the animals used in animal sacrifice have had a better and longer life than they would have had if left in their natural environment." **Brother Nero**

Cats, especially black cats, are frequently the victims of satanic ritualistic crimes. This is so prolific that many shelters and humane societies refuse to allow adoption of black cats during the entire month of October, because of the frequent torture and mutilation of cats over the Halloween period.

"We can judge the heart of a man by his treatment of animals." ~Immanuel Kant

Satanists already have numerous victims. Most of the sexual abuse and associated killings or murders committed are carried out on the "disappeared" infants, children or runaways. These acts are carried out as part of the rituals outlined in manuals of satanic organizations. A leading police association has received an expert estimate / opinion, which states that of all known murders, one in five is a ritual murder.

Maury Terry an award-winning reporter published "The Ultimate Evil: An Investigation of America's Most Dangerous Satanic Cult". In this he links mass murderers Charles Manson and David Berkowitz to a gruesome satanic network that crisscrossed America and ended in murdering untold numbers of people.

What Terry also shares in his book is how satanic cults film their human sacrifices and then proceed to circulate it among themselves / cults. These films are called "snuff films." It is said by Terry that one of the seven "Son of Sam" murders in New York City was actually filmed from a nearby parked van. The film was then purchased by a rich Satanist "Gimme Shelter," and the film has been watched by snuff film fanatics.

Satanism is the modern version of the rituals and human sacrifice in ancient Babylon, the societies such as Sumerian, Phoenician, Hittite, Egyptian, Canaanite and the Akkadian people, among many others across the world. Blood and sex are the corner stones of satanic rituals.

Satanists believe that the blood from a new-born baby holds magical properties that would cause the energy during rituals to be intensified. Some covens believe that the infliction of continuous pain on victims would greatly increase this energy.

"For instance, increasing the pain of an animal such as a goat would release adrenaline into the bloodstream so when the animal's throat was finally cut, and the blood drained into the ceremonial chalice, increased power could be extracted by drinking the blood mixed with certain drugs. Aleister Crowley experimented extensively at the Abbey of Thelema in Sicily. One approach was to have sexual intercourse with an animal and cut the it's throat at the time of the human's orgasm. The blood was ingested and a higher spiritual plane was reportedly reached."- **"The Coven" by Satanic Magus Aleister Nacht;**

When it comes to human sacrifices and rituals that are carried out using humans victims, they may be subjected to the following:

- Victims will be placed in actual or make-shift coffins.
- During rituals drug use (especially hallucinogens), is usually rampant - not just among the Satanists - but drugs are also given to the victims. These drugs heighten the frenzy during the rituals.
- Victims are sexually abused to destroy the victim's moral foundation.
- Where an entire family is involved in Satanism, incestuous sexual acts occur.
- Animal and human sacrifices are done.
- Cannibalism.

During Magical rituals, demons spiritually attached themselves to victims' personalities to terrorize and torment them, and to continually reinforce complex mind control. We can see how blinded Satanists are, they accuse Christians of mind control when, in fact, they are under mind control themselves.

One grotto master said "Satanic Magic is the most straight-forward approach to magic that there is". They state that there are only three steps Satanic Magic consists of; Goal, Method and Application.

Satanists do not bind themselves to the lunar moons in regards to their performing of rituals and practising magic. Although they recognise the increased energy during a full and new moon they do not believe that Satan and demons are bound to "full moon arrivals".

Tools that are used during rituals include a black robe, altar, symbols of Satan, candles, a bell, a chalice, a sword, a model phallus, a gong, parchment and some kind of elixir or drink.

There are three basic types of Satanic Rituals and three types of ceremonies incorporated in the practice of Satanic magic. Each of these resembles a basic human emotion. These rituals are aimed to invoke Satan's name for the purpose of calling on supernatural powers to bring an effect or change for the will of the Satanist.

A sex ritual: Commonly known as a love charm or spell. The purpose of this ritual is to make someone fall in love with you whom you want / desire or "to summon a sex partner to fulfil your desires".

A compassionate ritual: This is also known as a sentiment, this ritual is performed for the purpose of helping others, or helping oneself." Health, domestic happiness, business activities, material success, and academic expertise (just to name a few) are covered under a compassionate ritual.

A destruction ritual: This is known as a hex, curse, or destroying agent and is used for anger, annoyance, disdain, contempt, or just plain hate. The victim of a hex or curse is much more prone to destruction if they DO NOT believe in it!

This is a very important statement for believers to take note of. This is why Satan is very happy to have people believe that if "we leave the devil alone, he will leave us alone". Secondly, people think that if you are a saved child of God that you don't have to bother with curses, God will handle it for you.

What is very important to know is that Jesus gave us the authority to overcome the kingdom of darkness, and with authority comes responsibility. We need to stand in the Name of Jesus and break any curses that are sent our way. What good is authority if it is not used? We need to exercise our God given authority.

The curses sent through the spiritual realm in this case the Satanists, are the easiest to break but the hardest to detect if not for Holy Spirit and His discernment. These Statistic hexes and curses are actual demons called up through these occultic rituals. They are sent by the Satanist for a specific purpose, most definitely not for blessing! These curses should be broken in the Name of Jesus and the demons should be given the command to leave and go under the feet of Jesus.

[21] "far above all principality and power and might and dominion, and every name that is named, not only in this age but also in that which is to come. [22] And He put all things under His feet, and gave Him to be head over all things to the church, [23] which is His body, the fullness of Him who fills all in all."

Ephesians 1:21-23

Have a look at the warning that is given at the bottom of these rituals.

"A WORD OF WARNING!" "Concerning Destruction: Be certain you DO NOT care if the intended victim lives or dies before you throw your curse, and having caused their destruction, revel, rather than feel remorse." **Satanic Bible**

In Satanism great emphasis is placed on perfecting very complex ritual practices and obedience to the satanic calendar.

Making a Commitment to a satanic ritual, they first instruct a person to what they need.

- One or more black, blue or red candles (as many as you like)
- A sterilized needle or razor
- A piece of clean paper, large enough to write the prayer below
- A dry pen, where you sign your name in blood (dip the tip of the pen in your blood)

On the piece of paper they write a prayer they declare in front of Satan and his demons that they renounce any and all past allegiances to God, Jesus Christ and the Holy Spirit. Then they proclaim Satan / Lucifer as their only god and they promise to recognize and honour him in all things without any reservation and in return, Satan will then be the being to gain successes in what the person sets out to do.

When the person is ready they light the candle, prick the index finger on their left hand and squeeze out some blood. Once complete, the person must Sign their name in blood. The prayer can that be recited either in their head or aloud.

The paper should then be folded up and burnt in the fire of the candle. The person then has the option to meditate until the candle has burnt itself out. At the end of the ritual, the person closes with the words "So must it be" and a Big "HAIL SATAN!!"

Satanic rituals are real and binding...they are only done once.

The Black Mass

No other single device has been associated with Satanism as much as the black mass. The Black Mass is not just one single ritual but it is divided into five segments. It is more of a sequence of rituals which use the format of the Catholic Mass for the purpose to mock God and worship the devil. The Black Mass ceremony involves various criminal activities such as human sacrifice as well as obscenity and blasphemy of horrific proportions.

The first segment is the **"INTROIT"**; this segment closely follows the form of the Catholic Mass but the dedication has been reversed. Only the priest and his helpers or servers participate in this section. The priest has helpers who are a boy and girl child, traditionally past the age of seven, which is regarded as the theoretical age of reason. These two kids symbolise the altar-boy in the catholic mass. Therefore it should not be a surprise that in a Satanic Mass the use of both a boy and a girl takes place with the girl taking the most active part in a later stage of the ritual.

The naked woman who serves as the altar for the mass, has most probably taken her place by this time. An inverted cross hangs above the altar. A passage is recited and Satan is substituted for God and evil substituted for good.

"OFFERTORY"; this is the second segment where the priest and the worshippers participate.

The third segment is **"CANON"**. Up until this point the mass has made use of a lot of blasphemous language and paraphernalia and the worshippers have not yet displayed any abnormal or deviant behaviour. The tone is set by the priest for the acts to follow and the worshipper get ready for whatever is required from them to do.

The foul rite of the "sabbat" or the "black mass" is seen as part of the revenge of woman upon her male persecutors.

This is when acts such as the use of urine from a prostitute or servant take place and passages are recited to Satan. The priest and the congregation expose their genitalia to the image of Satan whilst more prayers are said. The girl servant or helper then presents herself and raises her robe to reveal her genitalia and urinates into it a small cauldron that the boy servant holds.

The cup of urine is held up to the image of Satan above the altar by the priest. More passage are recited to Satan

"CONSECRATION"; the fourth segment is blasphemy itself. Everything, however foul it may seem, was simply an introduction or a run-up to what is about to occur and which will cause any Christian to cry out in horror.

The priest and his congregation recite a mockery of the Lord's Prayer which, in its context, is the doctrine of the satanic rite. It is by now a foregone conclusion that the worst is soon to follow, much to the increasing excitement of the priest and the worshippers, that are at this stage so heavily intoxicated by the drugs ingested prior to and during the ritual, as the climax of the rite approaches.

In this segment, the second to last division of the Black Mass, the naked woman whom acts as the altar brings her genitalia into contact with the Body of Our Lord for the first time.

The last segment is the **"REPUDIATION".** The Repudiation is both the final dedication and the ultimate form of satanic rebellion. This is the time that human sacrifices are performed and the worshippers present at the ritual indulge in a sexual orgy.

The anonymous French writer in speaking of the black mass says "they couple monstrously." "The god of incest weds a son to his mother, a brother to his sister, a young bitch and an old greybeard, or conversely, a stripling and some toothless old woman." These, it must be remembered, are simply the heterosexual manifestations of the orgy.

More text is recited and lute acts combining the wafer, the representation of our Lord's body, and it touching the naked altar's breast and genitals follows during this segment. **Missa Niger - The Black Mass; text published by Aubrey Melech. To read more about this go to www.angelfire.com/az3/synagogasatanae/current.htm**

Other sources report on acts taking place such as the urine of a prostitute or blood being used and drunk out of a skull instead of wine. Mocking screams of "Beelzebub, Beelzebub, Beelzebub" instead of the holy words of consecration. Sacramental wafers that incorporate menstrual blood and semen are used or wafers stolen from a catholic church may be used. Feasting on roasted human flesh can also take place.

An invocation is done to Satan and various demons, such as Asmodeus and Astaroth, followed by an array of prayers and psalms that are chanted backwards or combined with rudeness... all performed within the confines of a "protective" pentagram drawn on the floor. New born babies are crucified alive or strangled and offered as a sacrifice to Satan. This is said to be the favourite sport of the Satanist; frenzied sexual orgies takes place and young boy's throats are cut to provide blood for the cup. Black candles made out of human fat are used. In some instances crosses are tattooed on to the soles of the feat of Satanists so that the symbol of Christ is continually trodden underfoot.

For Satanist, Occultists and Mother Earth worshippers there is no difficulty in understanding that it is very easy to have taken the Catholic mass and with a bit of "tweaking" form it into the Satanic Black Mass. Why? Because the Catholic Mass is basically an occult ceremony, a very powerful White Magic Satanic practice.

[24] For Christ has not entered the holy places made with hands, which are copies of the true, but into heaven itself, now to appear in the presence of God for us; [25] not that He should offer Himself often, as the high priest enters the Most Holy Place every year with blood of another [26] He then would have had to suffer often since the foundation of the world; but now, once at the end of the ages, He has appeared to put away sin by the sacrifice of Himself. [27] And as it is appointed for men to die once, but after this the judgment, [28] so Christ was offered once to bear the sins of many. To those who eagerly wait for Him He will appear a second time, apart from sin, for salvation.

Hebrews 9:24-28

Take a look at the verse above. Jesus offered Himself once and does not have to continually offer Himself. This is exactly what the Catholic Mass is doing. The Catholic Mass is considered as an actual sacrifice of Jesus each time it is celebrated.

"The Mass is the same sacrifice as the sacrifice on the cross, because in the Mass the victim is the same, and the principal Priest is the same, Jesus Christ." ("My Catholic Faith", p. 286). So creating and practising a ceremony, that sacrifices Jesus Christ repeatedly on a daily bases all over the world, violates God's decree.

Doc Marquis, a former Black Magic Satanist, says unequivocally that the Mass, when it is said in Latin, contains great occult power!

"Black magic witches in the early 6th Century discovered that the Roman Catholic Church had created a powerful White Magic ceremony in the Mass; therefore, they tried to capture this power for themselves by creating the infamous Black Mass, **said backwards**."- **The Cutting Edge Ministries**

It is important to note that rituals can differ greatly from group to group. In many satanic churches they will recite the Lord's prayer but they will start with "Amen" and say "Nema" and then recite the whole prayer backwards; a practise called "the law of reversal" taught by Aleister Crowley.

The Black Mass is not just a mockery of the Catholic Mass but it is also supposed to symbolise the death of Christ. Satan deceives humans by proclaiming that Christ was the ultimate sacrifice to him; that He defeated Jesus by killing Him at the cross.

[18] "No one takes it from me, but I lay it down of my own accord. I have authority to lay it down and authority to take it up again. This command I received from my Father."
John 10:18

[15] "Having disarmed principalities and powers, He made a public spectacle of them, triumphing over them in it."
Colossians 2:15

[34] "Who is he who condemns? It is Christ who died, and furthermore is also risen, who is even at the right hand of God, who also makes intercession for us."

Hélèné Fulton

Romans 8:34

Jesus is ALIVE, the grave is empty and He sits at The Right Hand of God and he did not just disarm Satan and his demons but Jesus made a spectacle out of them! Jesus laid His life down, no one killed Him!

When reading such horrible blasphemous rituals you cannot be surprised by the fact that, if high level Satanists do not have MPD (multiple personality disorder) they very often emotionally crack under the stress of the horrible blood rituals that are required. God did not create people to participate in such horrific acts. These are bad enough for those performing the rituals, but consider those being lured in or abducted and sacrificed.

Children and adults who are forced into the participation of human and animal sacrifices are severely traumatized, and if this was not bad enough, during the "Born again ritual" this entire trauma is followed by being buried alive with a corps. Before the child or person is placed in the coffin they are smeared with blood and / or faeces, and left in the coffin for hours or sometimes even for days.

The experiences that these victims have include suffocation, trauma to such an extent that the child / person leaves their body to survive the ordeal, starting to associate with the corps and actually becoming unconscious. If the victim / convert survive this they will then be saved by a person who dresses up as Satan. This act symbolises being born again into the satanic family.

Children and people who experience rituals like these, and others similar rituals, are gravely affected in a spiritual, psychological, physical and emotional way. Through the trauma gateways into the realm of the dead and the spirit of the dead are opened, demons will enter and attach themselves to all the functioning levels of a person. New personalities are born and when such a split in personality takes place there are more sides to the person that can be used, controlled and programmed by the Satanists.

Trauma such as what accrues during these incidents prevents people from remembering what had happened, and the effect of this has disastrous consequences in people's lives. People are cut off from their families and they become part of the new satanic family. Feelings of abandonment are coded into their minds and fear of abandonment and distrust is instilled.

These rituals make people feel unclean and contaminated and they have feelings of self-rejection. Out of body experiences are triggered or reinforced.

Holidays

DATE	Name of ritual	Type of ritual	Activity	Sex and age of victim
Jan 7	St Winebald's day	Blood rituals	Animal/Human sacrifices and dismemberment	Human; male Ages 15-33

Date	Ritual			
Jan 17	Satanic Revels	Sexual rituals	Oral/anal/vaginal intercourse	Human; female Ages 7-17
Jan 20-26	Sacrifice preparation	Kidnapping, holding and ceremonial preparation of person for human sacrifice. Blood and sex rituals		
Jan 26	The Da Muer ritual: Grand climax.		Human sacrifice and Sex rituals oral/anal/vaginal intercourse	Male child/woman/child female ages 7-17:
Feb	Candelmass and Satanic	Mass initiation of new	Animal/Human sacrifice oral/anal/v	Human: male ages

Date	Event	Type	Details	Victim
2	Revels	members and Blood and sexual rituals	aginal intercourse	15-33 Human; Female ages 7-17
Feb 7	Satanic Revels	Sexual	Oral/Anal	Human male
Feb 14	St Valentine's day	Sexual	Oral/Anal/Vaginal	Human female Virgin
Feb 25	St Walpurgis' day	Blood	Communion of blood and flesh	Animal
Mar 1	St. Eichatadt's	Blood	Involves the drinking of human blood for strength and paying homage to demons	Human male or female
Mar. 15	Eides			

Hélèné Fulton

',17				
Mar 20	Vernal Equinox; Sabbat Festival and a Major fertility Sabbat	Sexual Orgies	Oral/Anal/Vaginal	Human male or female
	Shrovetide - three days before Ash Wednesday which is a Witch Sabbat			
Easter Week-end: Black mass/black Sabbath				
DATE	**Name of ritual**	**Type of ritual**	**Activity**	**Sex and age of victim**
Date Varies	Good Friday Day of Passion; death of Christ To mock the death of Jesus Christ	Blood	Human sacrifice	Human Male A man is sacrificed on Good Friday
D	Name	Type	Activity	Sex

Hélèné Fulton

DATE	of ritual	of ritual		and age of victim
Date Varies	Easter Day; On Easter Sunday, known to Satanists as unholy Sunday	Blood	Human sacrificed followed by three days of fasting and chanting	Human Male or female
Apr 19-25	Abduction Ceremonial preparation of person for human sacrifice			
Apr 24	St. Mark's Eve	Divining and herb gathering		
Apr 26 - 1 May	Grand Climax	Sexual Da Meur	Oral/Anal/Vaginal Human Sacrifice Corpus De Baahl	Human female ages 1-25
A	Walpur	Bloo	Human or	Huma

pr 30	gisnacht/ Beltane; One of the most important nights on the satanic calendar	d	animal sacrifice	n male or female
May 1	Walpurgis' Day May Day Beltane	Coven Sexual Initiations	Oral/Anal/ Vaginal Druid Fire Festival	Human male or female very young
24 May	Ascension day;	Rituals to mock the ascension of Jesus Christ into heaven.		
Jun 17	Corpus Christi	Mocking with the body and blood of Jesus Christ		
Jun 21	Summer Solstice St. John's Eve	Orgies and blood	Oral/Anal/ Vaginal Human or Animal Sacrifice	Human or Animal of any age
Jul 1	Demon Revels	Blood	Druid Sexual Association	Human female of any age

Hélèné Fulton

Jul 17	St Alphonsis' Day	Blood	Human Sacrifice	Human of any Age or gender
Jul 20-26	Abduction Holding and ceremonial Preparation of Individual for Human Sacrifice	Blood	Human Sacrifice	Human of any Age or gender
Jul 27	Grand Climax; 5 weeks, 1 day after summer solstice	Da Meur sexual	Human Sacrifice Oral/Anal/Vaginal	Human female child or adult
1 Aug	Lammas' Day; SABBATH Festival	Blood	Animal or Human	Human Any age male or female
Aug 3	Satanic Revels and Satanic Magic	Sexual ritual	Oral/Anal/Vaginal	Human Female Ages 7-17
Aug	St. Egemon Day	Blood	Human Sacrifice	Human male any

Hélèné Fulton

9				age
Aug 10	Wilgemon Day	Blood	Human Sacrifice	Human Male Adult
Aug 24	St. Bartholomew's day; Great Sabbat and Fire festival	Sexual Rape	Conception of Twin	Human female
Sep 7	A Bride for the Beast/ Marriage to the Beast	Sexual	Sacrifice dismemberment	Infant - 21 (female)
Sept 21	Midnight Host	Blood	Human; Sacrifice/ Dismemberment of corpses: hands removed for hand of glory rituals. Cannibalism also occurs.	Human Female
Sept 2	Autumnl Equinox Orgies Michael	Orgies	Oral/Anal/ Vaginal	Human Male or Female

Hélèné Fulton

	2	mass			
Oct 13-30		Preparation for all Hallows Eve, Samhain (Halloween) Abduction, holding and ceremonial preparation of individual for human sacrifice 13th is Backward Halloween Date			
Oct 28-30		Satanist High Holy Day related to Halloween	Blood	Human Sacrifice Each day	Human male or female
Oct 31		All Hallows Eve; SABBATH; One of the two most important nigh	Blood and sexual	Animal/Human Sacrifice sexual climax association with demons	Human male/female any age and/or animal

Hélèné Fulton

	ts of the year			
Nov 1	Satanist High Holy Day	Blood	Human Sacrifice	Human male or female
Nov 4	Satanic Revels / Satanic Magic	Sexual	Oral/Anal/Vaginal	Humans female Ages 7-17
Dec 19	Immaculate Conception	Sexual	Oral/Anal/Vaginal	Human Female Ages 6-18
Dec 22	Yule Winter Solstice; Sabbat Festival, Feast Day; coven cele	Orgies	Oral/Anal/Vaginal	Human Male or Female

Hélèné Fulton

		bration			
Dec 24		Demon Revels High Grand	Da Meur Blood and sexual	High Grand Climax; Human Sacrifice	Any age (male or female, human and/or animal
Dec 25		Killing the Christ Child Climax	Blood	Animal/Human Sacrifice and also Receive body parts as Christmas gifts	Human Male infant

- Please take note that with satanic holiday dates, no group will perform every activity or use every date. The days change annually according to the regular calendar and differ from cult to cult
- The highest ritual holiday for a Satanist is his / her birthday.
- "The first and third of every month. Put 1 and 3 together and it makes 13, though ritual / worship can occur at any time, frequently coinciding with times of stress".
- All Fridays the 13th's are high satanic days.
- All full-moon nights are the easiest to move around without any difficulty and detection, making it a favourable time for major occult activity.

Over the Holy week, Palm Sunday to Easter Sunday, some satanic groups are thought to sacrifice, cook and eat a human baby on Easter Sunday

Satanic Wedding

In regards to marriage, Satanists believe anything goes. They believe that a Satanist or devil worshiper is free to decide what type of marriage suits them best and that it would be wrong and inappropriate for anyone to say that a certain form of marriage is wrong or unacceptable. All marriages in all forms are allowed, heterosexual, same-sex, polygamous and even open marriages are all allowed. Satanists say that the Christian moral code concerning polygamous and homosexual marriages is in direct conflict with a Satanists view. They recognise polygamy and same-sex marriages as a legitimate from of marriage. Satanists believe the most favourable time to get married is during a waxing moon. The Satanic Temple is decorated according to the couple's tastes. Modifications are made to suit each couple; the following is only a guideline:

The proceedings / ceremony is opened by the High Priest or Priestess with ringing a bell by drawing a pentagram in the air with his / her athame and the recites the following;…"In Nomine Dei Nostri Satanas, Luciferi Excelsi. In the Name of Satan, Ruler of the Earth, True God, Almighty and Ineffable, Who hast created man to reflect in Thine own image and likeness, we invite the Forces of Hell to bestow their infernal power upon us. Come forth to greet us and confer dark blessings upon this couple who desire to become as one in the eyes of Lucifer."

Then High Priest or Priestess proceed by drinking from a cup and invokes the Four Crowned Princes of Hell:

- Satan / Lucifer from the East
- Beelzebub from the North
- Astaroth from the West
- Azazel from the South

Then the following is recited by the High Priest or Priestess:

"We come together in the Name of our Father and Lord Satan to join_____and_____together in marriage."

A circle is draws by the High Priest or Priestess with his / her athame around the bride and groom.

Everyone at the ceremony should then visualize a blue light that is representing the "Powers of Hell".

Then the following is recited by the High Priest or Priestess. "Almighty Satan, look with favour upon your disciples _____ and _____. Both have come here of their own free will. They come before you to ask your blessings as they set forth on this very day as husband and wife. We ask that you bless this union with lust and the pleasures of life, that their mutual affection and desire for one another continues strong and enduring."

"Do you _____ desire of your own free will to take _____ as your lawfully wedded husband to love, honour and respect; to become as one in the eyes of Satan and before the powers of Hell?"

The bride will then answer

High Priest or Priestess will then ask the groom: "Do you _____ desire of your own free will to take _____ as your lawfully wedded wife to love, honour and respect; to become as one in the eyes of Satan and before the powers of Hell?"

The groom will then answer.

The bride and groom will then proceed to exchange rings.

High Priest or Priestess will then say: "In the Name of Satan and before all of the Demons of Hell, I pronounce you Husband and Wife. May your union be powerful, strong and abundant with pleasure. HAIL SATAN!!"

Everyone in the congregation will then shout "HAIL SATAN!!"

The High Priest or Priestess then recites, chants or vibrates the First Enochian Key:

After the reciting of the First Enochian Key the High Priest or Priestess then says the following: "Go forth as one, keep each other strong in Satan as you now walk together on the Left Hand Path. May Satan grant you many blessings along the way Ave Satanas!!"

Then the couple will say together: "Ave Satanas!!"

Then again High Priest or Priestess will say: "Hail Satan!! And the congregation will repeat: Hail Satan!!"

The High Priest or Priestess will then close off the ceremony or proceedings by ringing the bell once again. And after the ceremony intense celebrations are held.

"In Traditional Satanism there is no prohibition against having multiple sex partners in a relationship"- Rev Caesar 999 Satanic Bible.

Other

Anton LeVey and the Satanic Bible

Anton LaVey of the Church of Satan converted Christians by explaining that those in a "witchcraft group…practice the same basic philosophy as Christianity" without the guilt. **(The Satanic Bible).** He stated that the difference between Christian and Satanic philosophies is that Satanists admit that their actions please Satan and anger God.

LaVey served as a consultant to the producers of, and acted in, the Film Rosemary's Baby- A story of a woman impregnated by Satan.

The following statements are just some of the opening words of the Satanic Bible, published in 1969 and written by Anton LaVey. They are BASIC principles guiding LaVeyan Satanists. This document is © Anton Szandor LaVey, 1969

"Satan represents indulgence instead of abstinence; nothing is to be gained by denying oneself pleasure. Religious calls for abstinence most often come from faiths that view the physical world (and its pleasures) as spiritually dangerous. Satanism is a world-affirming, not world-denying, religion."

"[3] "For we ourselves were also once foolish, disobedient, deceived, serving various lusts and pleasures, living in malice and envy, hateful and hating one another."
Titus 3:3 NKJ

"For people will love only themselves and their money. They will be boastful and proud, scoffing at God, disobedient to their parents, and ungrateful. They will consider nothing sacred. They will be unloving and unforgiving; they will slander others and have no self-control. They will be cruel and hate what is good. They will betray their friends, be reckless, be puffed up with pride, and love pleasure rather than God."
2 Timothy 3:2-4

[9] "The heart is deceitful above all things, And desperately wicked; Who can know it? [10] I, the Lord, search the heart, I test the mind, Even to give every man according to his ways, According to the fruit of his doings.

Jeremiah 17:9-10

Satan represents kindness to those who deserve it (not) love wasted on ingrates; treating others as they treat you will form meaningful and productive bonds while letting parasites know that you will not waste your time with them.

[24] "And a servant of the Lord must not quarrel but be gentle to all, able to teach, patient"

2 Timothy 2:2

[32] "And be kind to one another, tender hearted, forgiving one another, even as God in Christ forgave you."

Ephesians 4:32

Satan represents vengeance instead of turning the other cheek; leaving wrongs unpunished merely encourages miscreants to continue preying on both yourself and others, and those who do not stand up for themselves end up being trampled.

[27] "But I say to you who hear: Love your enemies, do good to those who hate you, [28] bless those who curse you, and pray for those who spitefully use you. [29] To him who strikes you on the one cheek, offer the other also. And from him who takes away your cloak, do not withhold your tunic either."

Luke 6:27-29

[32] "But if you love those who love you, what credit is that to you? For even sinners love those who love them."

Luke 6:32

¹⁷ "Repay no one evil for evil. Have regard for good things in the sight of all men."

Romans 12: 17

¹⁸ "If it is possible, as much as depends on you, live peaceably with all men. ¹⁹ Beloved, do not avenge yourselves, but rather give place to wrath; for it is written, "Vengeance is Mine, I will repay," says the Lord. ²⁰ Therefore "If your enemy is hungry, feed him; If he is thirsty, give him a drink; For in so doing you will heap coals of fire on his head." ²¹ Do not be overcome by evil, but overcome evil with good."

Romans 12: 18-21

Satan represents man as just another animal...!

⁵ "For thou hast made him a little lower than the angels, and hast crowned him with glory and honour. Thou madest him to have dominion over the works of thy hands; thou hast put all things under his feet"

Psalm 8: 5-6

² "And the fear of you and the dread of you shall be on every beast of the earth, on every bird of the air, on all that move on the earth, and on all the fish of the sea. They are given into your hand.

Genesis 9:2

Anton LaVey compiled The Eleven Satanic Rules of the Earth in 1967, two years before the publication of the Satanic Bible. It was originally only meant for the eyes of The Church of Satan members, because the content was considered "too frank and brutal for general release".

The Eleven Satanic Rules of the Earth. This document is © Anton Szandor LaVey, 1967.

1. **Do not give opinions or advice unless you are asked.**

2. **Do not tell your troubles to others unless you are sure they want to hear them.**

3. **When in another's lair, show him respect or else do not go there.**

4. **If a guest in your lair annoys you, treat him cruelly and without mercy.**

[133] "Behold, how good and how pleasant it is for brethren to dwell together in unity!"
Psalm 133:1

[10] "Therefore, as we have opportunity, let us do good to all, especially to those who are of the household of faith."
Galatians 6:10

5. **Do not make sexual advances unless you are given the mating signal.**

A lot of "survivors" (some cases even growing up in a Satanic home or family) who manage to come out of the occult successfully, say that their childhood was filled with torture, sexual abuse, cannibalism and even murder. These acts are regularly conducted by the High Priests, often daily.

One Survivor describes a rituals as follows "There was a circle drawn and she was placed in the middle of the circle. There was fire burning around her. During that part she was told she had been married to Satan and would forever be a child of him. She was then pulled out beyond the fire and raped by the men in the cult".

6. **Do not take that which does not belong to you unless it is a burden to the other person and he cries out to be relieved**.

7. **Acknowledge the power of magic if you have employed it successfully to obtain your desires. If you deny the power of magic after having called upon it with success, you will lose all you have obtained.**

Spells, incantations, hexes and curses accomplish all the same purposes; that is, to summon a demon (or demons) to perform a given action.

The term "Placing a spell, hex, or curse on someone," refers to the act of calling up a demon and then sending it to the person to perform certain influences or damage. All spells, etc. are accomplished by demons, even the so-called "good" ones" – **"He came to set the captives free"; by Rebecca Brown. p 284**

In an interview with the "First Family of Satanism", Bob Larson asked Zeena LaVey, the daughter of Anton LaVey, to address the allegations of a curse her father, Anton LaVey, had placed on Sam Brody who died in a car crash with Jane Mansfield. She admitted that Anton indeed placed a ritual curse on Brody, but not on Jane. "Jane happened to be in the wrong place at the wrong time.....Jane had repeatedly been warned by Anton to stay away from Brody."

Jayne Mansfield, a devout follower of the church of Satan, was an American actress in film, theatre, and television, a nightclub entertainer, a singer, and one of the early Playboy Playmates. She was a major Hollywood sex symbol of the 1950s and early 1960s.

On June 29, 1967, Mansfield, Brody, a driver and three of Mansfield's children were travelling to New Orleans from Biloxi, Mississippi. On a dark stretch of road, just as their truck was approaching, a machine discharged a thick white fog used to spray mosquitoes, obscuring the truck from the drivers view. The car hit the trailer-truck from behind. The driver, Mansfield and Brody were all killed in the accident, while the kids, apparently sleeping on the back seat, survived.

The impact of the car was so severe that it completely sheared the top off of the car. The car was described as being, "crumpled like a piece of tinfoil after a cookout." The top part of Jayne's head had been ripped off. This does not mean decapitation. The death certificate reads "crushed skull with avulsion of cranium and brain." The dictionary definition of avulsion is the forcible tearing away of a body part by trauma or surgery.

"If you're going to do something wrong, do it big, because the punishment is the same either way."
Jane Mansfield

[11] "Therefore evil shall come upon you; You shall not know from where it arises. And trouble shall fall upon you; You will not be able to put it off. And desolation shall come upon you suddenly, Which you shall not know. [12] "Stand now with your

enchantments And the multitude of your sorceries, In which you have labored from your youth-Perhaps you will be able to profit, Perhaps you will prevail."

Isaiah 47:11-12

8. Do not complain about anything to which you need not subject yourself.

9. **Do not harm little children.**

10. **Do not kill non-human animals unless you are attacked or for your food.**

Ex-Satanists talk a great deal about the torture of loved ones, especially children, and it is seen as a very common tactic to ensure silence and obedience within the cults. Parents and siblings are forced to watch their loved ones beaten, brutally and sexually molested, raped or sacrificed.

Christie was as a teenager forced to participate in rituals. She even saw her twin brother sacrificed. She was also forced to watch a ritual of a little boy where the Satanists kept on telling this little boy "Don't cry this is what you were born for"- **Bob Larson "in the name of Satan"**

"Satanism is not like Christianity; a way of gathering sheep together in one place! We feel, for the best way to change the world in to a satanic arena, is to have strong individuals in different areas to do their own individual work. So joining the church of Satan you enter into the possibility of going into the higher echelon of the church of Satan" - **Nikolas Schreck, founder of the Werewolf Coven.**

The devil / Satan is alive and well, and is definitely real. He is even deceiving Satanists in the lie that HE does not exist and that he was the one who was victorious at the cross.

Satan proclaims that Jesus Christ was the ultimate sacrifice to him that he won over Christ, killing him at the cross. **He came to set the captives free, by Rebecca Brown, p74**

15 "Having disarmed principalities and powers, He made a public spectacle of them, triumphing over them in it."

Colossians 2:15

13 "But evil men and impostors will grow worse and worse, deceiving and being deceived."

2 Timothy 3:13

44 "You are of your father the devil, and the desires of your father you want to do. He was a murderer from the beginning, and does not stand in the truth, because there is no truth of it."

John 8:44

11 "Your pomp is brought down to Sheol, And the sound of your stringed instruments; The maggot is spread under you, And worms cover you."

Isaiah 14:11

Please read Isaiah 14:9-19

10 "The devil, who deceived them, was cast into the lake of fire and brimstone where the beast and the false prophet are. And they will be tormented day and night forever and ever."

Revelation 20:10

[4] "but the wise took oil in their vessels with their lamps."
Matthew 25:4

The Nine Satanic Sins:

1. Stupidity
2. Pretentiousness
3. Solipsism
4. Self-deceit (Also found in the "Nine Satanic Statements")
5. Herd Conformity (they few herd conformity as being like Christians)
6. Lack of Perspective
7. Forgetfulness of Past Orthodoxies
8. Counterproductive Pride
9. Lack of Aesthetics
   Video / computer and fantasy role-playing games.

[22] "Abstain from every form of evil."
1 Thesselonians 5:22

Occultic games have more and more become one of Satan's biggest tools. From occultic role-playing fantasy games such as Dungeons and Dragons to computer games like Mortal Combat and Diablo. More and more these games are becoming more blasphemous towards God and out rightly promote occultism and Satanism.

Within the last ten years there has been a dramatic increase in the satanic themes of these computer games. These games are more satanic than ever; so much so that a long-time video gamer has actually started to sound the alarm and is making people and parents aware of the new breed of satanically-themed video games that are hitting the market.

These games actually open doors for demons to demonically control people, and brainwash the young. The video game Assassin's Creed (version 1 and 2) might as well be called Satan's Creed for it is truly an anti-Christian video game that mocks and ridicules the Bible and God.

In the game, a weapon is introduced known as the Pieces of Eden. This weapon is used to brainwash and control the people. At a point in the game, it is revealed that the Pieces of Eden is the Word of God, the Bible, and it is depicted as being used in the game to deceive and control mindless people.

Other outright blasphemous lies that are told is that the Red Sea was never parted and that Moses used the Pieces of Eden, brainwashing the people with the Bible, in order to lead them.

Another is in reference to the New Testament; it says that the water was never turned into wine and it shows Jesus on the cross holding, yet again, a Piece of Eden. Depicting that Jesus brainwashes people. **Read more at http://godfatherpolitics.com/8344/assassins-creed-video-game-mocks-bible-and-christians/#38fUbJ0OGO2RkrfM.99**

Another blatant satanic video game is the Devil May Cry series. This gaming series, clearly promotes the occult, New World order and the satanic agenda to twist the version and truth of the Bible. The main

character is a Nephilim hybrid, the child of an angel and a demon. He battles a demonic king to save the world. Although it might seem as if this is going against the new world order message, the game is undoubtedly a shameless brainwashing into the occult. It is filled with satanic and occult imagery, such as a drink the "hero" drinks with the number 666 on it. The game also contains Illuminati symbolism.
To get more information concerning this game go to "Beginning and End website at www.beginnigand end.com/dmc-devil-may-cry-5-rise-of-satanic-video-games

These games target God and invites players to make pacts with the devil, and elevates Satan to hero status.

Other popular computer and video games with occultic and satanic messaging:-

- Dragon Age: Origins; in this game God is depicted
- Dragon Age: Awakening
- Tecmo's Deception: Invitation to Darkness (PlayStation). Players "make an unholy pact and sell their soul to Satan in exchange for power" with the object of the game being to ensure the resurrection of Satan and obtain his power. This game is in fact rated "T" for teen.
- Nocturne (Playstation 2). In this game the "hero" who is actually a demon, destroys the three archangels St. Michael, Gabriel and Raphael, then goes on to destroy God.
- Shadow Hearts (Playstation 2). Here the "hero" uses his power to intercept and destroy God and "save the world." Yet again some of the games in this series are rated "T" for teens.

- Dragon's Age Origins (Playstation 3 / Xbox 360). This game revolves around the story of God going mad and cursing the world. A witch attacks believers and players can "have sex" with her in a pagan act called "blood magic" so she can "give birth to a god." Another scenario allows player to have sex with a demon in exchange for a boy's soul.

Other well-known games with Satanic themes are Darksiders, Koudelka, Trapt, Bayonetta; Diablo 1, 2 and 3.

These are just some of several high-selling video games that distort the message of the Bible and continue the preparation of society for the arrival of the Antichrist.

Roll-play fantasy games such as Dungeons and Dragons can lead to demonic obsession, suicide attempts, recruitment vessel for occultism and witchcraft. It is very serious and very real. Do not be deceived, magic and sorcery are spiritual. Magic is a kind of spiritual lust. Magic is about the power to control and rebel.

Dungeons and Dragons has even been used in colleges as part of the curriculum in psychology. In some cases it is used as a group therapy technique for teenagers; but what it really is a crash course in witchcraft.

To people who are big into "gaming" it will definitely not disappoint. Satan is a lot cleverer and more cunning than we sometimes think. He knows that for new generation's, new thrills and new real experiences of a higher degree are required.

Dungeons and Dragons does not fail in offering a thrilling experience of creating mortal battles with spiritual consequences.

The "dungeon master" plans and creates the over-all outline for each game. Each game is an adventure in which many battles are fought with different "monsters" and "beings". Every one of these beings has their own abilities and characteristics. Every player must decide whether their character is either good or evil, lawful or chaotic. There are numerous manuals that contain a great deal of information about the abilities of all the various characters and even show pictures of the characters.

When playing the game players visualize the actions and happenings of the game in their minds. The better a person becomes at seeing the actions, being able to anticipate the next moves of the various "monsters" and fellow players, the more experienced and advanced the person becomes in the game.

There are a large number of "magic spells", magical devices, and satanic writings described in the various rule books (especially the more advanced manuals). These are used and taught to Satanists. What people don't realise is that the manufactures of these games want to make it as real as possible, just like the spells and characters in the Harry Potter books.

The monsters and deities are actually real demons. They are training themselves to see in the spirit realm and the better they can see the game the more in-tune they become with the spiritual world. Many people including Christians fall into this trap.

For the unsuspecting, unknowing person from the outside, it might not look as if this is such a dangerous or lethal game. On the grand scale of things, good is seen to be greater than evil and in some games it is as it is in real life - evil has consequences. Just the phrase "role-playing fantasy" should make us run in the other direction. This comes into stark contrast to what the word of God tell us to do with our minds.

[3] For though we walk in the flesh, we do not war according to the flesh. [4] For the weapons of our warfare are not carnal but mighty in God for pulling down strongholds, **[5] casting down arguments and every high thing that exalts itself against the knowledge of God, bringing every thought into captivity to the obedience of Christ**

2 Corinthians 10:3-5

Dungeons and Dragons is a game that lures the player into an entirely different fantasy world in which the power of magic and violence is unavoidable. We need to avoid such "games" at all costs.

Sadly people deny the impact of these "games" and say "Well I just see it as a game". They are playing with fire. Just because people think they are only playing a game doesn't mean that the evil spirits / demons regards it as a game.

Rock and Roll and its Satanic Roots

"We are instruments of evil we come straight from hell

We're the legions of the demons that are hunting for the kill

Cathedrals are now cemeteries doom is all you see

We have come to take the world and give you misery

We are pestilent and contaminate the world

And make tombs of your cities

We come bursting through your bodies, rape your helpless soul

Transform you into a creature merciless and cold

We force you to kill your brother eat his blood and brain

Shredding flesh and sucking bone 'till everyone's insane

We are pestilent and contaminate the world

Demonic legions prevail"

Rigor Mortis - Demons Lyrics

As Christians we should be especially concerned about music and the lyrics of songs we listen to. The problem with lyrics like these and others similar to them is that it is "Garbage in - Garbage out." Rock is not only one of the front running recruiters of Satanism, but it is a powerful weapon for Satanism. It is not surprising that Rock music is one of Satanism's biggest money-makers. We need to know that there is nothing spontaneous or accidental about "rock." Music is an undebatable spiritual weapon in the hand of Satan. Through music people are being inducted into Satanism. The message that is proclaimed through music is to murder, rape and hate. - See more at www.savethemales.ca/001799.html#sthash.Etool2ol.dpuf

Even without the drugs and sexual orgies which are characteristic features of hard-core rock affairs, repeated, frequent, hours-long exposure to constant repetition of "rock rhythms" produces lasting, drug-like effects on the mind of the victim.

One form of music that causes the greatest concern is the various types of "metal" music.

Metal can be classified into three categories.

First, is party metal: It represents the most popular style of music. Groups like Bon Jovi, Motley Crue, and Def Leppard are representative of party metal. They tend to glorify sexuality and the party spirit.
Bon Jovi sings in "Homebound Train":

"When I was just a boy
THE DEVIL TOOK MY HAND
Took me from my home
He made me a man . . .
I'm going DOWN, DOWN, DOWN, DOWN, DOWN
On the homebound train."

". . . I'd kill my mother for rock and roll. I WOULD SELL MY SOUL." **- Bon Jovi; Smash Hits magazine**

The second type is "trash metal": It is represented by groups like Metallica, Anthrax, and Megadeth. They primarily focus on "trash metal" such as violence and death.

The third type is known as "black metal": This music is overtly satanic. The lyrics encourage such activities such as incest, necrophilia, rape, torture, and human sacrifice. Black metal is represented by groups like Venom and Slayer.

Slayer sing of themselves, as:
"Warriors from the gates of hell . . .
In lord Satan we trust."
The following lyrics are from their song "Hell Awaits"
"Jesus knows your soul cannot be saved
CRUCIFY THE SO CALLED LORD
He soon shall fall to me
Your souls are damned
Your God has fell to slave for me eternally Hell awaits."

Satan is very cunning. It is relatively easy to avoid black metal and artist such as Marilyn Manson, whom not only proclaims that his purpose on earth is to rid it from Christianity, but also promotes witchcraft, drugs and suicide. The biggest wolf in sheep's clothing is the secular music. The spirit behind most secular music is Satanic and more and more of the average pop artists are selling their souls to the devil for fame and fortune. "Music is the strongest form of magic." — **Marilyn Manson**

A man that has played a significant role in rock is Aleister Crowley. He was a God-hating corrupt and immoral person, and was also greatly admired by Anton LaVey.

Aleister Crowley was a 33° Freemason, a bisexual Satan worshiping heroin-addict who asked people to call him "The Beast 666". It is said that Crowley killed his first cat at the age of 11, and was also linked to rumours of cannibalism and infanticide. Infanticide or also known as infant homicide is the intentional killing of new-borns.

Aleister Crowley might have been called the "the wickedest man in the world" by the press (back when he was still alive), but today is seen as one of greatest Britons of all time. **"100 great Britons"**

These were words spoken about Aleister Crowley when the details of his life were revealed in a courtroom during a lawsuit: "I have been over forty years engaged in the administration of the law in one capacity or another. I thought that I knew of every conceivable form of wickedness. I thought that everything which was vicious and bad had been produced at one time or another before me. I have learnt in this case that we can always learn something more if we live long enough. I have never heard such dreadful, horrible, blasphemous and abominable stuff as that which has been produced by the man who describes himself to you as the greatest living poet." Mr. Justice Swift

This man who called himself "The Beast 666" has been a great influence for many popular musicians throughout the 20th century, and although he might be deceased, he along with his teachings still has a great influence on Rock music with many musicians following his teachings.

Bands such as the Beatles took his teachings so seriously that Crowley was depicted on the cover of The Beatles' "Sergeant Pepper's Lonely Hearts Club Band" cover. He can be seen as the second from left on the top row. Frightening, and people think that this is all new.

Ozzy Osbourne, the Satanist musician of the music group Black Sabbath, was greatly influenced by Aleister Crowley. On his solo album Blizzard of Ozz he even went as far as to write a song about Crowley, titled "Mr. Crowley."

David Bowie's song "Quicksand", from his album Hunky Dory, makes the reference "I'm closer to the Golden Dawn, immersed in Crowley's uniform of imagery..."

It is also well known that the guitarist and co-founder of 1970s rock band Led Zeppelin, Jimmy Page, is another rock artist that had a great interest in Aleister Crowley. Crowley was also pictured on the cover of Led Zeppelins fourth album.

Besides the Satanic lyrics in secular music, satanic messages are also being embedded in rock recordings. Many people are fooled thinking that artists aren't serious, they're just selling records, but this mind set is exactly what Satan wants.

Jimmy Hendrix had this to say about music...

"Atmosphere is going to come through music, because music is a spiritual thing on its own. You can hypnotize people with music and when you get them at their weakest point, you can preach into their minds whatever you want to say"- **Jimmy Hendrix**

We see numerous famous musicians declaring themselves as being evangelists for Satan and saying that they derive their power from him or publically admitting receiving their music from spirits or selling their souls to the devil. Artist such as Eminem, Katy Perry, Snoop Dogg, Bob Dylan, Jim Morrison, Carlos Santana, Lady Gaga, Tori Amos, Michael Jackson, Beyoncé and many others.

Music is riddled with automatic writing and **backmasking.**

Some musician have even openly admitted that they get their music and inspiration from spirits or an outside power and are even in some cases merely channels (or pawns?) for demonic forces. This even happens during writing music and. performances. Some of them have actually identified this as demonic power.

"...you meditate and you got the candles, you got the incense and you've been chanting, and all of a sudden you hear this voice: 'Write this down' " - **Carlos Santana, Rolling Stone magazine, March 16, 2000, p. 41.**

"I wake up from dreams and go 'Wow, put this down on paper,' the whole thing is strange. You hear the words, everything is right there in front of your face. I feel that somewhere, someplace it's been done and I'm just a courier bringing it into the world"- **MICHAEL JACKSON, Rolling Stone, Feb. 17, 1983.**

Lady Gaga has said that the spirit of her dead aunt lives inside of her and that the spirit of Alexander McQueen wrote her song, "Judas", for her.

The lead singer of the notorious band Nirvana, Curt Cobain, had such a desire to be respected and accepted, that Cobain would sell his soul to the Devil for the price of fame. He was "obsessed with Anton LaVey" (**Mojo Magazine, Sept. 1999, p. 86.**) going as far as wanting LeVay to record a song with him.

"Backmasking"

One of the fundamental "laws" of Satanism is the "Law of Reversal," taught by Aleister Crowley. This technique of doing things backward is taught in his magic handbook, "Magick in Theory and Practice". Crowley himself practiced this, talking BACKWARDS as part of his Satanic-worship.

These are the instructions given to Satanists concerning "Backwarding"

". . .train himself to think BACKWARDS by external means, as set forth here following.

(a) Let him learn to write BACKWARDS. . .
(b) Let him learn to walk BACKWARDS. . .
(c) Let him . . . listen to phonograph records REVERSED
(d) Let him practise speaking BACKWARDS. . .

(e) Let him learn to read BACKWARDS. . ."

Aleister Crowley, Magick: Liber ABA, book four, 1994 Ordo Templi Orientis edition, p. 639

Let's take a look at other examples of this "Law of Reversal,".

• The Black Mass: The entire Roman Catholic liturgy of the Mass is performed backwards, or in reversed speech. The Cross that is hung above the naked woman altar is upside down. Upside down is the reverse from the cross being the right way up.
• The Anti-Christ: This signals the reverse or direct opposite of Christ.
• Heaven is the reversal of Hell. Heaven is up. Hell is down.
• God is Light and the Devil is Darkness

This "law of reversal" or Backwarding forms the basis for "Backmasking. Backmasking is the process of reversing an audio signal and placing it in something meant to be played forwards. When played normally the message will sound like gibberish, however, when the song is played in reverse the original message can be heard" **Top 10 Famous Cases of Backmasking Andrew C. August 28, 2011**

Backward masking is seen by a lot of people as just coincidental or going over the top (or overboard) with something but "Backmasking" is a proven and confirmed ploy by Satanism and Satan and a clear and very present danger in music in general.

JZ, a popular rapper and husband of Beyoncé, has often been linked to the illuminati and it is stated that he is satanic. When his song "Lucifer 9" from the album "Dangermouse's The Grey Album", was reversed Gibberish played normally was the message "666...murder... murder... Jesus...666" when played backwards.

You can go and listen to this at www.listvers.com

www.jesus-is-savior.com Aleister Crowley's Influence in Music

The black metal band Slayer's song "Hell Awaits" (lyrics showed earlier in chapter) not surprisingly, contains backwards messaging. When listing to it in a normal way one hears nothing but garbled noise, but when played backwards the real message "JOIN US, JOIN US, JOIN US" is heard over and over again.

In the book, "Satanic Rituals", a companion book to the Satanic Bible, Anton LaVey also a plays the "Law of Reverse" by writing that on the altar of the devil... up is down, pleasure in pain, darkness is light, slavery is freedom, and madness is sanity."

According to popular culture the **"Law of Reverse / backwarding"** is playing out in more than just speech, but in the way people live their lives today. What is good and noble and right in God's eyes has become exactly what is bad in the eyes of the world. This saying of Anton LaVey mentioned above was in essence acted out in full view of the world stage, applauded by all guests attending music's biggest night. In so doing, this year's Grammys proved we are truly in the last days when it reached a dark, new low.

Katy Perry, daughter of two preachers performed her latest single, "Dark Horse" at this year's Grammys. It was truly a dark and mysterious performance, a real 'Satanic' ritual laced with the lyrics and imagery filled with the Occult. The performance kicked off with a sinister voice saying: "She casts spells from crystal balls. Invoking spirits. She put me in a trance."

She started off the performance enclosed in a crystal ball dressed like a witch. While she sings, back-up dancers, dressed like four horned demon-like figures, rises above her, and they are all surrounded by darkness. A real scene out of the Salem witch trials. Let's take a look at some of the lyrics;

So you wanna play with magic
Boy, you should know what you're falling for
Baby do you dare to do this?
Cause I'm coming at you like a dark horse

Other phrases saying;
Mark my words
This love will make you levitate
Like a bird / Like a bird without a cage
But down to earth / If you choose to walk away, don't walk away
This love will make you **levitate** / Like a bird
Like a bird without a cage" and "It's in the palm of your hand now baby
It's a yes or no, no maybe". (This gives the impression of palm reading.)

She went on to portray herself as a witch burning at the stake. In an interview with Rayan Seacrest, prior to the Grammys she hinted that she had a big event in store for the Grammy performance. Saying "Let's just say, one of my favourite lines: 'Which witch is which?'

After Katy Perry's performance even the mainstream entertainment media commented on its occultic nature.

And if all the occultic rituals were not enough, the musicians Macklemore and Ryan Lewis took the stage. While they were performing their marriage equality anthem, "Same Love", with Madonna and Mary Lambert, Queen Latifa officiated 34 weddings to both gay and straight couples to a back drop that looked like a church. Complete with glass stained windows and "gospel choir" and the lyrics of the song…"Whatever god you believe in; we come from the same one."

More of a satanic sex ritual and an open declaration of Satanism and witchcraft one could not get. Some said that this was a political act, but others feel that this was a full-fledged spiritual war that went on that night. In the "Satanic Rituals" book, a companion book to the Satanic Bible, it says that on the altar of the devil…

"Up is down, pleasure is pain, darkness is light, slavery is freedom, and madness is sanity." What is good is seen as bad and that which is bad is now seen as good. God is good and stands for "all" that is good. Satan wants people to believe that what happened at the Grammys, the acceptance of same sex marriage, is inspired by God as God is love. According to the world going against Homosexuality, and denying same sex marriage would not be God. Did God changed his mind? **Resounding NO**. The word of God says He never changes His mind.

"God is not a man, that He should lie, nor a son of man, that He should repent. Has He said, and will He not do? Or has He spoken, and will He not make it good-
Numbers 23:19

Popular Christian gospel singer Natalie Grant walked out of the Grammys after witnessing these performances and the next day had the following to say: "We left the Grammy's early. I've many thoughts, most of which are probably better left inside my head. But I'll say this - I've never been more honoured to sing about Jesus and for Jesus. And I've never been more sure of the path I've chosen." - **Natalie Grant 27 Jan 2014**

Looking back in history, so often, we find famous musicians dying in such tragic ways and yet the cycle continues. The sad fact is that rock stars who willingly sell their souls to Satan for money and fame may receive all they want, but they also get a lot they do not expect. They literally pay with their lives and their souls. Satan will eventually destroy them.

The sad part is that although Nirvana means "any place of complete bliss and delight and peace" Kurt Cobain never experienced this and by looking at his life will never get the opportunity to experience it for eternity.

The day that Kurt decided to takes his own life he wrote a suicide note giving reasons for doing so. One of them was that the devil was no longer helping or supplying him with any musical inspiration. He wrote, "I haven't felt the excitement of listening to as well as creating music, along with really writing, for too many years now." The demonic forces that Cobain had aligned himself with were no longer giving him the powerful musical inspirations which he was so infamous for.

You see this is Satan's well thought out plan; people are desperate for fame, recognition, acceptance, affluence, power and then he uses them like pawns until he does not need them any longer when he simply discards them like old rubbish. If that is not enough, Satan and his demons have no qualm finishing the job by leading a person like Kurt Cobain to commit suicide. Satan hates God's creations even if they sell their soul willingly to him.

What a tragic end to a God created being whom He loved so much that He gave His only begotten Son for. Despite this, Kurt chose a live filled with drugs, hatred, vandalism, blasphemy and devil worship and rejected the love and blood of Jesus. Kurt Cobain died by the very sword he used in his lyrics.

"I Hate Myself and I Want to Die." - Album "In Utero"
"Rape Me"- from the Album "In Utero"
"Look on the bright side is suicide" Milk it lyrics. Album "In Utero"

It is said that young Satanists believe the lie that the strong will rule with Satan. After they have sold their souls to Satan they make a pact with him, and commit themselves to a future date when they will take their own lives by suicide. They believe that if they submit themselves to Satan in death, they will come back in another life as a stronger being and rule with him forever.

Sadly, Cobain along with his fans were deceived from the get go, and many other people and musicians continue to be entrapped by the same snare.

[27] "And as it is appointed for men to die once, but after this the judgment,"
Hebrews 9:27

[10] "For we must all appear before the judgment seat of Christ, that each one may receive the things done in the body, according to what he has done, whether good or bad."
2 Corinthians 5:10

In conclusion I think it is important to note that in Anton LaVey's last moments of his life, he was begging God to let him live long enough to repent: "Please don't let me die….I can't go there." This is not surprisingly widely disputed by Satanists. In my opinion, in those last moments, LaVey probably realized, in a moment of clarity, that his life of Satanism had led him to the jaws of hell and he could see Satan for the liar that he is. I believe he got a glimpse of the judgment he was about to face for the life that he had led. - **YouTube. Anton LaVey begs for God's mercy; uploaded by projectinsighter.**

Hélèné Fulton

Chapter 3: Yin and Yang

Written By: Sanet Gericke

Introduction.

The occult forces of Yin and Yang does not exist in reality. The symbol of yin and yang is seen at almost any place. It's used on book covers, in logos, in the New Age movement, by Wiccans, in the martial arts and by the homosexual community. "Yin and Yang" are considered to be opposites:- opposing forces.

Yin:- represents eternity, dark, feminine, left side of the body, etc. Yin is female, negative represented by the Moon.

Yang:- the opposite and represent history, light, right side of body, masculine, etc. Yang is male, positive represented by the Sun.

Yin / Yang meaning dualism is the underlying satanic doctrine behind all the following false religions:- Cheng- I, Chen-Ta- Tao, Fang- Shih, Five Pecks of Rice, Chau- Chen, Chaung- Tzu, Five Elements, Lao Tzu, Lieh Tzu, Northern Heavenly Masters, Shang Ching Mao Shan sect, Tai Ping Tao/ Yellow Turbans, Tien Shih Tao (The Way of the Heavenly Master), Wu- tou- Mi- Tao (Five Pecks of Rice), Hsuan Hsueh,

Ling-Pao, Peng-Lai, Southern Heavenly Master, Tai-i, Wicca, and Taoism.

History

The symbol dates back to the fourth century B.C., identified with the Eastern Philosophical religions of Buddhism, Taoism and Confucianism. The symbolism of myth, astrology, magic, and witchcraft has long been adopted in the Western World.

The book, Black Magic, White Magic, explains the Yin-Yang like this:
"Another ancient magical sign called the yin and yang first appeared sometime before the 3rd century B.C. in China. This emblem became a favorite of sorcerers and mystic throughout the Orient because it, too, embodies so many possible meanings. "

Belief

Yin Yang became associated with Taoism, a religion in China several hundred years before Jesus Christ's birth on earth. The Tao, is loosely translated as "the Way" or "the Path " is the ultimate reality and origin of all things. This concept is not to be grasped intellectually because it describes a reality beyond the intellect. According to the Taoist teachings, the truth of Tao can only be understood indirect or through enlightened living. By living in the flow of the Tao, which is the flow of the universe, you can gain happiness. They have no personal God.

Where does the Yin and Yang come in? "Through the dynamics of yin and yang, the female and male cosmic principles, the Tao creates all phenomena. Whereas the Tao is perfectly harmonious, the cosmos is in a state of constant disequilibrium" (Spirituality by The Numbers, George Feuerstein).

One well-known witch, Sybil Leek, who is called the "mistress of the occult," proclaims that the Yin Yang theory is an idea that inspired such things as, breath control used in yoga and meditating, Chinese boxing, some rather erotic sexual exercises designed to nourish the Yang with the Yin and the use of special herbs. She further adds that the idea of Yin and Yang is crucial to Taoism.

According to the ancient Chinese philosophers, in the beginning was Tao. But then Tao separated into two prime principles, yang and yin. And from the many combinations yang and yin everything else that is in the world has emerged.

I am Alpha and Omega, the beginning and the ending, saith the Lord, which is, and which was, and which is to come, the Almighty.
Revelation 1:8

Thus saith the LORD the King of Israel, and his redeemer the LORD of hosts; I am the first, and I am the last; and beside me there is no God.
Isaiah 44:6

Out of Yin and Yang came the 'five elements':-
- Metal
- Water
- Fire
- Wood
- Earth

Everything in life is in a constant flux. In fact, the only thing you can be sure of is that it will change. The Yang-Yin symbol is one of the easiest symbols to recognize and to understand. The two opposites represent the conflicting forces that is found in every action which is responsible for the dynamic universe. Yin –Yang operate primarily through the agency of the five elements: Water (Mercury), Earth (Saturn), Wood (Jupiter), Metal (Venus), Fire (Mars) in the universe. These elements under guidance of the moon and sun and the five planets form the seven rulers. Each element can be Yin or Yang, that there can be combinations of all these could produce a broad number of possibilities (sic) and astrological alternatives. Each of these has its own symbol which can be incised into jade.

Mine hand also hath laid the foundation of the earth, and my right hand hath spanned the heavens: when I call unto them, they stand up together.

Isaiah 48:13

He hath made the earth by his power, he hath established the world by his wisdom, and hath stretched out the heavens by his discretion.

Jeremiah 10:12

And they shall spread them before the sun, and the moon, and all the host of heaven, whom they have loved, and whom they have served, and after whom they have walked, and whom they have sought, and whom they have worshipped: they shall not be gathered, nor be buried; they shall be for dung upon the face of the earth.

Jeremiah 8:2

> (Seek him) that maketh the seven stars and Orion, and turneth the shadow of death into the morning, and maketh the day dark with night: that calleth for the waters of the sea, and poureth them out upon the face of the earth: The LORD (is) his name:
>
> **Amos 5:8**

In Chinese and other Eastern thought, **yin and yang** are the two opposing and complementary forces that make up all phenomena of life. Both proceed from the Supreme Ultimate and together they represent the process of the universe and all that is in it.

According to the *Encyclopedia Britannica*, "The significance of Yin Yang through the centuries has permeated every aspect of Chinese thought, influencing astrology, divination, medicine, art, and government."

Yin has the following characteristics:
- Earth
- Female
- Dark
- Passive
- Absorbing
- Even numbers
- Valleys and streams
- The Tiger
- The colour orange
- A broken line

Yang has the opposite characteristics:
- Heaven
- Male
- Light
- Active

- Penetrating
- Odd numbers
- Mountains
- The Dragon
- The colour (**Azure** is a shade of blue that falls between blue and cyan)
- An unbroken line

There are no absolutes in Yin Yang (NO SIN)

- There is no good or bad according to the Taoist / Yin- Yang view, only that what seems to be good or bad.
- There is no death or life- Life and death are one, right and wrong is the same.
- Opposites are not really opposites – they appear that way to us –we perceive through dualism and can't see that opposites are part of the whole. Opposites contain the essence of each other and in the end merge with each other. This is the origin of the holistic view of the world and the body, it remains the basis today of the body-mind connection.
- The universe is mystical connected and interplaying, so is every person, rock, tree, animal, river, etc. Through Yin Yang.
- Referring to Tao, Wen- Tzu states :- "the Way has no back or front, no right or left: all things are the same, with no right or wrong,"

Jesus saith unto him, I am the way, the truth, and the life: no man cometh unto the Father, but by me.

John 14:6

Even when we were dead in sins, hath quickened us together with Christ, (by grace ye are saved;)

Ephesians 2:5

In whom we have redemption through his blood, *even* the forgiveness of sins:

Colossians 1:14

So when they continued asking him, he lifted up himself, and said unto them, He that is without sin among you, let him first cast a stone at her.

John 8:7

Wherefore, as by one man sin entered into the world, and death by sin; and so death passed upon all men, for that all have sinned:

Romans 5:12

As it is written, There is none righteous, no, not one:

Romans 3:10

And God said, Let us make man in our image, after our likeness: and let them have dominion over the fish of the sea, and over the fowl of the air, and over the cattle, and over all the earth, and over every creeping thing that creepeth upon the earth.

Genesis 1:26

Groups that practice the concept of Yin and Yang

The yin and yang concept (also called Tai-gi-tu) plays an important role in many other occult practices like:

- ➢ Shu shu - Is the ancient Chinese system of divination , magic , and occult practices , including : dream interpretation ,astrology and the art of coordinating human affairs by the passive and active principles of the five elements (wu hsing) and the universe (yin yang), dream interpretation fortune telling using : stalks of the divination plant and tortoise shell and the regulating of forms and shapes of buildings, etc.

And the soul that turneth after such as have familiar spirits, and after wizards, to go a whoring after them, I will even set my face against that soul, and will cut him off from among his people.
Leviticus 20:6

- In Health: A Holistic Approach we find: The techniques of moxibustion apply needle, acupuncture, pressure, acupressure, or thermal (heat) stimulation respectively to the meridian points to effect a change in the orderly flow of Chi through the meridians. This helps the establishment of the Yin Yang balance by initiating normal energy flow in stagnant meridians. The choice of meridian points to be stimulated is reached by using specific laws directly from the five-element theory and knowing the order of Chi distribute in the meridians. The five-element theory is the practical, tangible application of the complementary opposites - yin and yang.

- Tai Chi Ch'uan – The system of physiotherapy, or therapeutic exercises of the Chinese practices.

This is a system of exercises performed in close co-ordination of regulated breathing. The exercises comprise of thirty – seven movement patterns composed of the principles of Yin Yang. The Tai Chi

Ch'uan philosophy is rooted in Taoisme, they advocate natural effort , in the I Ching, or Book of changes. The movements and inner teachings are derived from the complementary relationship between yin and yang, two forces that create and harmonize the universe by their interaction. Interaction of Yin and Yang is vital to the practice of Tai Chi Ch'uan because physically and mentally the practitioner is shifting continually between empty and full and hard and soft to achieve a proper evolving equilibrium. In fact Tai Chi is represented by the dark and light. (Yin and Yang)

Other techniques dependent upon Yin Yang are: polarity therapy, Shaitsu, zone therapy, Jin-Shin, macrobiotics, Do-In the martial arts(such as Kung Fu, Karate, Chi Kung and Tai Chi), etc.

Palmistry

This is the occult practice of foretelling the future by reading a person hand palm. This is also based on the Yin Yang theories and the Five Elements. In an occult book – the Chinese Art of Healing, written by a Buddhist monk, he explains the ancients relate message, which includes Reflexology, to the Five Elements and to palmistry. He states: "The thumb was associated with the spleen that belong to the earth element, the index finger with the large intestine (metal)…and so on …..The massage form known as: from the water element to the earth element, reminds people of occult concepts of this kind. The palm of the hand contains the secrets of life via the Oriental magicians. According to the ancient Chinese school of thought the hand palm is a replica of Yin and Yang and that it could provide information regarding one's entire fate, illness and good health.

There shall not be found among you (any one) that maketh his son or his daughter to pass through the fire, (or) that useth divination, (or) an observer of times, or an enchanter, or a witch,

Deuteronomy 18:10

Free Masons:

They use the concept of yin and yang in their symbolism only in a disguised form. Albert Pike says the black and white pavement symbolises the good and evil principles of the Egyptian and the Persian creed. It is the warfare of Michael and Satan, of the gods and Titans of Balder and Lok, between dark and light, which is darkness; night and day; disposition and freedom..... etc.

They also use the two triangles that represent the idea of opposites. In the Short Talk a pamphlet distributed in Lodges, they state that the triangles are symbolic of good and evil, day and night, the Chinese Yin and Yang. The two triangles joint together forming a hexagram indicates sexual union, this viewpoint is also associated with the Yin and Yang. In our Phallic Heritage we are told that the union of sexes is necessary to produce offspring, both sexes were represented in most religions. Representations of the genitalia of both sexes, or of the sex organs in union were worshipped in the crudest form of worship. The worship of the phallus-kteis in Greece and Egypt, the massebasher of Syria, the lingam-yoni in India, the yang yin in China, the yoseki-inseki in Japan and the baal-peor of the Canaanites in the Bible.

Masonic author, George Oliver writes:
The monad and duad were the phallus and kteis of the Greeks, the lingam and yoni of the hindos, the woden and fringa of the Goths, and yang and yin of the Chinese, and indeed, of the destructive and creative powers of every country under heaven.
This thought is repeated in the myths and symbols of the Indian art and civilization.

Lingam and yoni, Shiva and his goddess, symbolize the clashing yet co-operating forces of the sexes. The Sacred Marriage (Greek : hieros-gamos) is frequently figured in several traditions of world mythology. They are the standard parents, Father and Mother of the world. The first born of the pairs of opposites, the first division of the primal, cosmic reality, now reunited in productive harmony. Under the form of Mother Earth and Father Heaven they were known by the Greeks as Zeus and Hera, Gaia and Uranos, to the Chinese Yang and Yin and Tien and Ti.

And forgettest the LORD thy maker, that hath stretched forth the heavens, and laid the foundations of the earth; and hast feared continually every day because of the fury of the oppressor, as if he were ready to destroy? and where is the fury of the oppressor?

Isaiah 51:13

Yin Yang Promotes Homosexuality

Since there is some yang (Male) in the yin (female) that is represented in the little dot, and the yin in the yang, the concept of bisexuality is symbolised. At times efforts were made to make gods bisexual. [4]Hermaphrodite is the best example. He was the son of Aphrodite and Hermes and clasped onto a nymph called Salmamco, who pleaded with the gods to make them inseparable. The gods heard the plea and form out of the two a perfect being whom possesses the characteristics of both sexes. The term hermaphrodite comes from this mystical being. The next example was Omphale a queen of Lydiathe task-mistress of Hercules, presented by a lion's skin and a club, (male symbols) while Hercules wears her gown and spins for her. Omphale is presented as double sexed and so Hercules by his dress and work. Omphale means bisexual, coming from 'Om', he universal Mother and phallus, the male organ. Likewise, Janus of the Greeks not only had opposite faces but was double sexed.

The new age movement approves homosexuality. In alchemy the male and female in one body was considerate to be the image of human perfection and wholeness. Bly, Nin and Jung tell us that each person must achieve inner marriage of their feminine and muscular natures to encounter true balance.

Homosexuality and bi-sexuality are encouraged by the new age teacher. The unholy doctrine of reincarnation and the principles of Yin Yang are perfect excuses and rationale for homosexuality and other forms of the sexual immorality. New Age teachers believe that if

---

[4] In biology, a hermaphrodite is an organism that has reproductive organs normally associated with both male and female sexes.

you are homosexual or a lesbian in this lifetime you were a person of the opposite sex in a previous life or incarnation. The influence of that past life is simply retained in your brain and consciousness. The Yin Yang principle called unity, integration or polarity, says that a person is born with both masculine and feminine traits. New Age encourage adults and children to practice the harmony of opposites, teaching them to merge the two selves, man and woman.

[26] For this cause God gave them up unto vile affections: for even their women did change the natural use into that which is against nature:
[27] And likewise also the men, leaving the natural use of the woman, burned in their lust one toward another; men with men working that which is unseemly, and receiving in themselves that recompense of their error which was meet.
[28] And even as they did not like to retain God in their knowledge, God gave them over to a reprobate mind, to do those things which are not convenient;
[29] Being filled with all unrighteousness, fornication, wickedness, covetousness, maliciousness; full of envy, murder, debate, deceit, malignity; whisperers,
[30] Backbiters, haters of God, despiteful, proud, boasters, inventors of evil things, disobedient to parents,
[31] Without understanding, covenant breakers, without natural affection, implacable, unmerciful:
[32] Who knowing the judgment of God, that they which commit such things are worthy of death, not only do the same, but have pleasure in them that do them
Romans 1:26-32

Many of the gods and goddesses of paganism have dual sexual natures. Mercury, called the 'male-female' was an example. Lots of symbols contain this:

- dual nature
- The serpent's head and neck is distinctly a masculine symbol, but the serpent is sometime symbolized with its tail in the mouth , the body forms a circle that is feminine, the mouth is feminine, while the tail, which is in the mouth, is masculine. For two good reasons the serpent with its tail in its mouth represents both sexes. Sacred fire was often prepared on religious occasions by rotating a realistic wooden replica of the phallus into a wooden representation of the vulva, rotating being done by an apparatus resembling a bow. The cornucopia, or horn of plenty, was a symbol of double sexed nature. The horn was masculine and the inside was feminine, fruit inside symbolized productiveness of the female.
- The four-limbed cross had a different meaning, and represented the male and the female in union, in the act of creation. A line or object has been used to symbolize the phallus, and a horizontal line the vulva. The surface of water, a female element in creation, was horizontal, and women were practically in the horizontal position in the act of creation. The four-armed cross was an easy figure to make, being an intersection of two straight lines, and it became a symbol of expressing the reverence for the act. Some of the Asherahs of the Bible represented Baal in union with Astoreth. The union between the sexes resulted in a new life. Separately, man and woman were incomplete, important, and barren, but in their union they became a perfect soul, realizing the immortality of life.

Rituals

- Yin Yang and Wicca Witchcraft: The witches themselves employ the demonic teachings of Yin and Yang. Wiccans do NOT believe in sin. Rather, is only what one appears to be wrong. Consequently, the whole concept of right and wrong within Wicca is relative. With Yin Yang, there are NO absolutes. What one person think is wrong, might not appear wrong to another. Just the fact that homosexuals and witches would cleave to the teachings of Yin and Yang reveal its dark nature.
- "YIN YANG: The Wicca circle is divided in four sections: earth, air, fire, and water. Each section has Yin Yang connections: earth and water = yin, fire and air = yang. The Yin Yang symbol is divided in half, one half the beginning and end of the yin energies, and the other half, the beginning and end of yang energies. This Yin Yang division represents both sides power, and is brought together by the High Priest and High Priestess. Yin and yang is two sides, not four, hence the passive powers of earth and water must be grouped on one half of the circle, and the active powers of air and fire must be grouped on the other half. - Yin Yang is used in Witchcraft ceremonies. Witchcraft is a sin according to the Word of God. Few believers today are aware of the evils of Yin and Yang, but there's no time like the present to learn the truth.

Hélèné Fulton

For rebellion is as the sin of witchcraft, and stubbornness is as iniquity and idolatry. Because thou hast rejected the word of the LORD, he hath also rejected thee from being king

1 Samuel 15:23

Groups Using the Yin Yang Symbol

A group that knows the sexual implications of the Yin Yang and uses it as their official symbol is The Sex Information and Education Council of the United States (SIECUS). They promote extensive sex education in schools. SIECUS Statements reveal the following: It is the believe of SIECUS that contraceptive services should be available to all that includes minors who should have the same rights of free and independent access to contraceptive care as others. It is the opinion of SIECUS that the use of explicit sexual materials (pornography) can serve a variety of important needs in the lives of many individuals. Another group using the Yin Yang (knowingly or unknowing) is the Girls Scouts. In the Girl Scout Badges and Signs book, the Yin Yang symbol is used for the World in My Community proficiency badge. In the Junior Girl Scout Handbook Yoga exercises are explained. The Year of Magic was their theme for their 1987 program. Many holistic groups, dealing with natural remedies uses the occultic principles of Yin Yang. Many people accept the body-mind connection of holism because they know that our attitudes often affect our health or recovery from illness. Attitudes and the contemporary mystical holistic view are two separate things. The holistic view of the body and of health is based in monism, that one is all and all is one, and a universal force (referred to as chi or qi) connects us and flows through the body. Holism today says that all illness is an imbalance of or blockage of the chi and/or the Yin Yang forces in the body, and that the state of one's health is a reflection of this spiritual imbalance or blockage.

The I Ching (Book of Changes) is another occult practice that incorporates the use of the Yin Yang. Geoffrey Parrinder writes: "The Yin Yang dualism entered into Confucian orthodoxy by its incorporation into the I Ching - a late compilation from, and rational arrangement of, earlier works on divination."

William Spear teaches astrology and macrobiotics and has been using the I Ching for 20 years? He states: "Taoism, inseparable from the philosophy of the I Ching, is based on the complimentary yet antagonistic principles of Yin and Yang which mutually create and destroy each other by the ceaseless rearrangements of their relationship. The basic rule they obey is life's only certainty change." One ad for a book by Diane Stein on the I Ching (also called Kwan Yin) tells us: "The Kwan Yin Book of Changes is a wonderful book, finding admirers, with not only new agers, and feminists, but others such as pagans, divination fans, goddess worshippers, and those involved with Eastern philosophy. "Of course Diane Stein isn't the only pagan who uses the I Ching.

A witchcraft magazine, Circle Network News, gives an extensive ritual to be used in connection with the I Ching. Part of the witchcraft instructions are: "An altar should be set up in the middle of a room facing north. Lay the stalks in the middle of the altar along with the I Ching book that you are going to use and your I Ching journal. Include on the altar other ritual tools and symbols that you feel you need. They must include burning incense. Ritually purify yourself and the space with techniques you choose. Ground and center. Call the quarters and spirit in a fashion that feels appropriate. Once you have determined the hexagram, draw it in your journal. Look it up within the text of your I Ching book. When you feel complete with your answer and have recorded all relevant information in your journal, pay respects to the I Ching in whatever way you feel comfortable. Thank the demons, and the quarters for helping with your work. New Ager, Jeffrey S. Stamps, uses the Yin Yang in a slightly different form. He calls his symbol the Emergent Tao. He explains: The ridgepole symbolizes the line of the roof, separating heaven from earth. As a line, the ridgepole is unity, but it also generates duality - a right and left, front and back, above and below - in a word, the world of opposites.'..."As a symbol of change, Tao, too, may change. To compress my thought of many pages to a single symbol, I offer Emergent Tao...This symbol extends the traditional T'ai chi symbol of the circle with a ridgepole dividing the complements of yin and yang. I have added the spiral curves between the outer circle and the two inner circles. With these lines, the symbol clearly expresses emergence and levels: the circle of the whole and the "higher" and "lower" smaller circles/levels. Emergent Tao expresses the essence of Holonomy: complements, levels, and unitary process."

Emergent Tao

The Word of God Condemns Yin Yang. The Yin Yang symbol is quite appropriate today for humanists, New

Agers, witches, Satanists, etc. As Michael Tierra, a proponent of the Yin Yang theory, states: "The Yin Yang theory is a teaching method and does not define anything absolute."

There are seven laws concerning the Yin Yang, one of which is:
Everything changes. This is an important item to notice. The idea that "everything changes" does not agree with the Bible.

Jesus Christ the same yesterday, and to day, and for ever.
Hebrews 13:8

Every good gift and every perfect gift is from above, and cometh down from the Father of lights, with whom is no variableness, neither shadow of turning.
James 1:17

For **I am the Lord, I change not**;
Malachi 3:6

Another law is that all antagonisms are complementary. Again, this is contradictory to Scriptures. This would make Jesus and Satan complementary to each other! What blasphemy!

But the fruit of the Spirit is love, joy, peace, longsuffering, gentleness, goodness, faith,
Galatians 5:22-23

Now the works of the flesh are manifest, which are (these); Adultery, fornication, uncleanness, lasciviousness,
Galatians 5:19-21

Yet another law is the extreme of any condition will produce signs of the opposite. Again applying this to Christ would mean that because He is the extreme in goodness, mercy, compassion, etc., that He will produce signs of hate, injustice, unconcern, etc. This also would make Satan eventually become kind, loving, obedient, and so forth. The Bible warns: Which justify the wicked for reward, and take away the righteousness of the righteous from him.

Woe unto them that call evil good, and good evil; that put darkness for light, and light for darkness; that put bitter for sweet, and sweet for bitter!

Isaiah 5:20

Woe unto them that are wise in their own eyes, and prudent in their own sight!

Isaiah 5:21

In addition to the seven laws of Yin Yang, there are twelve theorems. One of these is: 8. Nothing is solely Yin or Yang; everything involves polarity. This states that nothing is entirely good or entirely evil. This again contradicts the Scripture.

Thou art of purer eyes than to behold evil, and canst not look on iniquity

Habakkuk 1: 13

The Bible also tells us that there is no truth in Satan.

Ye are of your father the devil, and the lusts of your father ye will do. He was a murderer from the beginning, and abode not in the truth, because there is no truth in him. When he speaketh a lie, he speaketh of his own: for he is a liar, and the father of it.

John 8:44

The Yin Yang theory is not consistent with God's Word. There are probably hundreds upon hundreds of groups that have used the Yin Yang in their logo or symbolism. Some groups do so innocently, the majority of them know exactly what they are doing and what the occult symbolism means.

Chapter 4: Pieter L White
"People of Jesurene"

Written By: Matthew Dean

There is a sect in the Western Cape province of South Africa called the People of Jesurene. The sect leader is Pieter L White. They are based on a farm called Grootdam, some 100km north of the sleepy town of Ceres. In other words, very far away from civilisation! My most recent knowledge of them – and indeed all I can trace on the Internet – dates back to 2010. See the local news article. The article is from January 2010. The experience I will write about is from February-March 2010, which is after the police involvement.

[5]South Africa: 'White Supremacy Cult' Trio in Court
By Lavern De Vries (Crime Writer), 21 January 2010

Three men, who allegedly belong to a religious cult that believes in white supremacy, have appeared in the Ceres Magistrate's Court on attempted murder charges.

Peter White, 45, Johan Pretorius, 30, and a 17-year-old youth, who cannot be named as he is a minor, also face charges of assault with the intent to do grievous bodily harm (GBH), and crimen injuria.

The three, as well as a woman, Linda Koertzee, were tenants in holiday cottages on Grootdam farm.

---

[5]http://www.iol.co.za/news/south-africa/white-supremacy-cult-trio-in-court-1.471130

Hélèné Fulton

All four were arrested in December after a spat on the farm resulted in a gun being fired.

Police spokesman Inspector FC van Wyk said police were called and arrested farm owner Jan Roodt after he allegedly fired the shot.
Roodt, 66, then lodged complaints against three men, resulting in the charges against them of attempted murder, assault GBH and crimen injuria.

A day later police, acting on a tip-off, searched the farm and found 17 firearms of different calibres as well as two boxes of ammunition.
Police said the tenants were also found to be in possession of religious literature in which a sect, named the People of Jesurene, proclaim their superiority over all people of colour.
It is understood that the group refused to associate themselves with other race groups.

But Roodt's lawyer, Zirk Mackay, called the issue "a storm in a teacup".
Roodt, who was arrested for the illegal possession of the firearms, appeared in court last week.
He also faces a charge of attempted murder as a result of the spat, and is out on bail of R1 000.
He is expected to appear in court again on May 14.
White, Pretorius and the 17-year-old, who have since moved from the farm, appeared in court on Tuesday.
They were granted bail of R6 000 each.

They are expected to appear in court again on February 17.

Koertzee, who appeared separately from the three men, was found guilty of assault and was fined R1 500 or six months in prison.

It is understood that Roodt allowed them to stay on the farm as they were friends of his wife.

None of the suspects has been linked to other previous or current criminal cases.

I had a friend back then; female, 24 years of age and single. To protect her, I will not name her. But here is the background. She grew up in a remote village all her life; a year prior to this case her family moved to a part of Johannesburg and she joined them. She found it hard to make proper friends here, so turned to social network websites and instant messaging programs – especially Mxit. For those who do not know Mxit, it is an instant messaging program most often used on mobile phones. Some people use it for good – I have heard of people trying to spread the Good News this way – but often it is used for terrible purposes; in some cases, rape and kidnap. At the time I used Mxit but stopped using it a long while ago and absolutely advise against this horrible network, due to the level of sexual sin and danger that it leads many of its users to.

So, she was lonely; she was in a new, strange city; she had also had a bad experience with an ex-boyfriend. Although she was living with her parents, she felt really lonely. She was a Christian (Baptist) so did have some scriptural background at least.

I got to know this person from a social network site, and we used Mxit to chat regularly. One day she told me about a friend of hers in the Western Cape who was professing his love for her. He was showering her with affection and compliments and on such a regular basis that she would get annoyed about it. His name was Pieter L White. She would say how she would not bother having contact with him. But she still did. She saw the newspaper article (see the second paragraph of this article) so knew he was bad news.

She gave me his Facebook details so that I could check him out. So I approached him directly to find out who he was and what he believed. In his first response to me, he was very friendly and amicable, but without prompt launched into a long attack of the King James Bible. He claimed that because the word [6] "trinity" is not in the KJV, it is a Catholic lie that a Holy Trinity exists. This is a stereotypical cult/sect

---

[6] The Bible, God's Word, proclaims that there is ONE God, Who has revealed Himself to mankind in three distinct Persons; namely, God the Father, God the Son and God the Holy Spirit. Although the term "Trinity" is not found in the Scriptures, the word "Godhead" most certainly is — in 3 places!

[19] because what may be known of God is manifest in them, for God has shown it to them. [20] For since the creation of the world His invisible attributes are clearly seen, being understood by the things that are made, even His eternal power and Godhead, so that they are without excuse

Romans 1:19-20

[29] Forasmuch then as we are the offspring of God, we ought not to think that the Godhead is like unto gold, or silver, or stone, graven by art and man's device.

Acts 17:29 (KJ)

[9] For in him dwelleth all the fulness of the Godhead bodily.

Colossians 2:9 (KJ)

characteristic and I saw through it. When I replied to tell him that the Bible *does* speak of the Holy Trinity – albeit not with the word "trinity" – his next reply was short and aggressive: "Just go onto my site and read my stuff". So I did. I cannot find his website right now, so I hope the police eventually got to him. But to describe it; it looked almost like the website of a regular church. It spoke of charity work, it gave SARS (inland revenue) references as a non-profit organisation; it "looked" above board. But it was most definitely not.

That was my one and only direct interaction with him. So my former friend knew full well that he was a sect leader and would just laugh it off and makes jokes about him. But she refused to break contact with him, despite apparently knowing the dangers of getting involved with a sect.

He later told her that he has a wife, other wives, and wanted her to be his wife too as he loved her. She would make fun of him to me, then said she was invited to visit him and she was going. She claimed that she wanted to go there just to learn more about him, and to expose his sect to the world. But the day before she left, she was in a terrible state; it boiled down to "at least he cares for me, who else does". I was very concerned so pleaded with her to keep my contact details handy in case of trouble.

She was booked for a two-week visit to him in "Cape Town". He specifically did not tell her *where* in Cape Town. Her flight went there on the Wednesday. Because he was under house arrest following the police involvement in January 2010*, he was not there in person to meet her. There, she was met by his wife and some other followers who fetched her at the airport. She went to stay on the farm and honestly believed she was somewhere in the Cape Town area.

*I discovered that he had since met an acquaintance of mine in mid-2011, in Johannesburg; assumedly the house-arrest was lifted?

On arrival, Pieter L White showered her with affection and love. On the Thursday he walked with her for hours, again showering her with affection and love; and said he would marry her, besides his current wives. At the compound there were at least two other young women being groomed for marriage to him. She was also subjected to "Bible study" lasting many hours, where he only read and quoted from the book of Numbers.

On that Thursday, she was forbidden by him to have any contact with any other males; after all, he was supposed to marry her! Luckily though, she remembered what I said, so changed my listed name on Mxit to a female name. This later proved to be crucial in getting her out of there. Because I know that sect leaders hate followers having contact with the outside world, and are liable to confiscate her mobile phone and even send messages on her behalf to say "I'm fine, leave me alone", we agreed on using a password during every form of contact. If she didn't use it, I'd know there was trouble.

On the Friday and Saturday, she was subjected to many hours of "Bible study" which again came only from the book of Numbers, twisted to suit Pieter L White's crazy ideas. By Saturday evening, she was starting to realise the possible danger involved, so gave me her sister's contact details just in case.

More cause for concern was when I asked about how she got to Cape Town and where she was. It emerged that the flight tickets were paid for with cash – in other words, no debit or credit card mentioned on the ticket and therefore not traceable to an address. The tickets were also not in her actual possession anymore. Clearly Pieter L White was intent on keeping her there for longer than the supposed two weeks! Also, she had no idea whatsoever where she was. She didn't even know the name of the compound! Apparently, when she was picked up in Cape Town, those in the car constantly talked to her, which diverted her attention from the time it took to get to the compound, and distracted her from looking at signposts along the road. I was the one who told her where she was, and she was shocked – 100km north of Ceres on the Grootdam farm.

By Sunday morning it was going bad. She was starting to get a bit worried and I managed to get her mother's contact details. She had been having "sex lessons" – not physically, but she was being taught how to have sex! I instantly phoned her mother to warn her of what was going on. I also got in touch with Friedrich Griess, an international sect expert.

On the Monday, it got serious. In the morning she was told that in the afternoon they would be having lessons to teach them how to have an orgasm. For me, that was an instant red flag that she was about to be raped soon. I immediately phoned the police in Ceres to tell them what had been going on. They told me that

Pieter L White was being investigated by the Falcons (a special unit) but would go check them out immediately. I also phoned her mother to tell them what had happened and gave both her and the police each other's details. They arranged for a relative of hers in Cape Town to drive to the farm and fetch her. She was, therewith, rescued. After spending a few days with her relative, she returned to Johannesburg. After explaining to Friedrich Griess what had happened, he confirmed that she would have almost certainly been raped and held at the compound against her will.

I am really grateful that we managed to get her out of that sect. Initially she was furious with me for getting the police involved and having her removed from the compound, but eventually seemed to be grateful. We continued being friends for a few months, but she eventually stayed very quiet, even ignoring me. If I ever asked if something was wrong, she would tell me I'm her best friend. Yet she kept ignoring me, and now I have no means of contacting her. These things happen; it is very sad, but at least I know she is safe to pursue her life; it could have ended far worse.

As for Pieter L White, I have no idea what has happened since. A few months after the rescue, I received a very strange phone call. It lasted about a minute and there was lots of background noise; it sounded like a group of women in distress, but not actually at the phone. The strange thing is that the area code was from around the Ceres area. I told my former friend, but she didn't know the number – and though we tried afterwards to phone the number back, there was no answer.

But what is interesting is this: last year there were all kinds of websites related to him. There was his own website for a start. Now when I look with Google, there is no such website anymore. There are a few related blog sites, and an incredible amount of social network sites where he is a member of, but at a glance they haven't been touched in a while. I really hope and pray that this monster is in jail as you are reading this.

So be on your guard my friends! There are still all kinds of demonic sects out there, even here in South Africa. If you know somebody who has the characteristics of being vulnerable – far away from home, lonely, depressed, no real life outside of work, longing to be loved – help them. Let them know you care about them and love them. Let them know that God loves them more than anything else. Invite them to your house or socialise with them. But don't just do nothing; sect leaders are on the prowl. In this case there was a good ending, but next time they could be successful!

Finally, just a light hearted part of this story. Pieter L White apparently knew that I was giving my former friend information about cults and sects. He was apparently very concerned about me knowing about him, and believed I was a sect specialist from Interpol. To my knowledge, nobody told him otherwise.

Note (2 December 2011) - *About 2 weeks after originally publishing this piece, I received a rather nasty comment on my guestbook, calling me a liar, then asking for contact. I e-mailed the person, who claimed to be a woman. First the woman made an* *intimidating threat that Pieter White wants to sue; ater more contact claimed "she" was being sued "too", then changed her story and harassed me to meet "her" to "get more information" but I mustn't tell anybody. Highly suspicious.*

To be safe, I removed the article temporarily. I then handed all the e-mails, as well as my article and all supporting written evidence and sources over to the authorities. I also ran the same via a lawyer to make sure I'm fine. And indeed, here is the article again, unedited from the original. Besides this, my site does have a disclaimer and I'm aware of the various applicable laws, and I am still safe on this one. Intimidation will not work.

10 January 2013 - *I had mentioned this in April but somehow that update got lost on the website. My bad! But I had spoken with a friend, who met Pieter in person and debated him in 2011, in Johannesburg - hence it would appear the house arrest no longer stands. The debate was apparently interesting, with Pieter claiming the "mark of Cain" doctrine (that is, the idea that when God marked Cain, He actually made him black, hence black people would be cursed). When replied to with "how's that even possible because there were only 8 people on the ark during the flood, his response was that he "had a vision from God telling him so". Oh Really?.*

20 February 2013 - *I have learned that he is indeed free from house arrest and is back in the Strand (Cape Town); still trying to charm ladies despite being married - one of them informed me. Remember, the aim is 7 wives…*

# [7]Chapter 5: Scientology

L. Ron Hubbard quote:
"Writing for a penny a word is ridiculous. If a man really wants to make a million dollars, the best way would be to start his own religion"

Reader's Digest reprint, May 1980, p.1

Hubbard later created the Church of Scientology...

2 But there were also false prophets among the people, even as there will be false teachers among you, who will secretly bring in destructive heresies, even denying the Lord who bought them, *and* bring on themselves swift destruction.

2 Peter 2:1

Scientology is a false religion, founded in 1953, which leads people into Hell.

According to a quote from www.scientology.org Frequently Asked Questions section on What is Scientology About?
......Scientology further holds man to be basically good, and that his spiritual salvation depends upon himself and his fellows and his attainment of brotherhood with the universe.

[23] for all have sinned and fall short of the glory of God

Romans 3:23

[12] Therefore, just as through one man sin entered the world, and death through sin, and thus death spread to all men, because all sinned

---

[7] For this Chapter we used the King James Version

Romans 5:12

⁸ For by grace you have been saved through faith, and that not of yourselves; *it is* the gift of God, ⁹ not of works, lest anyone should boast.

Ephesians 2:8-9

This is in sharp contrast with the Word of God which states that mankind is inherently sinful and cannot save himself.

Man is not sinful because he sins; man sins because he is sinful by nature. When Adam sinned, he opened the gate for sin and death to enter the human race. Mankind is basically evil and is totally incapable of saving himself through any self-righteous efforts

⁵ not by works of righteousness which we have done, but according to His mercy He saved us, through the washing of regeneration and renewing of the Holy Spirit

Titus 3:5

Scientology and the Occult

Carefully notice the two Illuminati pyramids in the Scientology logo to the right, with a big "S" passing through them.

To gain a perspective on the significance of this, please read Appendix 1 & 2. Anytime you see those Illuminati pyramids, you know the Devil is involved. Scientology is simply repackaged New Age heresy.

Hélèné Fulton

The goal of New Age doctrine is to homogenize the world's religions into a universal, undefined, ambiguous, false religion. The basic idea behind New Age is that there are many paths to the "light"; but that light is Lucifer. Truth is truly stranger than fiction my friend.

The following quote is from www.scientology.org.

What is Scientology?

Introduction to Scientology ...

Scientology is the study and handling of the spirit in relationship to itself, others and all of life. The religion comprises a body of knowledge extending from certain fundamental truths. Prime among these:

Man is an immortal, spiritual being. His experience extends well beyond a single lifetime. His capabilities are unlimited, even if not presently realized — and those capabilities can be realized. He is able to not only solve his own problems, accomplish his goals and gain lasting happiness, but also achieve new, higher states of awareness and ability.

In Scientology no one is asked to accept anything as belief or on faith. That which is true for you is what you have observed to be true. An individual discovers for himself that Scientology works by personally applying its principles and observing or experiencing results.

Through Scientology, people all over the world are achieving the long-sought goal of true spiritual release and freedom.

That is exactly what the New Agers such as Oprah Winfrey teach. Says Oprah, "One of the most important books I've read is Eric Butterworth's (a New Age Unity leader), *Discover the Power Within You*." In the book Butterworth blasphemes God by stating ... "*Jesus did not come to teach us how divine He was but to teach that divinity was within us.*" Later Oprah said that "*It* (claiming exclusive Divinity) *would make Jesus the biggest egotist that ever lived.*"

New Agers such as Oprah believe that mankind can be elevated to divine status through self-improvement, enlightenment, and spiritualism. Oprah's close friend and show guest, Shirley MacLaine, described on a show how to meditate, by going inside yourself, asking your own "intuitive Self" to seek answers to life's questions. Oprah responds, "You know, that is the same as the Bible says, 'Ask and it shall be given, seek and ye shall find'." Shirley confirms. Do you see how subtle Satan's false prophets are ... even twisting the Word of God around in an attempt to deceive people? New Age is damnable heresy folks, and it's the exact same garbage that Scientology teaches.

In the Scientology quote above, we read ... "*Man is an immortal, spiritual being ... He is able to not only solve his own problems, accomplish his goals and gain lasting happiness, but also achieve new, higher states of awareness and ability.*" There's not a dime's difference between the ultimate goal of New Age and Scientology-man can become his own god!

Satan is the god of this world

⁴ In whom the god of this world hath blinded the minds of them which believe not, lest the light of the glorious gospel of Christ, who is the image of God, should shine unto them.

2 Corinthians 4:4

and he controls the false religions of this world. The Illuminati pyramid is the symbol of an organization's allegiance to Satan. The agenda behind all of this is to brainwash the masses into accepting and following the Antichrist when he comes. The world's masses are being conditioned for Satan.

¹⁰ And with all deceivableness of unrighteousness in them that perish; **because they received not the love of the truth, that they might be saved.**

2 Thessalonians 2:10

The above verse from scripture tells us why so many people will be deceived.

Scientology: A Thriving Greedy Cult

The following quote is from *Time Magazine*; May 6, 1991; Page 50; Special Report (cover story); by Richard Behar; *The Thriving Cult of Greed and Power* ...

The Church of Scientology, started by science-fiction writer L. Ron Hubbard to "clear" people of unhappiness, portrays itself as a religion. In reality the church is a hugely profitable global racket that survives by intimidating members and critics in a Mafia-like manner. At times during the past decade, prosecutions against

Scientology seemed to be curbing its menace. Eleven top Scientologists, including Hubbard's wife, were sent to prison in the early 1980s for infiltrating, burglarizing and wiretapping more than 100 private and government agencies in attempts to block their investigations. In recent years hundreds of longtime Scientology adherents - many charging that they were mentally of physically abused - have quit the church and criticized it at their own risk. Some have sued the church and won; others have settled for amounts in excess of $500,000. In various cases judges have labeled the church "schizophrenic and paranoid" and "corrupt, sinister and dangerous."

Scientology boasts of some famous members in Hollyweird…

In Hollywood, Scientology has assembled a star-studded roster of followers by aggressively recruiting and regally pampering them at the church's "Celebrity Centers," a chain of clubhouses that offer expensive counseling and career guidance. Adherents include screen idols Tom Cruise and John Travolta, actresses Kirstie Alley, Mimi Rogers, and Anne Archer, Palm Springs mayor and performer Sonny Bono, jazzman Chick Corea and even Nancy Cartwright, the voice of cartoon star Bart Simpson. Rank-and-file members, however, are dealt a less glamorous Scientology.

The musician and congressman, Sonny Bono, was also a longtime Scientologist. Elvis Presley's widow and daughter, Priscilla and Lisa Marie, are also Scientologists. The cult appeals to the rich and famous because God is undefined, and man can become his own god if he so chooses. In sharp contrast, the Word of God defines God by name ... Jesus Christ!

⁶ For unto us a child is born, unto us a son is given: and the government shall be upon his shoulder: and his name shall be called Wonderful, Counsellor, The mighty God, The everlasting Father, The Prince of Peace.

Isaiah 9:6

1 In the beginning was the Word, and the Word was with God, and the Word was God.

John 1:1

¹⁴ And the Word was made flesh, and dwelt among us, (and we beheld his glory, the glory as of the only begotten of the Father,) full of grace and truth.

John 1:14

³³ The Jews answered him, saying, For a good work we stone thee not; but for blasphemy; and because that thou, being a man, makest thyself God.

John 10:33

⁹ For in him dwelleth all the fulness of the Godhead bodily.

Colossians 2:9

¹⁶ And without controversy great is the mystery of godliness: God was manifest in the flesh, justified in the Spirit, seen of angels, preached unto the Gentiles, believed on in the world, received up into glory.

1 Timothy 3:16

⁸ I am Alpha and Omega, the beginning and the ending, saith the Lord, which is, and which was, and which is to come, the Almighty.

Revelation 1:8

Jesus is God Almighty!
Scientology is a front religion for a continuation of Aleister Crowley's Luciferian teachings and dogmas. Thus, the cult is supported by many famous Hollywood actors and celebrities. Even mass-murderer Charles Manson was once a devout follower of Scientology.

The Church has long opened its door to artists, musicians, writers and actors to get a spiritual look at their lives and careers, and state that Scientology can help them be more successful in their lives. Among the most well-known celebrity Scientologists are Tom Cruise, John Travolta, Juliette Lewis, Kirstie Alley, Leah Remini, Catherine Bell, Nancy Cartwright, Beck, Kelly Preston, Elisabeth Moss, Erika Christensen, Jason Lee, Edgar Winter, Giovanni Ribisi, Jenna Elfman, Anne Archer, Chick Corea and opera singer Julia Migenes. The January 14, 2008, issue of The New Yorker magazine included a feature by Dana Goodyear, "Château Scientology," on the topic of Scientology and Hollywood celebrities.

According to prosecuting attorney Vincent Bugliosi in his 1974 book Helter Skelter, American serial murderer Charles Manson had been an avid Scientologist in the mid-1950s, claiming for years to be proud of his Theta Clear status.(10) Bugliosi referenced Manson's interest in Scientology several times during his trial as a basis for some of Manson's psychologies about human culture and behavior.
SOURCE: [8]Scientology and celebrities

---

[8] https://en.wikipedia.org/wiki/Scientology_and_celebrities

Hélèné Fulton

L. Ron Hubbard's Bizarre Claims and Teachings

Any reasonable person has to wonder what Scientology's founder, L. Ron Hubbard, was smoking.

Hubbard is documented to have written about past life memories that include all stages of human evolution since the clam (see [9]Scientology History of Man), lives on past planets as other life forms, and real and implanted memories from the alien spirits that [10]Xenu trapped on Earth 75 million years ago.

SOURCE: [11]WIKIPEDIA, *Scientology Beliefs and Practices* - past lives

Past lives, evolution, implanted memories from aliens? Whoa! Hubbard even claimed that he had experienced life on other planets in different life forms! The amazing thing is that millions of victims have been foolish enough to even follow Hubbard ... and make him filthy rich!

The following information is from http://www.sweenytod.com/cos/#IntroScn ...

Scientology is a religion invented by L. Ron Hubbard, a science fiction writer who died in 1986. It is a mixture of the 'science of mental health' and religious philosophy. They believe that through their technologies and practices they can, through their own effort, achieve immortality and spiritual fulfillment.

The official numbers put the church as "ministering to some 8 million people in more than 100 countries", although how many of those 8 million are active Scientologists is not mentioned.

---

[9] http://en.wikipedia.org/wiki/Scientology_History_of_Man
[10] http://en.wikipedia.org/wiki/Xenu
[11] https://en.wikipedia.org/wiki/Scientology_and_celebrities

The upper teachings of Scientology are similar to those of a UFO based religion. They teach that Earth is a prison planet, home to the souls of millions of murdered intergalactic beings. They teach that an evil galactic overload named Xenu had them all killed in order to solve a massive overcrowding problem. This is known as Incident 2. This is not a joke. These are the actual teachings of Scientology. Ex-members have confirmed it. For a complete analysis of Incident 2, please see http://www.xs4all.nl/~kspaink/fishman/ot3.html.

The following information is from http://www.sweenytod.com/cos/#CompatReligion.

Scientology claims to be compatible with all religions.

This section looks at that claim, with a special focus on how it relates to orthodox Christianity.
L. Ron Hubbard, the creator of Scientology, the following:
- Claim that man invented God.
- Claim that there **was no Christ.**
- The Christian faith is part of an implant, a false memory planted by an evil space alien.
- Say that because Scientology and Christianity disagree, the Christian religion cannot be true.
- Claim to have been nearly run down by a train on Venus (yes, the planet Venus - I kid you not).
- A number of other things, that you'll just have to [12]listen to yourself!

Clearly, Ron Hubbard was NO Christian! Hubbard was a wolf in Sheep's clothing, and the cult of

---

[1212] http://www.sweenytod.com/cos/Sounds/index.html

Scientology is straight out of the pits of Hell. Unbelievably, Scientologists today claim that Christianity and Scientology are compatible. The honest truth is that Christianity is diametrically opposed to the damnable false religion of Scientology. The following writings of the lunatic, L. Ron Hubbard - the ideals and policies that he developed for the Church of Scientology to blindly follow, clearly prove that the *Church of Scientology* is NOT in any way compatible with Christianity:

- "There are gods above all other gods, and gods beyond the gods of the universes." (Scientology, 8-8008, pp. 72-3)

- "The whole Christian movement is based on the victim ... A Scientologist is not a victim ... We can win by converting victims. Christianity succeeded in making people into victims. We can succeed by making victims into people" (HCO Bulletin, 18 July 1959).

- "Neither Lord Buddha, nor Jesus Christ were O T's according to the evidence. They were just a shade above clear" (Ability, No. 81, 1959).

- Scientology claims that it alone "brings man to total freedom and truth" (A Description of the Scientology Religion, p. 57). The Word of God teaches that Jesus Christ shed His blood upon the cross to set us free (Galatians 5:1; 1st Peter 1:18-19).

- "It is despicable and utterly beneath contempt to tell a man he must repent, that he is evil"

(Professional Auditor Bulletin (PAB) #31, 23 July 1954). In sharp contrast, Romans 3:23 declares ... "For all have sinned."

- "Nobody but the individual can die for his sins" (HCO Bulletin, 2 January 1960). Hubbard is a liar! Unsaved men who die in their sins without Christ will die the second death, paying for their sins forever in the Lake of Fire (Revelation 20:11-15, 21:8). 1st Corinthians 15:3 proclaims ... "For I delivered unto you first of all that which I also received, how that Christ died for our sins according to the scriptures."

- "It is a basic tenet of Scientology that man is basically good ... Sin is composed ... of lies and hidden actions and is therefore untruth" (What is Scientology? p. 546). Romans 3:10 states the exact opposite.

- "Hell is a total myth, an invention just to make people unhappy and is a vicious lie" (PAB #130, 15 Feb. 1958). Is L. Ron Hubbard being punished in Hell at this moment for his rejection of Christ.

- "Religion ... being basically a control mechanism used by those who have sent the preclear into a body. You will find the cross as a symbol all over the universe, and the Christ legend as an implant in preclears millions of years ago" (PAB #31, 23 July 1954).

- In Scientology's Class 8 course, lecture 10, (3 October 1968) Hubbard taught, "Somebody somewhere on this planet, back about 600 B.C.

found some pieces of R6, and I don't know how they found it, either by watching madman or something. But since that time they have used it and it became what is known as Christianity. The man on the cross. There was no Christ" (Corydon and Hubbard, L. Ron Hubbard, Messiah or Madman? p. 362). (Note 1)

- "Also the Christian church used (and uses) implanting ... They took over the Nicene Creed before the year zero, invented Christ (who comes from the crucifixion in R6 75M years ago, and implanted their way to power" (HCO Bulletin, 23 September 1968, Class VIII). (Note 1)

- Hubbard claimed that through "scientific research," not opinion, he went to Heaven. He wrote, "For a long while some people have been cross with me for my lack of cooperation in believing in a Christian Heaven, God, and Christ. I have never said that I didn't disbelieve in a Big Thetan, but there was something very corny about Heaven, et. al ... There was a heaven ... Yes, I've been to Heaven. And so have you. You have the pattern of its implants ... The Symbol of the crucified Christ is very apt indeed. It's the symbol of a [13]thetan betrayed ... The place is so full of lies by implant that the preclear becomes quite confused.... somebody discovered ...and utilized them to install religious mania and pin Thetans down to 'one life' and planets" ("Routine 3", HCO Bulletin, 11 May, A.D. 13 (pub. 1963) pp. 1-3).

---

[13] http://en.wikipedia.org/wiki/Thetan

- "But I imagine when we finally manage to communicate with beetles under rocks and free them, we'll no doubt find the Creator of Heaven who 43+ trillion years ago designed the Pearly Gates and entrapped us all. Good Lord, I'd hate to be guilty of that overt" (Ibid., p.4)

- August Murphy, president of the Church of Scientology of San Francisco wrote, "Another basic concept Scientology shares with universal religious thought is reincarnation. Like Buddhism, Hinduism, and early Christianity, Scientology believes that the individual as an immortal being has assumed many bodies in his evolution in the physical universe toward an ultimate realization and freedom from material bondage" (The News-Herald, 27 July 1992 p. 5). Reincarnation is a lie of the Devil.

- Hubbard claims that reincarnation was a belief held by the early Christian church and was removed by "four monks" at the "synod of Constantinople" in 553 A.D. (Have You Ever Lived Before This Life? p. 2).

- L. Ron Hubbard created an entire universal cosmology that includes an evil Galactic Ruler named Xenu. He places humans on other planets in the Solar System, including Mars and Venus. He populates billions of planets in the universe with people. Do they all have Jesus for their redemption? The Bible doesn't mention any of them. (OT III, see http://www.xenu.net/)

- L. Ron Hubbard claims that Scientology can give people supernatural powers including the power to heal the sick, both body and mind. Hubbard also created a ritual he called "touch assist" which is a Demonic version of the laying on of hands which does not call upon God's power (e.g. See *The Road to Xenu*, by Margery Wakefield).

So what do you think about the Church of Scientology's claim that their religion is somehow compatible with Christianity?

Note 1: The Church of Scientology claims that the documents which comprise "Operating Thetan Level 8" are forgeries. It is therefore surprising to note that when the Church of Scientology raided the home of Arnie Lerma for alleged copyright violations, the Church of Scientology identified copies of the OT8 documents as copyrighted materials belonging to their Church. Was that an error or does the Church of Scientology disavow L. Ron Hubbard's ideals and policies out of both embarrassment and the fact that his goal is to covertly lead as many people away from Jesus and redemption as possible?

The Satanic and Occult Influence in Scientology

Carefully notice the Illuminati pyramid in Aleister Crowley's hat to the right. The following information is from
http://www.sweenytod.com/cos/
#Occult ...
Aleister Crowley was a Satanist, and described himself as "The Beast." Crowley said this about Satan, the Devil:
"I was not content to believe in a personal devil and serve him,

in the ordinary sense of the word. I wanted to get hold of him personally and become his chief of staff." - Aleister Crowley, *The Confessions of Aleister Crowley*, chapter 5 (1929; revised 1970).

To the best of my knowledge, Mr. Hubbard was not a disciple of Crowley, but he was a fan. Crowley on the other hand is reported to have been in despair over Hubbard and his followers, calling them idiots. L. Ron Hubbard made reference to him in several of his lectures, and even called Crowley "my good friend" at least once.

Another interesting thing to look at is the Scientology cross. This is their symbol. You can see the huge similarity between Crowley's cross and the one Mr. Hubbard adopted for his new religion.

This clearly shows that the founder of Scientology was so impressed by A. Crowley's work, that he adopted his symbol.

The fact that L. Ron Hubbard was enamored with the occult needs to be kept in mind when evaluating what they teach. The techniques and processes used by Scientologists all over the world come from L. Ron Hubbard, a man influenced by the occult and Aleister Crowley, a Satanist who openly worshipped Lucifer. The Bible exposes Lucifer, who appears as an angel of light, as Satan.

[13] For such are false apostles, deceitful workers, transforming themselves into the apostles of Christ.

[14] And no marvel; for Satan himself is transformed into an angel of light.
[15] Therefore it is no great thing if his ministers also be transformed as the ministers of righteousness; whose end shall be according to their works.

2 Corinthians 11:13-15

For a much more exhaustive study on the subject, please refer to this report written by Jon Atack. These are a long read, but worth the effort if you're interested in the subject.

- [14] L. Ron Hubbard and the Occult, Part 1
- [15] L. Ron Hubbard and the Occult, Part 2
- [16] L. Ron Hubbard and the Occult, Part 3
- [17] L. Ron Hubbard and the Occult, Part 4

[18] I **strongly** recommend everybody who is serious about studying Scientology, L. Ron Hubbard and his relationship with other world religions to read this rather long page. It is heavy going, but worth the effort. I don't know of a better examination of the subject.

L. Ron Hubbard (founder of Scientology) calls Crowley, "My very good friend"

---

[14] http://www.sweenytod.com/cos/huboccult1.html
[15] http://www.sweenytod.com/cos/huboccult2.html
[16] http://www.sweenytod.com/cos/huboccult3.html
[17] http://www.sweenytod.com/cos/huboccult4.html
[18] http://www.sweenytod.com/cos/Theology/Theology/index.htm

[19]Chapter 6: Episcopal Church

The Episcopal Church is the American Counterpart of the Church of England or Anglican Church of England. There are 75 million worldwide and 2.3 million in the USA, with the Episcopal Church being formed in America in 1789 in Philadelphia. Membership is on the decline, with a 28% since 1965. Headquarters in America is in New York for the Episcopal Church.

Background and Formation

This church was formed in 1534 when it broke away from the Anglican Church over the matter of a king who wanted to divorce his wife and the pope wouldn't let him! As church historian A. A. Davis notes - "There does not seem to have been any doctrinal matter involved at all when the Church of England was born. Luther objected to the doctrines and the practices of Rome, but the Church of England seems to have come about purely by accident. King Henry VIII of England had become dissatisfied with one of his wives, and incidentally he only had six of them. I learned a little ditty many years ago concerning the fate of the wives of Henry VIII. It went like this "Divorced, beheaded, died, divorced, beheaded, survived." He divorced the first one; he beheaded the second one; the third one was fortunate to die a natural death; the fourth one he divorced; the fifth one he beheaded; but, the sixth one outlived him. He had fallen in love with beautiful Anne Boleyn. He wanted a

---

[19] For this Chapter the King James Version was used for all scripture

divorce from Katherine. The pope claimed the right, as he has until this day, as supreme authority in domestic affairs. When the prime minister chided the king regarding his desires, and the pope would not grant him a divorce, Thomas Cromwell said to him: "You are the King of England. Why don't you just write a letter to the pope, and in your own way, tell him to go jump in the lake, then organize a church of your own; write yourself a bill of divorcement, go marry the woman of your choice." He said it was a pretty good idea. That is just about what happened in history. He wanted another wife and he got her. And the world got another church. That is just as plain and blunt as I know how to put it. There is not a historian of any reputation that will refute one statement that I have made. Now do not misunderstand me. There were no doctrinal matters involved at the time of the Church of England's birth, but after it was instituted, there were many good and needed reforms instituted. They threw overboard some of the most repulsive Catholic doctrines; the chief one was the celibacy of the priesthood. They do permit their ministers. They did away with the Catholic idea of purgatory and limbo; and in the main as a doctrine, did away with confessional policy. Though in some instances, they have sought to return it. But they brought with them from Rome, their mother church these same doctrines, infant baptism, and a state religion." It was the Church of England, under the enforcement of their laws, that imprisoned John Bunyan, kept him in jail for 12 long years, during which time he gave to the world that matchless piece of literature, "The Pilgrim's Progress." It was written by a Baptist preacher in Bedford prison. He was imprisoned not by the Catholics or the Lutherans, but imprisoned by the Church of England people because he preached against the baptism of infants. They offered him his freedom several different times if he would promise not to preach against the baptism of infants. (The Trail of Blood pg. 87)

[20]Beliefs and Practices

"Though not under papal authority, many Catholic practices remain intact in the Church of England, or Episcopal Church."

The Episcopal Church is facing real struggles with liberalism within its ranks. Most no longer believe the Bible to be God's inerrant word, and many church leaders do not believe in the Deity of Christ.

The Episcopal Church believes in a Sacramental Salvation.

The Episcopal Church believes, like Roman Catholicism, in a "sacramental" salvation. It is taught that salvation is achieved by performing the 7 sacraments, beginning with baptism as an infant, then confirmation, Eucharist, penance, holy orders, matrimony, and unction. Unlike most other Protestant Churches which believe the elements of the common service (grape juice or wine, and bread) are merely symbolic, the Episcopal Church believes in the real presence of Christ in these elements. (Mead's pg. 134, 11 ed.)

The Anglican Church practices infant baptism, teaching that infants receive the Holy Spirit and are regenerated through baptism. Baptism is by pouring,

---

[20] From Mead's Handbook of Denominations

sprinkling, or immersion. Baptism, as one of the Sacraments and channels of grace is necessary for salvation in the Episcopal Church. "The 39 Articles allow for teaching baptismal regeneration" Religious Bodies of America (pg. 290)

The Episcopal Church, as Roman Catholicism, does not believe in the Eternal Security of the Believer and does not teach that one can have assurance of salvation and know he is going to heaven during this lifetime.

The 'Real Prescence' of Christ is spiritually present in the elements. This is known as 'Consubstantian', in contrast to Roman Catholic's Transubstantiation.

Anglican church government is the Episcopal system - the local church is governed by outside control through a hierarchy of priests and bishops. The highest Anglican bishop is called the Archbishop of Canterbury. The Episcopal Church has Nuns and Monks like Catholicism has (Mead pg. 135)

Since 1976 the Charismatic movement has 'swept thru' the Episcopal Church. Episcopal Sources claim that 1/3 of all Episcopal priests are charismatic and speak in tongues. (Religions of America, Leo Rosten, p591) (New and Revised Edition)

The Anglican Church (Episcopal Church) has a highly ritualistic form of worship. Some Episcopal churches are "high", with elaborate ritual and ceremony; others are described as low, with less involved ceremony and more of an evangelistic emphasis. This has been called the church of beauty, and it is an apt description. Its prayer book is eloquent in the literature of religious worship, containing the heart of both New Testament and Old Testament devotions. Members have built stately cathedrals in the U.S.; the Cathedral of St. John the Divine in New York City, the third largest in the world; and the Cathedral of Saints Peter and Paul, the national cathedral in Washington, D.C., sometimes called the American Westminister Abbey. Stained-glass windows, gleaming altars, vested choirs, and a glorious ritual are not only beautiful, but also give the worshiper a deep sense of the continuity of the Christian spirit and tradition. Next to the stress on episocopacy, its liturgical worship is a distinguishing feature, varying in degree according to high-or low-church inclinations. Its roots are in the Church of England and include the reading, recitation, and intonation by priest, people and choir of the historic general confession, general thanksgiving, collects, psalms, and prayers.

For the past two decades or more many Anglican leaders, including the archbishops, have been attempting to reconcile the Church of England with the RCC. The Episcopal Church is very active in all ecumenical ventures and is a member of both the National Council of Churches and The World Council of Churches.

Episcopalians believe that it is the right of a woman to have an abortion.

During 2003 a homosexual priest was ordained as Bishop of the Episcopal Church in America. In 1993 a survey revealed that 75% of Episcopalians believed that it is possible for a sexually active homosexuals to be faithful Christians.

The Way of Life Encyclopedia of the Bible and Christianity says on page 20: In this century liberalism has largely taken over the Anglican denomination. A large percentage of its bishops and pastors are modernists who deny the miracles of the Bible. Former Archbishop of Canterbury Robert Runcie illustrates this sad trend. In an interview with a newspaper the editor picked up in London on Easter 1982, Runcie was asked about the meaning of the cross. He replied, "As to that, I am an agnostic." Runcie was not certain of the meaning of the cross! In the same interview he said he felt Buddhism is a proper way to God and that Christians should not say that Jesus Christ is the only way of salvation. Anglican bishop David Jenkins openly questions every major teaching of the Bible. Of Christ's resurrection, this Church of England bishop says, " The Christian is not bound up with freak biology or corpses getting up and walking around." Of Chris's virgin birth, Jenkins says, "As for the virgin birth, they're the sort of stories that get told after you already believe somebody is very important. You don't have to believe in the virgin birth....."

Other Distinguishing Beliefs

Here are beliefs that differ from the Roman Catholic Church that it broke away from:

No Celibacy required for priests

No RCC purgatory & limbo, but they do pray for the dead(?)

Hélèné Fulton

No confession to a priest

They do have nuns and monks Like the RCC does.

They also believe in Apostolic Succession as the RCC does

Chapter 7: Anglican Church

Their own Official Anglican Statement of Faith condemns them! According to the 39 Articles of Religion of the Anglican Church of Canada from *The Book of Common Prayer*, 1959, pg. 698-714...
XXVII. *Of Baptism.*

Baptism is not only a sign of profession, and mark of difference, whereby Christian men are discerned from others that be not christened, but it is also a sign of Regeneration or new Birth, whereby, as by an instrument, they that receive Baptism rightly are grafted into the Church: the promises of forgiveness of sin, and of our adoption to be the sons of God by the Holy Ghost, are visibly signed and sealed; Faith is confirmed, and Grace increased by virtue of prayer unto God. The Baptism of young Children is in any wise to be retained in the Church, as most agreeable with the institution of Christ." (The 39 Articles of Religion of the Anglican Church of Canada from *The Book of Common Prayer*, 1959, pg. 698-714).

Heresy! They state above, "*...they that receive Baptism rightly are grafted into the Church: the promises of forgiveness of sin...*"

There is NOT one verse in the entire Bible that requires a person to be baptized to have their sins forgiven. When Jesus said to the man sick of palsy in Mark 2:5, "*Son, thy sins be forgiven thee*," He didn't tell the man to get baptized. Jesus forgave and healed that sick man on the spot, without baptism! How foolish are those unscrupulous Bible teachers who fail to study the Word of God, to understand its true meaning.

Baptismal regeneration is of the Devil, i.e., the heresy that a person must be baptized to go to Heaven.

It is so simple people. No one in the Old Testament was ever required to be baptized; but rather, we read in

> [6] And he believed in the LORD, and He accounted it to him for righteousness.
> **Genesis 15:6**

that Abraham "believed God" and it was counted unto him for righteousness.

> [5] But to him that worketh not, but believeth on him that justifieth the ungodly, his faith is counted for righteousness.
> **Romans 4:5**

plainly states, "*But to him that <u>worketh not</u>, but believeth on him that justifieth the ungodly, his faith is counted for righteousness.*" What is there not to understand? Listen my friend, you'd better forget, and forsake, the 39 articles of the Anglican faith, and rather obey the Word of God! In fact, there is a Scripture which tells us exactly that in

> [4] God forbid: yea, let God be true, but every man a liar; as it is written, That thou mightest be justified in thy sayings, and mightest overcome when thou art judged.
> **Romans 3:4**

Men are liars, who tell you that you must be baptized in order to be saved. The entire purpose of 1 John being written, according to 1 John 5:13, was so that we could KNOW that we have eternal life.

> [13] These things have I written unto you that believe on the name of the Son of God; that ye may know that ye have eternal life, and that ye may believe on the name of the Son of God.
>
> **1 John 5:13**

Carefully notice - NO MENTION is ever made of being baptized. In fact, the words "baptize," "baptism," or "baptized" is NOT mentioned in 1st, 2nd, or 3rd John. If baptism were necessary for salvation, surely the Apostle John would have mentioned it.

When Jesus witnessed the Gospel to Nicodemus in John Chapter 3, He never mentioned baptism. When Jesus witnessed the Gospel to the Samaritan woman, at the well, in John Chapter 4, He never mentioned baptism. In Acts 16, when a Roman prison-guard fell at Paul's feet and asked, "What must I do to be saved," Paul responded ... "*Believe on the Lord Jesus Christ, and thou shalt be saved, and thy house.*" Again, no mention was made of being baptized.

Salvation is of the heart. Only by believing upon Jesus Christ, because of the precious blood which He shed for us, can we be saved. Jesus said He is the Door into Heaven (John 10:9). Salvation is as simple as walking through a Door, and that Door is Jesus. Simply trust Him now, to forgive all your sins, believing upon Him as your personal Savior.

Chapter 8: Islam

Written By: Leeanne Naicker

Belief

"Islam" is an Arabic word that means "acceptance," "surrender," "submission," or "commitment," and is closely related to the Arabic word for peace (salaam; in Hebrew, shalom). Islam, which when translated from Arabic, means "to submit to the will of Allah," worshippers of this religion are known as Muslims, which means "one who submits to the will of Allah."

Muslims believe in one, unique, incomparable God - Allah, who has neither son nor partner, and that none has the right to be worshipped but him alone. He is the true God, and every other deity is false.

No one has the right to be invoked, supplicated, prayed to, or shown any act of worship, but their God alone. Muslims believe that God is not Jesus, and Jesus is not God and that there is no trinity.

Islam rejects that God rested on the seventh day and also rejects the attribution of any human form to God. They consider these to be blasphemous as God is far removed from every imperfection.

Muslims believe in the existence of angels and that they are honoured creatures. The angels worship God alone, obey him, and act only by his command. Among the angels is Gabriel, who brought down the Quran to the prophet Mohammed. Muslims believe that God revealed books to his messengers as proof for mankind and as guidance for them. Among these books is the Quran, which God revealed to the Prophet Mohammed. They also believe in the prophets and messengers of God, starting with Adam, including Noah, Abraham, Ishmael, Isaac, Jacob, Moses, and Jesus. Muslims believe that the Prophet Muhammad is the last prophet sent to the world.

Islam sets out that Abraham was one of God's most important messengers who were called by God to leave his home in Ur (in present-day Iraq). Abraham (whose name means "Father of Many Nations") is revered in the scriptures of Judaism, Christianity, and Islam as the ideal model of pure faith in the one true God. Abraham's belief in Islam is believed to be exemplary since he followed God's instructions in everything, and was even willing to sacrifice his own son because God had commanded it. The sacred story of Islam tells of how Abraham and his son Ishmael (Arabic, Ismail) built the Kaaba (literally "House of God") in Mecca, the centre of Muslim worship.

Muslims believe in the Day of Judgment or the Day of Resurrection at which point all people will be resurrected for God's judgement according to their beliefs and deeds. They also believe that God has given human beings freewill and this means that they can choose right or wrong and that they are responsible for their choices. The Quran says that terrible events will proclaim that the end is near. The people will gather at the bridge called Sirat. Sirat spans the fires of hell. Those bound for paradise will find the crossing easy. But for those bound for hell, the bridge will be as thin as a razor, and the condemned will fall into the flames. Hell, called Jahannam, is a horrifying inferno. The flames roar, scorching hot winds blow, and black smoke chokes the air. The skin of the suffering sinners is continually refreshed so that they will feel the pain of burning, with no relief. Their thirst is unquenchable, and yet they drink disgusting fluids in an effort to alleviate their suffering. Boiling water is poured over their heads. If they try to flee, iron hooks drag them back. In contrast, paradise is a blissful garden where the blessed are at peace and are content. The conversation is pleasant, the wine has no ill-effects, and the food is endlessly abundant.

The faithful, dressed in silk robes, relax on beautiful couches while servants tend to their every need. Men and women are attended by beautiful and handsome young members of the opposite sex. Choirs of angels sing in Arabic and all the bounties of heaven are enjoyed endlessly. No one is ever full.

Every Muslim is expected to follow these rules of the Five Pillars of Islam, in order to lead an ethical life:

- **Shahadah** - Confession of Faith: The belief that "there is no God but Allah, and Mohammed is His prophet."
- **Salat** - Prayer: Muslims must pray five times per day, facing towards Mecca.
- **Zakat** - Charity: Muslims must give donations to the poor, and support the local Mosque by donating a portion of their income.
- **Sawm** - Fasting: During the Ramadan, the ninth month of the Muslim calendar, all Muslims must

fast during daylight hours, except the very young or sick.
- **Hajj** - Pilgrimage: Where possible, each Muslim must make a hajj, or holy pilgrimage, to the city of Mecca.

When it Started - Origins

Essentially Islam was started by the prophet Mohammed. The prophet Muhammad gave the name Islam to the religious movement he founded. Muslims believe that the prophet Mohammed received the word of God, or Allah, through the angel Gabriel while living in the city of Mecca. Around 590CE, Muhammad, then in his twenties, entered the service of a merchant widow named Khadijah and actively engaged with trading caravans to the north. Sometime later he married her, and had two sons, neither of whom survived, and four daughters by her. In his forties, he began to retire to meditate in a cave on Mount Hira, just outside Mecca, where it is said that the first of the great events of Islam took place. An angelic being, later identified by Mohammed as Archangel Gabriel, appeared to him and commanded him to "recite" in the name of God. Mohammed did not respond immediately, and the angel took him by the throat and shook him as he repeated his command to "recite." Again Mohammed did not react, so the angel choked him until Muhammad agreed to do as he was told. So began Mohammed's years as a prophet, first to the Meccans and ultimately to all of Arabia.

At first Mohammed divulged his experience only to his wife and his immediate circle. But, as he began to proclaim the oneness of God universally, his following grew, at first among the poor and the slaves, but later, also among the most prominent men of Mecca. The revelations he received at this time, and those he did later, are all incorporated in the Quran, the Scripture of Islam. The town's people of Mecca soon became fearful of the Mohammed's preaching and he began to receive threats. As a result, he fled to the nearby city of Medina, where people began to believe in his message. The flight of Mohammed from Mecca to Medina was instrumental to the founding of the religion of Islam, and is known as the Hegira. Thus, in 622 CE Islam was founded and this date became the starting point for the Islamic calendar. Geographically Islam developed on the Arabian Peninsula and quickly spread to other regions.

Still, monotheism was not unknown, as there were Christian and Jewish tribes in Arabia. They too had received guidance from God's messengers, recorded in sacred writings such as the Torah (Moses), the Psalms (David), or the Gospel (Jesus). They were "People of the Book," or people who possessed sacred scripture. But from the perspective of Mohammed and his followers, God's message in these scriptures had become corrupted, whether by time or self-interest.

Mohammed and his followers later returned to Mecca and declared a jihad, or holy war, after which he captured the city. Under Mohammed's leadership, the basic teachings of Islam were established, which are known as the Five Pillars of Islam.

Islam is currently the second most practiced religion in the world, and experts predict that it will overtake

Christianity as the most popular religion in the world in a short amount of time given the rapid pace at which it is growing worldwide.

Islam has several branches and much variety within those branches. The two divisions within the tradition are the Sunni and Shi'a, each of which claims different means of maintaining religious authority.

Traditions

The Quran does not mention many practices that are prevalent in the Muslim world today. Instead, the traditions, sayings, and stories of Prophet Mohammed and his companions provided basis for today's traditions and practices that are called the Hadith.

> - Hajj, or Pilgrimage to Mecca
>   One of the most important in Islamic traditions is the Hajj. Hajj is the pilgrimage to the holy city of Mecca in Saudi Arabia, which every adult Muslim, men and women, is expected to make at least once in his or her lifetime. The hajj is incumbent on every Muslim who is physically and financially able to make the pilgrimage, but only if his absence will not place hardships on his family. A person may perform the hajj by proxy, appointing a relative or friend going on the pilgrimage to "stand in" for him or her. The hajj is the fifth of the fundamental Muslim practices and institutions known as the Five Pillars of Islam. At the beginning of a pilgrimage, a pilgrim must enter into state of, or the spirit of, Ihram before crossing the pilgrimage boundary, known as Miqat. This is done by

performing the cleansing rituals and wearing the prescribed attire.

A pilgrim is a person who undertakes a pilgrimage. This is traditionally a visit to a place of some religious or historic significance, and a considerable distance is often traveled.

- Sawm, or Siyam - Fasting in Islamic Tradition
  Aside from the five-times-daily prayer, fasting during the month of Ramadan is the most visible and recognizable of Muslim acts the world over. During the 30-odd days of Ramadan, Muslims are required to fast during daylight hours, neither food nor drink nor smoke, and abstain from sexual pleasures. The focus is on humility, spiritual oneness with God and social oneness with the ummah, or Islamic community, across the globe.
- Pronouncing God's Name before Eating or Drinking
  The pronouncement of God's name before eating or drinking is with a twofold purpose. One: to recognize the countless blessings by God and two: as a supplication for the continuation and abundance of blessings in the future. The prophet Mohammed is reported to have stressed strict adherence to this etiquette.
- Using the Right Hand for Eating & Drinking
  After pronouncing God's name before starting to eat or drink, a Muslim should use his right hand for eating and drinking. This practice is a continual reminder for Muslims to strive to be among those, who - on the Day of Judgment - shall get their records in their right hands. Adherence to this practice, on behalf of the individual symbolizes his desire and commitment to be among the people of 'right hand' on the Day of Judgment.

- Eating Etiquette
  Followers are not allowed to sit for food unless they are hungry and must chew their food in your mouth well. It is reported that the prophet always used to have salt before and after meals, and said that a person who does this act is protected from 70 types of diseases (curses), among which leprosy is the minor one. Islam made this calling because of the benefits of salt (sodium chloride) to the physiology and the human energy system, in particular when taken before and after meals, when it has the most merit during the digestion process.
- Consumption of Food & Beverages
  All practising Muslim believers obey God Almighty by eating the allowed foods (halaal) and avoiding the forbidden foods (haram) which are mentioned in the Qur'an and in the saying of the final prophet Mohammed. The following are a list of Muslim dietary practices. Muslims follow these because it in the Qur'an.

The Qur'an prohibits Muslims from eating and drinking the following:

- Dead Meat: These are the dead bodies of animals which died naturally, (i.e. without being Islamically slaughtered) or by being strangled, or by falling from a high place, or by being partly eaten by a wild animal, and were not slaughtered before being dead.
- Also, those animals slaughtered by other than Muslims, Jews or Christians.
- The meats of dead sea animals are not forbidden.
- Blood poured forth.

- Flesh of the Pig (pork).
- Meat which when slaughtered, had the name of anything or anyone other than Allah invoked upon it, or that was slaughtered to glorify anyone other than Allah.
- The meat of beasts of prey, such as lions, dogs etc. and those of preying birds that attack with their claws, such as eagles, vulture etc.
- The meat of domestic donkeys and asses
- The meat of animals that feed on filthy things, except if they are isolated and fed clean food for sufficient time.
- Any food spoiled by filth until it is cleaned by water if it is possible.
- Wine and all kinds of intoxicants.
- Foodstuffs containing toxic elements which are harmful to our bodies.

Muslim Greeting & its Response

At the time of meeting a Muslim should greet each other with the words: "Assalaam `alaikum". The addressees should subsequently respond with the words: "Wa `alaikum Assalaam". These words are, in fact, a supplication for the addressee for peace and blessings. These words have been referred to in the Qur'an as well as in sayings of the prophet Mohammed. The young are required to greet the old, the passer-by should first greet the one who is sitting and the smaller group should greet the larger group first.

Keeping the Nose, the Mouth & the Teeth Clean

As a part of elevating the religious tastes and developing a strong sense of purification and cleanliness among their followers, cleaning the nose, the mouth and the teeth has been a permanent feature of the teachings of the prophets of God. Maintaining cleanliness and hygiene, especially, keeping the nose, the mouth and the teeth clean has been mentioned in the history of the Arabs, since pre-Islamic times, as an accepted religious tradition. The prophet Mohammed is reported to have strictly adhered to the practice of rinsing his mouth and his nose every time he performed his bathing. In the same manner, he also greatly stressed the importance of keeping the teeth clean.

Washing after Urination and Defecation

The Arabic word "Istinjaa" is used as a term for cleaning the related organs after urination and defecation. "Istinjaa", was also strictly adhered to by the Arabs, since pre-Islamic times. Depending upon the circumstances, "Istinjaa" may be performed with water, with pebbles of dry earth or with any other suitable thing. It is believed that when the prophet would go to relieve himself (i.e. to urinate or defecate), he perform Istinjaa with the water and brush his hand on the earth.

Reciting 'Adhaan' in the Right Ear of a Newly Born

This tradition was initiated by the prophet Mohammed. The words of the Adhaan as fixed by the prophet according to God's directive, entail the complete summarized message of Islam. The Adhaan - the call to prayers is, in fact, a call to Islam - a call to complete submission to God's will. Every Muslim is continually being called toward the message entailed in the Adhaan. This message is being delivered through mosques five times during every day.

Recitation of the Adhaan in the right ear of a new born child symbolizes, on behalf of the parents, that like their respective physical contributions in the formation of the child, they have also, through the deliverance of God's message, initiated the transmission of their spiritual beings to the child.

Islamic Dress Code

Islam prescribes a more conservative minimum dress code for both men and women. In Islam, both men and women are expected to dress simply, modestly, and with dignity. A man must always be covered in loose and unrevealing clothing from his navel to his knee. This is the absolute minimum covering required. He must never, for example, go out in public wearing a short bathing suit. When leaving the home, a Muslim woman must at least cover her hair and body in loose and unrevealing clothing, obscuring the details of her body from the public; some also choose to cover their face and hands (hijab). The wisdom behind this dress code is to minimize sexual enticement and degradation in society as much as possible for both men and women. Obeying this dress code is a form of obedience to God. Islam forbids any sex appeal and physical allurement outside of marriage. In contrast, Islam encourages sex appeal and physical attraction for both men and women within the privacy between married couples.

Hélèné Fulton

Forbidden Deeds - Haram

These deeds and their doers will be punished by God. Anything that is prohibited in Islam is called 'Haram'.

- To associate (in worship) anything or anyone with Allah.
- To be disobedient to parents.
- To give false testimony.
- To kill a person whom Allah has forbidden to, except by Law (Legally).
- Adultery and fornication.
- To steal.
- To take anything, unjustly, from the property of an orphan.
- To desert the battle-field while fighting unbelievers.
- To falsely accuse with adultery or fornication a chaste Muslim woman or man.
- To take others' wealth illegally, by means of bribery, robbery, trickery, or deceit.
- To bribe in order to take others' properties illegally or to obtain what is not rightfully a person/so.
- To marry mother, daughter, sister, paternal aunt, maternal aunt, and brother's daughter, sister's daughter, whether they are through blood or foster relationship, father's wife, son's wife, wife's mother or daughter.
- A Muslim man is not permitted to marry a non-Muslim woman unless she becomes Muslim; but he can marry a Christian or a Jewish woman.
- A Muslim woman is not permitted to marry a non-Muslim man, even a Christian or a Jew, unless he becomes a Muslim.
- To take part in gossiping, back-biting or scandals.

Hélèné Fulton

Rituals

Halaal

The word Halaal, means permitted or lawful. It is a broad term covering what is allowed in the context of Islamic law, but is often used in conjunction with the issue of how meat is dealt with. The opposite of halal is haram, meaning "forbidden".

The name of Allah is pronounced over the meat as thanks during the slaughter process, any animal slaughtered in another idol's name can never be halaal. Dhabiha is the name for the halal method of slaughter, which requires that animals are killed with a swift incision to the throat from a razor sharp blade. The animal must never see another animal being slaughtered nor must it ever see the blade being sharpened. Animals must be checked prior to slaughter to ensure they are healthy and given clean water to drink, once they have drunk they are turned to face Mecca, the name of Allah is spoken and then the throat is cut and the blood drained from the carcass. When carried out correctly the sudden drop in blood pressure to the brain renders the animal brain dead within seconds and many researchers have found Dhabiha to be less stressful and painful to the animal than modern western methods of slaughter. The intention behind all of this is to ensure that the meat is fresh and free of impurities, the animal is given proper respect and Allah is thanked for providing Muslims with food.

Ritual Prayers

Prayer, in the ritual sense, is an obligation of the faith, to be performed five times a day by adult Muslims. According to Islamic law, prayers have a variety of obligations and conditions of observance. However, beyond the level of practice, there are spiritual conditions and aspects of prayer which represent its essence.

The five times of obligatory ritual prayer are:

- From dawn to sunrise;
- From noon until mid-afternoon;
- From mid-afternoon to sunset;
- From sunset to early evening;
- From early evening to the middle of the night. These times coincide with the significant temporal changes that are part of each day's cycle on earth as the planet moves through its various stations in relation to the Sun. The Sun, which is the focal point of the solar system, thus becomes a guiding light for the worshiper, indicating the beginning and ending of each prayer's interval. The worshipper faces the Kaabah, the holy shrine of Islam, as determined to the best of his or her ability by simple means. This directional focus is called the qiblah.

The Kaabah is the House of Allah, located in the holy city of Mecca in present-day Arabia. It is the goal of the pilgrimage, which is the fifth pillar of Islam. In Islamic teachings, the Kaabah is said to mark the location where the Divine House in the Seventh Heaven, beyond which stands the Supreme Throne, which angels constantly circle in praise and worship of

Allah, descended to Earth after the first man and woman, Adam and Eve, were cast out of Paradise for their mistake. In the time of Noah's flood, this heavenly sanctuary was taken up to heaven again. Millennia later, Abraham and Ishmael built the Kaabah in the same location, where it stands until today, the first house of worship dedicated to Allah. Each Muslim aims and hopes to reach that holy location at some point in her or his life by facing this location in prayer.

The first and foremost fundamental part of the ritual prayer is intention (niyyah). As in all Islamic worship, the worshipper intends the prayer as a fulfillment of Allah's Order done purely for God's sake. The prayer is initiated by the consecratory magnification of Allah (takbīr), followed by multiple cycles, each of which follows the same series of postures and recitations: first standing, then bowing, brief standing, prostrating, a brief sitting, a second prostration, and in the even cycles, sitting after the second prostration. Each of these positions also involves specific recitations. While standing, the first chapter (Sūratu 'l-Fātiħa) and other portions of the Holy Qur'ān are recited, either silently or aloud, depending upon the time of prayer. In bowing, the brief standing, prostration and the brief sitting, Allah is glorified and praised in short formulas. While sitting, the testimony of faith (tashahhud) is recited, along with greetings to and prayers for prophet Mohammed, prophet Abraham and their families. In addition, there are a variety of supplemental invocations and recitations that are traditionally part of the practice of most worshippers. Each obligatory prayer has a prescribed number of cycles to be observed. These are:

Hélèné Fulton

Prayer	Number of cycles
Maghrib (sunset)	3
Isha	4
Fajr	2
Dhuhr	4
Asr	4

A Muslim must perform wudu (ablution) before prayer and pray in a clean place. Many new prayer mats are manufactured or made by weavers in a factory. The design of a prayer mat is based on the village it came from and its weaver. When praying, a niche at the top of the mat must be pointed to the Islamic centre for prayer, Mecca. All Muslims are required to know what direction Mecca is from their home or where they are. The prayer rug has a very strong symbolic meaning and traditionally taken care of in a holy manner. It is disrespectful for one to place a prayer mat in a dirty location (as Muslims have to be clean to show their respect to God) or throw it around in a disrespectful manner. The prayer mat is traditionally woven with a rectangular design, made asymmetrical by the niche at the head end. Within the rectangle one usually finds images of Islamic symbols and architecture.

Decorations not only are important but also have a deep sense of value in the design of the prayer rug. One of the most important prayers is that of the Night Vigil (Qīyām al-layl). The ideal time for voluntary prayer and indeed for spiritual endeavours in general, is at night—preferably after midnight. This is the time when the world is asleep, but the lovers and seekers of God are awake and traveling towards reality and their divine destinations. It is under the veil of the night that the plane of consciousness is clear from the chaos of worldly affairs (dunyā), for it is a time when the mind and heart operate most effectively. Prayer before midnight, whether supplicatory or ritual, is very slow; after midnight, it is very fast.

Funerals and Ceremonies

There are primarily two sects within Islam (Shi'a and Sunni) that hold different views on a number of religious issues. For the most part, however, Muslims commonly believe that the good deeds one does in life will yield entry into Paradise on the Day of Judgment, also called the Last Day, when the world will be destroyed. Many Muslims believe that until the Last Day the dead will remain in their tombs and those heading for Paradise will experience peace while those heading for Hell will experience suffering.

- When death is imminent
  When a Muslim is approaching death, family members and very close friends should be present. They should offer the dying person hope and kindness, and encourage the dying person to say the "shahada," confirming that there is no God but Allah. As soon as death has occurred, those present should say, "Inna lillahi wa inna ilayhi raji'un" ("Verily we belong to Allah, and truly to Him shall we return"). Those present should close the deceased's eyes and lower jaw, and cover the body with a clean sheet. They should also make

"dua'" (supplication) to Allah to forgive the sins of the deceased.

- When to hold a Muslim funeral
  According to Islamic law ("shariah"), the body should be buried as soon as possible from the time of death, which means that funeral planning and preparations begin immediately. A local Islamic community organization should be contacted as soon as possible, and they will begin to help make arrangements for the funeral service and burial, assist the family in identifying an appropriate funeral home, and coordinate with the funeral home.

- Organ donation
  Organ donation is generally acceptable for Muslims, as it follows the Qur'an's teaching that "Whosoever saves the life of one person it would be as if he saved the life of all mankind." If there is any question as to whether or not organs may be donated, it is best to consult with an imam (religious leader) or Muslim funeral director.

- Autopsies
  Routine autopsies are not acceptable in Islam as they are seen as a desecration of the body. In most cases, the family of the deceased may refuse to have a routine autopsy performed.

- Embalming
  Embalming and cosmetology are not allowed unless required by state or federal law. Because of the prohibition on embalming and the urgency with which the body must be buried, it is not possible to transport the body from one country to another. Many Muslims living in America have a desire to be buried in the country of their ancestry, and this cultural practice, while acceptable in some

communities, is in conflict with shariah. An imam or Muslim funeral director should be consulted if there are any questions on the matter.

- Cremation
Cremation is forbidden for Muslims.
- Preparing the body
To prepare the body for burial, it must be washed ("Ghusl") and shrouded ("Kafan"). Close same-sex family members are encouraged to give Ghusl, though in the case of spousal death the spouse may perform the washing. The body should be washed three times. If, after three washings, the body is not entirely clean, it may be washed more, though ultimately the body should be washed an odd number of times. The body should be washed in the following order: upper right side, upper left side, lower right side, and lower left side. Women's hair should be washed and braided into three braids. Once clean and prepared, the body should be covered in a white sheet.

To shroud the body, three large white sheets of inexpensive material should be laid on top of each other. The body should be placed on top of the sheets. Women should, at this point, be dressed in an ankle-length sleeveless dress and head veil. If possible, the deceased's left hand should rest on the chest and the right hand should rest on the left hand, as in a position of prayer. The sheets should then be folded over the body, first the right side and then the left side, until all three sheets have wrapped the body. The shrouding should be secured with ropes, one tied above the head, two tied around the body, and one tied below the feet. The body should then be transported to the mosque ("masjid") for funeral prayers, known as "Salat al-Janazah."

- Viewing, wake, or visitation before a Muslim funeral
  When a Muslim dies, the body should be buried as soon as possible after death, thus there is no viewing before the funeral.
- The Muslim funeral service
  Salat al-Janazah (funeral prayers) should be performed by all members of the community. Though the prayers should be recited at the mosque, they should not be recited inside the mosque; instead, they should be performed in a prayer room or study room, or in the mosque's courtyard. Those praying should face the "qiblah"—that is, toward Mecca—and form at least three lines, with the male most closely related to the person who died in the first line, followed by men, then children, then women.
- Interment
  After Salat al-Janazah has been recited, the body should be transported to the cemetery for burial. Traditionally, only men are allowed to be present at the burial, though in some communities all mourners, including women, will be allowed at the gravesite. The grave should be dug perpendicular to the qiblah, and the body should be placed in the grave on its right side, facing the qiblah. Those placing the body into the grave should recite the line "Bismilllah wa ala millati rasulilllah" ("In the name of Allah and in the faith of the Messenger of Allah"). Once the body is in the grave, a layer of wood or stones should be placed on top of the body to prevent direct contact between the body and the soil that will fill the grave. Then each

mourner present will place three handfuls of soil into the grave. Once the grave has been filled, a small stone or marker may be placed at the grave so that it is recognizable. However, traditionally, it is prohibited to erect a large monument on the grave or decorate the grave in an elaborate way.
- Post-funeral reception
After the funeral and burial, the immediate family will gather and receive visitors. It is customary for the community to provide food for the family for the first few days of the mourning period (usually three days). Generally, the mourning period lasts 40 days, but depending on the degree of religiousness of the family, the mourning period may be much shorter.
- Muslim mourning period and memorial events
Widows are expected to observe a longer mourning period, generally of four months and ten days. During this time, widows are prohibited from interacting with men whom they could potentially marry (known as "na-mahram"). However, this rule may be overlooked in cases of emergency, such as when the widow must see a doctor.
It is acceptable in Islam to express grief over a death. Crying and weeping at the time of death, at the funeral, and at the burial are all acceptable forms of expression. However, wailing and shrieking, tearing of clothing and breaking of objects, and expressing a lack of faith in Allah are all prohibited.

Festivals and Holidays

The Islamic Calendar
The Islamic calendar is a lunar calendar, whereas the rest of the world uses the Gregorian calendar, and

months begin when new moon is sighted. The Islamic lunar calendar year is 11 to 12 days shorter than the solar year.

The Islamic months are named as follows:
1. Muharram or Mu_arram al Haram
2. Safar ,or _afar al Muzaffar
3. iRabii al-Awwal, Rabi I
4. Rabi' al-thani or Rabi al Thani, or Rabi al-Akhir, Rabi II
5. Jumada al-Awwal Jumada I
6. Jumada al-thani or Jumada al-Akhir, Jumada II
7. Rajab, or Rajab al Murajab
8. Sha'aban or Sha'aban al Moazam
9. Ramadan ,or Ramzan, long form: Ramadan al Mubarak
10. Shawwal or Shawwal al Mukarram
11. Dhu al-Qi'dah
12. Dhu al-Hijjah

Ramadan

Ramadan is the ninth month of the Islamic lunar calendar. It begins with the sighting of the new moon after which all physically mature and healthy Muslims are obliged to fast for the complete month. Fasting is done as an act of worship and obedience to Allah (God). Between dawn and sunset, Muslims abstain from all food, drink and any kind of sexual contact. In addition to this physical component, the spiritual aspects of the fast include an added emphasis on refraining from gossip, lies, obscenity and in general, any sinful act. Muslims focus during this month on strengthening their relationship with the Creator. It is a time for spiritual reflection, prayer and doing of good deeds. Fasting is intended to inculcate self-discipline, self-restraint and generosity.

During Ramadan, mosques are full of worshippers and acts of charity increase, ties of brotherhood strengthen, anger and temper are controlled and an atmosphere of peace prevails.

Eid

The first Eid of the year is known as Eid Al-Fitr also called Feast of Breaking the Fast. It marks the end of the month of Ramadan, which is the month in which Muslims fast every day from sunrise to sunset. The entire community comes together for special prayers and to congratulate each other. The rest of the day is typically spent visiting friends and family, enjoying time together. Eid al-Fitr is celebrated for one, two or three days. Typically, practicing Muslims wake up early in the morning—always before sunrise— offer Salatul Fajr (the pre-sunrise prayer), and in keeping with the traditions of the prophet Mohammed, clean their teeth with a toothbrush, take a shower before prayers, put on new clothes (or the best available), and apply perfume.

The second and final Eid celebration of the year is called Eid Al-Adha. It commemorates the completion of the Hajj pilgrimage. Although only pilgrims in Mecca participate in the Hajj fully, Muslims around the world join them in celebrating Eid Al-Adha.

Islamic New Year - Muharram

The month of Muharram marks the beginning of the Islamic liturgical year. The Islamic year begins on the first day of Muharram, and is counted from the year of the Hegira (anno Hegirae) the year in which Mohammed emigrated from Mecca to Medina (A.D. July 16, 622). The Islamic New Year is celebrated relatively quietly, with prayers and readings and reflection upon the hegira.

Prophet Mohammed's Birthday – Mawlid al-Nabi

This holiday celebrates the birthday of Mohammed, the founder of Islam. It is fixed as the 12th day of the month of Rabi in the Islamic calendar. Mawlid means birthday of a holy figure and al-Nabi means prophet. The day is commemorated with recollections of Muhammad's life and significance. Fundamentalist Muslims, such as the Wahhabi sect, do not celebrate it.

Wedding Ceremonies

From the United States to the Middle East to South Asia, Islam stretches across a diverse terrain of politics and culture with followers and practices as varied as the countries from which they hail. Marriage in Islam is viewed as a religious obligation, a contract between the couple and Allah.

The only requirement for Muslim weddings is the signing of a marriage contract. Marriage traditions differ depending on culture, Islamic sect, and observance of gender separation rules. Most marriages are not held in mosques, and men and women remain separate during the ceremony and reception. Since Islam sanctions no official clergy, any Muslim who understands Islamic tradition can officiate a wedding.

Pre-marriage rituals are conducted separately in the bride and the groom's house. Prospective bride and the groom have limited interaction during these rituals. Once the boy and the girl give the consent for the marriage, the pre-wedding rituals begin.

Ishtikara

Before starting separate rituals in the bride and the groom's house, the Maulvi or the religious head seeks permission from the Almighty to perform the wedding. This tradition is known as Ishtikara. Ishtikara is usually held in the mosque, in presence of the respective fathers of the bride and the groom and other senior members of the family. After reciting, the verses from holy Quran and seeking the permission from Almighty, the Maulvi and the father of the bride and the father of the groom have a consensus on the marriage date.

Imam-Zamin

Now starts the bevy of events that are filled with fun and excitement. On a fixed day, Groom mother and senior members from the groom's family visit the bride and her family. They carry fruits, dates, incense, perfumes and gifts for bride and her family members. Groom's mother also carries a silver coin or gold coin wrapped in a silken cloth with her. This coin is tied to the bride's arm and it signifies the marking of the bride as the future daughter-in-law. This ceremony is known as Imam-e-Zamin. Imam-E-Zamin is similar to the shagun ceremony in the Indian weddings. Few days after Imam-Zamin, the date of Mangni or the engagement is fixed. Traditionally Mangni involves exchange of gifts between the bride and the groom's family. In the modern day, Muslim bride and the groom may also exchange rings to mark the engagement. Both the parties make themselves busy in the wedding preparation after the Mangni. In the days to come, bride is pampered by her friends and relatives. Traditionally, Muslim brides were bathed in essential and aromatic oils to make their skin soft and smooth. Jasmine extracts are applied to the bride's hair to add luster and fragrance to her hair. Special food and bride's favorite dishes are cooked to pamper her. This period also involves the shopping frenzy. The bridal lehenga or the wedding outfit is chosen by the mother in law and is presented to the bride along with jewelry, perfume, dates, and fruits. Now there pre-marriage rituals are in full force at the bride's place.

Mehndi ki Raat

Mehndi ceremony is organized two to three days prior to the wedding night. Mehndi ceremony is one of the most exciting ceremonies in the Muslim Wedding. During this ceremony, the family members of the bride revel in music, song and dance. A paste of fresh turmeric is applied on bride's skin by her family, relatives and friends. This is done, in order to bring in natural glow to her face. Beautiful Arabic Mehndi designs are drawn on bride's hands and feet. The first dot of henna is applied by the bride's mother on bride's palm. Family members also have Arabic

Mehndi designs or intricate Mehndi designs drawn on their hand. This ceremony is dominated by women. Bride is fed by her mother with her own hands. Cousins of the bride might engage in fun and frolic and resort to teasing the bride about the groom. Mehndi ki Raat is much awaited ceremony in Muslim weddings. Many traditional Muslim families believe that the darker the shade of henna on the bride's hand, happier is her married life. Muslim brides do not step out of their house after the Mehndi ceremony until the day of their wedding.

Mahr or Baraat

This ritual takes place on the wedding day, the groom arrives at the bride's house or the wedding venue with the Baraat. Baraat refers to the marriage procession that includes friends, relatives, musicians etc. On reaching, the wedding venue, the groom shares a sherbet (sweet drink similar to juice) with the bride's brother or her relatives. Bride's sisters and cousins resort to slapping the groom and his friends playfully with a bouquet of flowers. Groom is then welcomed by the bride's parents.

Hélèné Fulton

Meher

The marriage contract includes a meher - a formal statement specifying the monetary amount the groom will give the bride. There are two parts to the meher: a prompt due before the marriage is consummated and a deferred amount given to the bride throughout her life. Today, many couples use the ring as the prompt because the groom presents it during the ceremony. The deferred amount can be a small sum - a formality - or an actual gift of money, land, jewellery, or even an education. The gift belongs to the bride to use as she pleases, unless the marriage breaks up before consummation. The meher is considered the bride's security and guarantee of freedom within the marriage.

Nikah

The marriage contract is signed in a nikah ceremony, in which the groom or his representative proposes to the bride in front of at least two witnesses, stating the details of the meher. The bride and groom demonstrate their free will by repeating the word qabul ("I accept," in Arabic) three times. Then the couple and two male witnesses sign the contract, making the marriage legal according to civil and religious law. Following traditional Islamic customs, the bride and groom may share a piece of sweet fruit, such as a date. If men and women are separated for the ceremony, a male representative called a wali acts in the bride's behalf during the nikah.

Vows and Blessings

The officiant may add an additional religious ceremony following the nikah, which usually includes a recitation of the Fatihah - the first chapter of the Quran - and durud (blessings). Most Muslim couples do not recite vows; rather, they listen as their officiant speaks about the meaning of marriage and their responsibilities to each other and to Allah. However, some Muslim brides and grooms do say vows.

Ruksat

After the Nikaah is solemnized, bride is bid farewell by her teary eyed relatives. This ceremony is called the Ruksat. During the Ruksat, the bride's father places his daughter's hand in the hand of the groom and tells him to be her protector and her guide. Groom's mother welcomes the bride in their new house. A copy of Holy Quran is held over the bride's head during the welcoming ceremony. Bride seeks blessings from the elders in the groom's family. The bride visits her home on the fourth day of her wedding. She receives a warm welcome from her family and relatives.

Walima

Groom's family hosts a wedding reception at a chosen venue on the fifth day of the wedding ceremony. This reception is formally known as Daawat-e-Walima. Both the families, relatives and friends join the Daawat-e-Walima; they celebrate the unison of the couple, and wish them a happy married life.

Hélèné Fulton

Other

Role of Women in Islam

The role of Muslim women in the Islamic world is one that is prone to much discussion and assumptions; unfortunately the discussion is more often than not a negative one. The most common perceptions are of women living under the oppressive dictatorships of their husbands and fathers, forced into marriage, and of course suffocated under the veil. In terms of her contribution and role in society the caricature is one of the women restricted to five metres away from the kitchen sink.

However the women's role of being a mother and a wife are not her only roles. Islam permits the women to perform Hajj (pilgrimage), to exercise the vote, engage in politics, to take up employment and even run her own business.

The Quran mentions that men and women are equal in Gods sight. The only difference is that of piety, of gaining reward and of obeying God. A basic understanding of the life of Mohammed and knowledge of the wives of the prophet show examples of women excelling in their fields of knowledge. Both men and women are the slaves of Allah and have a duty to worship and obey Him. Men and women have to pray, fast, give charity, go on pilgrimage, refrain from adultery, avoid the prohibited, enjoin the good and forbid the evil, and so on. Because of women's roles as mothers, a role which does not end at a specific time but is a round-the-clock career, they have been exempted from attending the Mosque for the five daily prayers or for Jumuah (Friday) prayer.

Nevertheless, if they wish to attend the Mosque, no one has the right to stop them.

The battlefield is a place, which frightens many men let alone women. Due to the aggressive and violent nature of war, only men have a duty to participate in Jihad (holy fighting in Allah's cause) while women are exempted.

Jihad in Islamic Culture

Jihad is the Arabic for what can be variously translated as "struggle" or "effort," or "to strive," or "to exert," or "to fight," depending on the context. In the West, the word is generally understood to mean "holy war," and the terms are given, inaccurately, exclusively military connotations. The Qur'an does call for "jihad" as a military struggle on behalf of Islam. But the Qur'an also refers to jihad as an internal, individual, spiritual struggle toward self-improvement, moral cleansing, and intellectual effort - the difficult effort that is needed to put God's will into practice at every level, personal, family, social, business, and political. It is said that Prophet Mohammed considered the armed-struggle version of holy war "the little jihad," but considered the spiritual, individual version of holy war — the war within oneself — as "the great jihad." Still, "jihad" is considered to be every Muslim's duty — be it the struggle to improve society, preventing the exploitation of the poor or vulnerable, or improving oneself before the Day of Judgment.

Mujahideen in Islamic culture

A Mujahid is Arabic which means "struggler." The plural is Mujahideen. It is a person involved in a jihad. Muslims who engage in the defense of Muslim lands, or who take up a struggle in defense of the oppressed, the poor or the exploited, or against the oppression of the state or foreign invaders, consider themselves to be mujahidin, or mujahideen.

Caliphate

The title, or term, Caliph is the head of state in a Caliphate, and the title for the leader of the Islamic Ummah (an Islamic community). It is a transliterated version of the Arabic word Khalifat (or, Khalif), which means "successor" or "representative."
In Islamic culture the early leaders of the Muslim nation following Muhammad's death were called "Khalifat Rasul Allah," which means the political successors to the messenger of God. Caliphs were also often referred to "Commander of the Faithful", or Imam al-Ummah, "leader of the Muslims." The Caliphate has two lesser titles. Most historical Muslim governors were called either sultans (meaning "strength", "authority", or "ruler ship") or amirs (also known as "emir" to denote a military title, roughly meaning "general" or "commander"). These titled positions gave allegiance to a caliph.

Sheik

Sheikh (also written as Sheik, Shaykh, Shaikh, Cheikh, and other variants) is an honorific term which in the Arabic language means "elder." It is commonly used within the Muslim world to denote an elder of a tribe, a revered wise man, or an Islamic scholar.

Al-aqsa Mosque

Al-Aqsa Mosque, or al-Masjid al-Aqsa; meaning, "the Farthest Mosque." It is also known as al-Aqsa. It is an Islamic holy place in the Old City of Jerusalem. The mosque itself forms part of the al-Haram ash-Sharif, or "Sacred Noble Sanctuary," along with the Dome of the Rock. This is a site also known as the Temple Mount, and considered the holiest site in Judaism, since it is where the Temple in Jerusalem once stood.

Widely considered as the third holiest site in Islam, Muslims believe that the prophet Muhammad was transported from the Sacred Mosque in Mecca to al-Aqsa during the Night Journey. Islamic tradition holds that Muhammad led prayers towards this site until the 17th month after the emigration, when God ordered him to turn towards the Kaaba.

Ayatollah

Ayatollah (meaning, "Sign of God") is a high ranking title given to Shi'a clerics. Those who carry the title are experts in Islamic studies such as jurisprudence, ethics, and philosophy. They teach usually in Islamic seminaries. The title is currently granted to top Shia mujtahid after completing specific studies in the hawza. A mujtahid is an Islamic scholar, competent to interpret divine shari'a law in practical situations using ijtihad (independent thought). Hawza is a seminary of traditional Shi'a Islamic studies.

By then he would be able to issue his own edicts from the sources of religious laws: Qur'an, Sunnah, "intellect" (rather than the Sunni principle of Qiyas). Most of the time, a certificate is issued, attested by his teachers. The ayatollah can then teach in hawzas according to his specialty, can act as a reference for their religious questions, and act as a judge. There is an important difference from Shi'a ayatollahs and "saints" in other religions and Sunni Islam. They are not regarded as enlightened by God Himself, but by the Word of God.

The name "ayatollah" originates from the Qur'an where human beings can also be regarded as signs of God, the literal translation of the title. 51:20-21 of the Qur'an states: |On the earth are signs (Ayat) for those of assured Faith. As also in your own selves: Will ye not then see?"

Kaaba

Kaaba (also known as, Ka'aba, Ka'bah, Kabah, and Caaba) is the center of the holiest place of worship in Islam. It is located inside the Sacred Mosque of Mecca, Al Masjid Al-Haram. Its name is an Arabic word that means "a home, or a room, that looks like a cube." It is believed to be built by Prophet Abraham as a landmark for the House of God, for the sole purpose of worshipping Allah alone.

Kaaba is the center of the procession (known as the "tawaf", which means, "to walk around") performed during the pilgrimage (known as "hajj"), and it is toward the Ka'aba that Muslims face in their prayers (known as "salat"). Before Prophet Mohammed's Islam religion, Meccans who lost the religion of

Abraham, worshipped many idols. The Black Stone, possibly of meteoric origin, is located at one of its outside corners. It has been used by the pilgrims as a landmark to count the number of circumambulations. Some traditional Muslims, in defiance of their religion, consider the stone holy, and put emphasis on touching it and kissing it.

The Ka'aba is a large masonry structure roughly the shape of a cube. It is made of granite from the hills near Mecca, and stands upon a 10 inch marble base, which projects outwards about one foot. It is approximately 43 feet high, with sides measuring 36 feet by 42 feet. The four corners of the Ka'aba roughly face the four cardinal directions (meaning, north, south, east, and west) of the compass. The Ka'aba is covered by a black silk and gold curtain known as the kiswah, which is replaced yearly. About two-thirds of the way up runs a band of gold-embroidered calligraphy with Qur'anic text, including the Islamic declaration of faith, the Shahadah. The actual structure of the Ka'aba has been demolished, and rebuilt several times in the course of its history. Around the Ka'aba is a restricted area (known as the "haram" area) extending in some directions as far as 12 miles, into which only Muslims may enter.

Islamic Symbols

The name Allah

The words "Allah" in Arabic script or characters can be regarded as visually representing Islam as a symbol. There are many Christian scholars, anointed Men of God who state that in the book of Revelation's John didn't see 666. He wrote down what looked like the Greek numbers for 666, but what if they weren't really Greek numbers? What if they were really Arabic script that just looked like Greek numbers?

Where did John see the image of 666 that he wrote in the Bible? What was he looking at? The bible says in the Book of Revelation 13…

Here is wisdom. Let him that hath understanding count the number of the beast: for it is the number of a man; and his number is Six hundred threescore and six.

Revelation 13:18

The Crescent Moon and Star

Hélèné Fulton

Many non-Muslims think of the hijab (veil) or the sword as symbols of Islam, but these are not symbols the Muslims themselves use. Nor is the symbol of the crescent moon and star universally accepted by Muslims, although it is widely regarded as an international symbol of the faith. The symbol of the crescent moon and star is older than Islam, probably dating to pre-Christian Byzantium. When the Ottoman Turks conquered the Byzantine Empire and captured its capital city, the Ottoman Empire adopted the city's existing flag and symbol of crescent moon and star as its own. In the modern world, a number of Islamic nations have a version of the crescent moon and star on their flags, including Algeria, Malaysia, Pakistan, Turkmenistan, and Turkey.

The Colour Green

The colour green is also traditionally associated with Islam. Although the origins of this are obscure, by the time of the Crusades, the European Crusaders avoided using the colour green in their coats of arms so that they would not be mistaken for Muslims during battle. Some believe that the colour green was the colour of Mohammed's tribe, the Quraysh, while others believe that green was the Prophet's favourite colour, and that he always wore a green turban. Others associate the colour green with a hadith attributed to Mohammed, which says that "Three things of this world are acceptable: water, greenery, and a beautiful face." Still others find special status attributed to the colour green in the Quran, which says in surah 18:31 that in paradise, the blessed will wear garments of green silk. Covers of green silk cover the graves of Sufi saints, and Qurans are bound in green. A number of flags of the Islamic world are green, including those of Iran and Libya.

Flag of the Organization of Islamic Conference

The flag of the Organization of the Islamic Conference coordinates several of the central symbols of Islam, including the color green, the Red Crescent on a white disk, and the words "God is great" (Allahu akbar) in Arabic calligraphy. The Organization of the Islamic Conference, with 57 member states, is an international organization with a permanent delegation to the United Nations.

Jesus Christ in Bible and Qu'ran

Jesus Christ as seen in Christianity and Islam, the sources are mainly the Bible, and Quran. These are just a few excerpts from both the Bible and Quran.

Hélèné Fulton

Christianity (Bible)	Islam (Quran)
"God created man in his own image, in the image of God he created him; male and female he created them." ***Genesis 1:27***	"The similitude of Jesus before Allah is as that of Adam; He created him from dust, then said to him: "Be": and he was." ***Quran 3:59***
The Birth	
..."the time came for the baby to be born, and she gave birth to her firstborn, a son. She wrapped him in cloths and placed him in a manger"... ***Luke 1:6-7***	"So she conceived him, and she retired with him to a remote place. And the pains of childbirth drove her to the trunk of a palm-tree: she cried (in her anguish): "Ah! would that I had died before this! would that I had been a thing forgotten and out of sight! But (a voice) cried to her from beneath the (palm-tree) :"Do not grieve! for your Lord has provided a rivulet beneath you; "And shake toward yourself the trunk of the palm-tree: it will let fall fresh ripe dates upon you." ***Quran 19:22-5***
Prophet	
"They were all filled with awe and praised God, "A great Prophet has appeared among us," they said. "God has come to help his people." This news about Jesus spread throughout Judea and the surrounding	..."Jesus, the son of Mary, said: "O Children of Israel! I am the Messenger of Allah (sent) to you, confirming the Law (which came) before me"... ***Quran 61:6***

country." ***Luke 7:16-7***	
He was Sent by God	
..."I have not come on my own; but he (God) sent me." ***John 8:42***	"O People of the Book! commit no excesses in your religion: nor say of Allah anything but the truth. Christ Jesus the son of Mary was (no more than) a Messenger of Allah, and His Word"... ***Quran 4:171***
It is not my will!	
"For I have come down from heaven not to do my will but to do the	"And behold! Allah will say: "O Jesus the son of Mary! Did you say to men, 'worship me and my mother as gods in derogation of Allah'?" He (Jesus) will say: "Glory to You! Never could I say what I had no right (to say). Had I said what is in my heart, though I do not

know what is in Yours. For You know in full all that is hidden. **"Never said I to them anything except what You commanded me to say**, to wit, 'Worship Allah, my Lord and your Lord'; And I was a witness over them whilst I dwelt amongst them; when You took me up, You were the Watcher over them, and You are a Witness to all things."
Quran 5:116-7

Chrislam

Many are not aware but Chrislam is a Nigerian syncretic religion which mixes elements of Christianity and Islam. Founded by Tela Tella in the 1970s, the sect once predominantly existed in Lagos, Nigeria. Its followers recognise both the Bible and the Qur'an as holy texts, and practice "running deliverance," a distinctive practice of spiritual running which members liken to Joshua's army circling Jericho, or the Muslim practice of circumambulating the Kaaba.

However, the recent years has seen a Chrislam as the fastest growing religions in America. Chrislam is the merging of apostate christianity and the ideology of Islam, and it is truly a pit of serpents and devils. One of the main founders of Chrislam and one of its main drivers is Rick Warren from Saddleback Church in Southern California. Warren at the same time passionately denies his connection with Chrislam while at the same time promoting it through his many ministries and outlets.

To understand where it all started, one has to journey back to 2009 where Rick Warren addressed the annual meeting of the Islamic Society of North America. He opened by telling the audience how much he had in common with Muslims and the ideology of Islam. He preached a pro-globalization message of uniting together at any cost by laying down our differences. He quoted no scripture from the bible, and only mentioned the Name of Jesus Christ once in passing. But what he did repeat over and over was how Muslims and Christians needed to "band together" and start work right away on "interfaith projects".

A number of Christian leaders today are attempting to bridge the gap between Muslims and Christians. While perhaps well intentioned, the foundation of this new mantra, often called Chrislam is that "we all worship the same God". At the heart of this movement and perhaps the most dangerous issue is that these Christian leaders suggest that because we use similar terms such as "God" and "Jesus" - there is a form of shared belief. What we mean by the words we use matters and when no one defines the terms we are using - deception can slip in (which is why lawyers will fill page after page of small print defining the terms in a contract). Whether intentional or not, many Christian leaders are leading their followers into believing Chrislam is acceptable.

24 For there shall arise false Christs, and false prophets, and shall shew great signs and wonders; insomuch that, if it were possible, they shall deceive the very elect. 25 Behold, I have told you before. 26 Wherefore if they shall say unto you, Behold, he is in the desert; go not forth: behold, he is in the secret chambers; believe it not. 27 For as the lightning cometh out of the east, and shineth even unto the west; so shall also the coming of the Son of man be.

Matthew 24:24

The first thing Jesus mentioned when He answered the disciples' questions about the signs of His coming and the end of the age was to watch out for religious deception.

Hélèné Fulton

And Jesus answered and said unto them, Take heed that no man deceive you.

Matthew 24:4

Another type of deceiver also exists. This type is a smooth talker just like the people on TV and radio, who speak so well and this is typically what we see on mainstream media, these very people who claim to be followers of Christ but instead use their charm, wit and smooth words to lure and deceive the children of God.

For they that are such serve not our Lord Jesus Christ, but their own belly; and by good words and fair speeches deceive the hearts of the simple.

Romans 16:18

Chapter 9: New Age

Written By: Sanet Gericke

Introduction

The New Age Movement is unlike most formal religions, it has no holy text, central organization, membership, formal clergy, dogma, creed, geographic centre etc. The New Age is a free-flowing spiritual movement. A network of practitioners and believers that share some similar practices and believes, that they add on to whatever their formal religion they follow. Their Conventions, Seminars, book publishers, informal groups and books takes the place of religious services and sermons.

Quoting John Naisbitt
"In turbulent times, in times of great change people head for the two extremes: fundamentalism and personal, spiritual experience……with no membership lists or even a coherent philosophy or dogma, it is difficult to define or measure the organized New Age movement. But in every major U.S. and European city, thousands who seek insight and personal growth cluster around a metaphysical bookstore, a spiritual teacher or an education centre."

The New Age is definitely not of the same sort of individuals, most of them craft some New Age believes into their regular religious believes. A recent survey of U.S. adults indicates many Americans hold some New Age believes:

- ➢ 8% - Believe in astrology as a method of foretelling the future.

  Give no regard to mediums and familiar spirits; do not seek after them, to be defiled by them: I *am* the Lord your God.
  Leviticus 19:31

- ➢ 7% - Believe in crystals as a source of healing or energizing.

  Behold, I will bring it health and healing; I will heal them and reveal to them the abundance of peace and truth.
  Jeremiah 33:6

  who Himself bore our sins in His own body on the tree, that we, having died to sins, might live for righteousness—by whose stripes you were healed.
  1Peter 2:24

- ➢ 9% - Believe tarot cards are reliable for life decisions.

  Trust in the Lord with all your heart,
  And lean not on your own understanding
  Proverbs 3:5

  So Saul died for his unfaithfulness which he had committed against the Lord, because he did not keep the word of the Lord, and also because he consulted a medium for guidance. ¹⁴ But *he* did not inquire of the Lord;
  1Cronicles 10:13-14

- ➢ 1 in 4 – Believe in a non-traditional concept of the nature of God, often associates with New Age thinking.

- ➢ 11% - Believe God is " a state of higher consciousness that a person may reach"

- ➢ 8% - of them define God as "total realization of personal, human capability."

- ➢ 3% - believe each person is God.

> For the invisible things of him from the creation of the world are clearly seen, being understood by the things that are made, (even) his eternal power and Godhead; so that they are without
>
> **Romans 1:20**

> Thus saith the LORD the King of Israel, and his redeemer the LORD of hosts; I (am) the first, and I (am) the last; and beside me (there is) no God.
>
> **Isaiah 44:6**

> Tell ye, and bring (them) near; yea, let them take counsel together: who hath declared this from ancient time? (who) hath told it from that time? (have) not I the LORD? and (there is) no God else beside me; a just God and a Saviour; (there is) none beside me.
>
> **Isaiah 45:21**

New Age religion classify religious believes in 7 faith groups from the largest to the smallest:

- ➢ Cultural Christianity (Christmas and Easter)
- ➢ Conventional Christianity.
- ➢ New Age Practitioners.
- ➢ Biblical Christianity (Fundamentalists, Evangelical.)
- ➢ Atheists / Agnostics.
- ➢ Other.
- ➢ Jewish.

A study from 1991 – 1995 shows that New Agers represent 20% of the population, the third largest group.

History of the New Age Group.

The New Age teachings gain popularity in the 1970's, the reaction of the failure of Christianity and Secular Humanism to provide ethical and spiritual guidance for the future. Their roots are traceable to many sources like:

- Astrology
- Channelling
- Hinduism
- Gnostic traditions
- Spiritualism
- Taoism
- Theosophy
- Wicca
- And often Neo-pagan traditions

The movement started in the 1960's in England where many of these elements were well established.
The Findhorn Community in Iverness and the Wrekin Trust were of the groups that were formed, this movement quickly became international. A New Age milepost in North America was a "New Age Seminar" by the Association for Research and Enlighten, the establishment of the East-West Journal in 1971. Shirley MacLaine the actress was their most famous figure. In the 1980's and 1990's the movement where criticized by various groups. Seminar and group leaders were criticized for fortunes made from New Agers, channelling was ridiculed. The uncritically

believe in the "scientific" properties of crystal was out ruled as groundless. During the past generation the movement became well established and a major force in North American religion. The New Age Movement is expected to expand, promoted by the social backlash against logic and science.

The version of the New Age that does not exist.

Major confusions generated by academics, fundamentalists, counter-cult groups and traditional Muslim groups and other evangelical Christians, etc. About the New Age Movement are:

- Many of the groups dismissed Tasawwuf (Sufiism) as a New Age cult. Sufiism historically has been an established movement in Islam; they have always existed in a state of tension with the divisions within Islam. There is no connection with the New Age Movement.
- Some Christians believe that there is a massive organization underground a highly coordinated New Age Movement that organise the infiltration of schools, governments, media, and churches. That is not true.
- Some conservative Christians don't differentiate among the Satanism, Wicca, occult, and other neo-pagan religions. Some people seem to regard all as forms of Satanism that performs criminal acts on children. Other says New Age, Neo-pagan religions rune readings, channelling, tarot card readings and working with crystals is recruitment for Satanism. The occult, Satanism, neo-pagan religions are very different and unrelated. Dr. Carl Rashke, professor of religious studies at the

University of Denver explains New Age practises as the spiritual version of AIDS, New Age destroys a person's ability to cope and function.

History of the New Age Movement:

The New Age teachings gained popularity in the 1970's the reaction of the failure of Christianity and secular Humanism to provide ethical and spiritual guidance for the future. Their roots are traceable to many sources like:

- Astrology
- Channelling
- Hinduism
- Gnostic traditions
- Spiritualism
- Taoism
- Theosophy
- Wicca
- Other Neo-pagan traditions

The movement started in the 1960's in England where many of these elements were well established. The Findhorn Community in Iverness and the Wrekin Trust were of the groups that was formed, this movement quickly became international, a New Age milestone was a New Age "Seminar" held by the Association for Research and Enlighten establishment of the East-West Journal in 1971. Shirley MacLaine the actress is their most famous figure. In the 1980's and 90's the movement where criticized by various groups. Seminar and group leaders were criticized for fortunes made from New Agers, channelling ridiculed, the uncritical belief in the "scientific" properties of crystals was out ruled as groundless. During the past generation the movement become well established and a major force in North American religion. The New Age Movement is expected to expand, promoted by the social backlash against logic and science.

New Age Believes:

The number of fundamentals that are held by many - but not all – New Age Followers; they are encouraged to "shop" for the practises and beliefs they feel comfortable with:

- **Monism** – All that exists derives from a single source of divine energy.

  > Thou art worthy, O Lord, to receive glory and honour and power: for thou hast created all things, and for thy pleasure they are and were created
  >
  > **Revelation 4:11**

- **Pantheism** – God is all that exists – all that exist is God. This leads to a concept of the individual's divinity – that we are all god's. They don't seek God as exists in heaven or in a divine secret text; they seek God through the universe within self.

  > For the invisible things of him from the creation of the world are clearly seen, being understood by the things that are made, even his eternal power and Godhead; so that they are without excuse:
  >
  > **Romans 1:20**

  > Tell ye, and bring them near; yea, let them take counsel together: who hath declared this from ancient time? who hath told it from that time? have not I the Lord? and there is

no God else beside me; a just God and a Saviour; there is none beside me

Isaiah 45:21

Thus saith the Lord the King of Israel, and his redeemer the Lord of hosts; I am the first, and I am the last; and beside me there is no God.

Isaiah 44:6

- ➢ **Reincarnation** – Rebirth and living another life after death – this repeats itself many times. This is similar to the concept of transmigration of the soul in Hinduism.

Thou hidest thy face, they are troubled: thou takest away their breath, they die, and return to their dust.

Psalms 104:29

O spare me, that I may recover strength, before I go hence, and be no more.

Psalms 39:13

Then shall the dust return to the earth as it was: and the spirit shall return unto God who gave it.

Ecclesiastes 12:7

- ➢ **Karma** – At the end of your life you are rewarded or punished according to your karma. The good and the bad deeds you have done add or subtracts from your record – your karma – being reincarnates in a good or painful new life, this is linked to reincarnation, that derives from Hinduism.

For by grace are ye saved through faith; and that not of yourselves: it is the gift of God:
Not of works, lest any man should boast.

Ephesians 2:8-9

- **Aura** – I an energy field surrounding the body, most people can't see it, some sees a multi-coloured field or shimmering around the body. Those skilled to detect and read aura's can diagnose a person's state of mind, and their spiritual and physical health.

  Behold, I will bring it health and cure, and I will cure them, and will reveal unto them the abundance of peace and truth.
  Jeremiah 33:6

- **Personal Transformation** – This Intense mystical experience will lead to acceptance and use of New Age practises and beliefs, hypnosis, guided imagery, (sometimes) the use of hallucinogenic drugs and meditation are useful to enhance and bring about this transformation. The believers hope to develop new potentials within themselves: - ability to heal others and oneself, a new understanding of the working of the universe, psychic powers. When sufficient numbers of people achieved these powers, a major physical, spiritual, cultural, psychological planet –wide transformation is expected.

But the fearful, and unbelieving, and the abominable, and murderers, and whoremongers, and sorcerers, and idolaters, and all liars, shall have their part in the lake which burneth with fire and brimstone: which is the second death.
Revelation 21:8

¹⁰ There shall not be found among you any one that maketh his son or his daughter to pass through the fire, or that useth divination, or an observer of times, or an enchanter, or a witch.
¹¹ Or a charmer, or a consulter with familiar spirits, or a wizard, or a necromancer.
¹² For all that do these things are an abomination unto the Lord: and because of these abominations the Lord thy God doth drive them out from before thee.

Deuteronomy 18:10-12

➢ **Ecological Responsibility** – This belief in the importance of the uniting to preserve the health of Mother Earth (Gaia).

The earth is the Lord's, and the fulness thereof; the world, and they that dwell therein.

Psalms 24:1

For thus saith the Lord that created the heavens; God himself that formed the earth and made it; he hath established it, he created it not in vain, he formed it to be inhabited: I am the Lord; and there is none else.

Isaiah 45:18

For, behold, I create new heavens and a new earth: and the former shall not be remembered, nor come into mind.

Isaiah 65:17

➢ **Universal Religion** – All religions are simply different paths to the ultimate reality – all is God the only reality existing. The universal religion can be seen as a mountain with many spiritual paths to the summit, some easy, some hard. There is not only one path correct; all eventually leads to the top of the mountain. They have anticipation that a new universal religion with all current faiths will start, **and** will be accepted world wide.

Then said Jesus unto them again, Verily, verily, I say unto you, I am the door of the sheep.
John 10:7

- **New world order** – As the ages of Aquarius unfolds, a New Age is standing up. This will reveal a utopia where an end to hunger, wars, diseases, pollution, poverty and a world government religion, gender and racial discrimination will end. Allegiance to one's own tribe or nation will shift to concern for the entire world and its people.

Thus he said, The fourth beast shall be the fourth kingdom upon earth, which shall be diverse from all kingdoms, and shall devour the whole earth, and shall tread it down, and break it in pieces.
Daniel 7:23

New Age Rituals and Practices

Among New Agers many practises are found. A typical practioner is only active in a few areas.

- **Channelling** – It's nearly the same method the spiritualists use to conjure a spirit of a long dead person. Only difference is that the Spiritualist believe that one's soul remain relatively the same after death, most channellers believe that the soul evolves to a higher planes of existence. Channelers usually try to make contact with only one spiritual evolved being. This being's consciousness is channelling through the medium and then relays information and guidance through the medium's voice to the group. Channelling exists frohe 1850's, many groups consider themselves on their own not dependant on the New Age Movement. The most famous channelling event was the popular "A Course in Miracles." Over an 8 year period it was channelled through Dr. Helen Schucman (1909 –1981) a Columbia University psychologist. In no way she regarded herself as a New Age believer, she was an atheist. She took great care in recording the words she received accurately.

And he caused his children to pass through the fire in the valley of the son of Hinnom: also he observed times, and used enchantments, and used witchcraft, and dealt with a familiar spirit, and with wizards: he wrought much evil in the sight of the Lord, to provoke him to anger.

2 Chronicles 33:6

And the soul that turneth after such as have familiar spirits, and after wizards, to go a whoring after them, I will even set my face against that soul, and will cut him off from among his people.

Leviticus 20:6

> **Crystals** – Materials which have their molecules arranged in a highly, specific and ordered internal pattern, is called crystals. These are reflected in the crystal's external which has typical symmetrical planar surfaces. Many common substances form crystals like: salt, sugar, diamonds and quartz. These substances can be shaped to vibrate at a specific frequency and they are used in computing devises as well as in radio communications. The New Agers believes that the crystal has healing powers.

Who his own self bare our sins in his own body on the tree, that we, being dead to sins, should live unto righteousness: by whose stripes ye were healed.

1 Peter 2:24

Is any sick among you? let him call for the elders of the church; and let them pray over him, anointing him with oil in the name of the Lord

James 5:14

- ➢ **Meditating** – Is a process of blanking out your mind and releasing oneself of the conscious thinking. This is often aided by focussing on an object or repetitive chanting of a mantra.

But his delight is in the law of the Lord; and in his law doth he meditate day and night.

Psalms 1:2

When I remember thee upon my bed, and meditate on thee in the night watches.

Psalms 63:6

This book of the law shall not depart out of thy mouth; but thou shalt meditate therein day and night, that thou mayest observe to do according to all that is written therein: for then thou shalt make thy way prosperous, and then thou shalt have good success.

Joshua 1:8

- ➢ **New Age Music** – The music is used as an aid in massage therapy, in healing and general relaxation. The music is gentle, inspirational, melodic involving the harp, lute, human voice, flute etc.

Let the word of Christ dwell in you richly in all wisdom; teaching and admonishing one another in psalms and hymns and spiritual songs, singing with grace in your hearts to the Lord.

Colossians 3:16

Speaking to yourselves in psalms and hymns and spiritual songs, singing and making melody in your heart to the Lord;

Colossians 5:19

➢ **Divination** – Various techniques being used to foretell the future: Pendulum movements, I Ching, Scrying, runes and tarot cards.

➢ **Astrology** – Believing in astrology is common amongst the New Age people, but not limited to them alone. The orientation of the planets at one's time of birth and the location of one's birth predicts one's future and personality.

Thy word is a lamp unto my feet, and a light unto my path.

Psalms 119:105

For I know the thoughts that I think toward you, saith the Lord, thoughts of peace, and not of evil, to give you an expected end.

Jeremiah 29:11

And we know that all things work together for good to them that love God, to them who are the called according to his purpose.

Romans 8:28

➢ **Holistic Health** – A collection of healing techniques diverged from the traditional medical model. It tries to cure mind disorders, spirit and body, and try to promote balance and wholeness in an individual. For example acupuncture, homeopathy, crystal healing, massage, iridology, polarity therapy, various meditation methods, psychic healing, therapeutic touch and reflexology etc.

> And heal the sick that are therein, and say unto them, The kingdom of God is come nigh unto you.
> **Luke 10:9**

> ➢ **Human Potential Movement (Emotional Growth Movement)** – A collection of therapeutic methods involving group working and individual methods, using both physical and mental techniques. The idea is to help people to advance spiritually. Examples: EST, Gestalt therapy, Esalen Growth Centre, Transactional Analysis, Primal scream Therapy, joga and transcendental meditation.

According to the Canadian Census of 1991 only 1,200 people (0,005% of the Canadian population) identified their religion as New Age. However that is no way to indicate the influence of New Age ideas in that country. Many individuals identify with other religions and Christianity, but incorporate a lot of new age concepts in their faith.

Indigo Children

Some people in the New Age Movement belief that children with indigo coloured auras and special powers has been born in recent years. This is a global phenomenon that effects over 95% of new-borns since 1995 according to Nancy Anne Tappe reader of

aura's. She writes: "As small children, Indigo's are easy to recognize by their unusually large and clear eyes. Extremely bright, precocious children with an amazing memory, a strong desire to live instinctively, these children of the next millennium gifted, sensitive souls with an evolving consciousness, who came here to help change the vibrations of people's lives and create one globe, one land and one species. They are the bridge to the future.
Some New Ager's feel that with the Indigo children's special personalities they're being diagnosed as ADD or ADHD by therapists not understanding the children's special needs and qualities.

And now, Lord, what wait I for? my hope is in thee.
Psalms 39:7

Blessed is the man that trusteth in the Lord, and whose hope the Lord is.
Jeremiah 17:7

The Following is a Testimony from one of my spiritual sons, Gert Zaayman.

[2] I am the LORD thy God, which have brought thee out of the land of Egypt, out of the house of bondage.
[3] Thou shalt have no other gods before me.
[4] Thou shalt not make unto thee any graven image, or any likeness of any thing that is in heaven above, or that is in the earth beneath, or that is in the water under the earth.
[5] Thou shalt not bow down thyself to them, nor serve them: for I the LORD thy God am a jealous God, visiting the iniquity of the fathers upon the children unto the third and fourth generation of them that hate me;
[6] And shewing mercy unto thousands of them that love me, and keep my commandments.

Hélèné Fulton

Exodus 20:2-6

⁷ Then came in the magicians, the astrologers, the Chaldeans, and the soothsayers: and I told the dream before them; but they did not make known unto me the interpretation thereof.
⁸ But at the last Daniel came in before me, whose name was Belteshazzar, according to the name of my God, and in whom is the spirit of the holy gods: and before him I told the dream, saying,

Daniel 4:7-8

³⁰ And I will destroy your high places, and cut down your images, and cast your carcases upon the carcases of your idols, and my soul shall abhor you.

Leviticus 26:30

²⁶ For all the gods of the people are idols: but the LORD made the heavens.

1 Chronicles 16:26

³⁶ And they served their idols: which were a snare unto them.

Psalm 106:36

¹⁹ The burden of Egypt. Behold, the LORD rideth upon a swift cloud, and shall come into Egypt: and the idols of Egypt shall be moved at his presence, and the heart of Egypt shall melt in the midst of it.

Isaiah 19:1

³ And the spirit of Egypt shall fail in the midst thereof; and I will destroy the counsel thereof: and they shall seek to the idols, and to the charmers, and to them that have familiar spirits, and to the wizards.

Isaiah 19:3

> [16] They shall be ashamed, and also confounded, all of them: they shall go to confusion together that are makers of idols.
>
> **Isaiah 45:16**

> [4] And your altars shall be desolate, and your images shall be broken: and I will cast down your slain men before your idols. [5] And I will lay the dead carcases of the children of Israel before their idols; and I will scatter your bones round about your altars. [6] In all your dwelling places the cities shall be laid waste, and the high places shall be desolate; that your altars may be laid waste and made desolate, and your idols may be broken and cease, and your images may be cut down, and your works may be abolished.
>
> **Ezekiel 6:4-6**

This article will give some light on the dangers of New Age, false religions, Reiki and Ascended Masters and how easy it is to get involved in these false practices by deception.

The above verses are but a few concerning idols, false gods, wizards, magic.

I've got involved in New Age theology 4 years ago by reading a chapter on a website claiming that the owner of the website talks to Jesus every day. What he did was actually "channeling". A spirit will either contact him or he will contact a spirit. The problem is the spirit that is contacting him are demons or familiar spirits they know everything in the spiritual world, if there is something that you do not understand in the bible, this demon then will give you a very thoroughly explanation of the Bible, he will twist it and sugar coat it for you. What this mean is – all the channeling that gets done is specifically directed against Christianity in its total form. Within this major plan of deception of Satan is the lie because he is the father lies.

[44] Ye are of your father the devil, and the lusts of your father ye will do. He was a murderer from the beginning, and abode not in the truth, because there is no truth in him. When he speaketh a lie, he speaketh of his own: for he is a liar, and the father of it.
John 8:44

The questions that will be asked ranged from everything what Jesus did 2000 years ago, whether Jesus was in Tibet or not, whether Jesus was married, what happened after his resurrection and how He performed miracles. The other Celestial bodies this guy talked to was so called Ascended Masters like Mother Mary, Jesus (a false Jesus), Gautama Budha, Kuthumi, Saint Germain, Maitreya, Merlin, Sanat Kumara, Kuan Yin, Serapis Bey, these are all so-called Ascended Masters, who have been reincarnated a lot of times up until a stage where their karma was more than 51% and then to ascend into heaven never to return to the earth again. Some of these practices have their origin in Hinduism and Eastern Religions. Then there is the Order of Melchizedek not the one mentioning in the Bible a false one and the "White Brotherhood" just to mention a few. Another "cool thing" to do before the end of 2012 was the upgrade of your current 12 strand DNA to 24 then 48 and even higher to hold more light. This was all the stuff I was involved with. I said mantras of Hindu gods more than a thousand times a day to be more enlightened. These false gods would be shiva, kali, mahalakshmi, sarasveti just to mention a few.

Now all these false gods was actually demons for thousands of years and still is.

Hélèné Fulton

The problem with all these New Age stuff is that it is a deception. Just like in Christianity where you have the Holy Trinity so does the devil has his holy trinity, someone masquerading as the father, the son, and holy spirit, this will either be 3 demons fulfilling the job or Satan himself. What does the Bible says about all this New Age nonsense:

[9] When thou art come into the land which the LORD thy God giveth thee, thou shalt not learn to do after the abominations of those nations.
[10] There shall not be found among you any one that maketh his son or his daughter to pass through the fire, or that useth divination, or an observer of times, or an enchanter, or a witch.
[11] Or a charmer, or a consulter with familiar spirits, or a wizard, or a necromancer.
[12] For all that do these things are an abomination unto the LORD: and because of these abominations the LORD thy God doth drive them out from before thee.
[13] Thou shalt be perfect with the LORD thy God.
Deuteronomy 18:9-13

What happened with me was there were decrees and prayers given by these so called Ascended Masters straight from the spiritual realm right down to earth. These decrees and prayers are directed against the evil of today (deception). There are decrees against the devil himself that he may not tempt you (deception), decrees for spiritual growth in Christianity, Mother Mary's rosary, Archangel Michael rosary's, decree's to the seven rays of God, decrees for Archangel Gabriel, Archangel Uriel, Archangel Raphael, Archangel Metatron. All these Ascended Masters and Archangels speak of light and love, peace for humans on earth and the terrible evil we have to face every day on earth because God? loves us, this is the deception that hooked me. The other thing that new age confirms is reincarnation and karma. In all the websites that I used 4 years ago there was a strong link between Hinduism, Buddhism, Zoroastrianism and their so called false Christianity and in all the web sites channeling was used, all the information that was channeling from these Ascended Masters (demons) correlated 100%, meaning that if you read on a website about Mother Mary all her sayings it DOES NOT contradict itself to rest of ALL the new age channelings on the web.

This is scary! Because if there is a contradiction people will see the difference and will not believe it. What this mean is in the spiritual order of Satan his plans with this new age is very well planned. What I am going to say now may shock you, so hold on to your chair, you might fall off. In one of the websites I primarily used for decrees and prayers, this so called jesus said that it is fine to serve another Master (Ascended Master) and this Master you can serve and pray to because he is already Ascended to heaven and he can also save you and he will help you for your ascension. This means since everyone is still reincarnating this false Master or any other one, can help you to balance your karma to a point where you have 51% good and 49% bad karma on earth, you can qualify for ascension, only if you use the decrees and prayers given by these Ascended Masters(demons). This is shockingly against the sound doctrine of true Christianity.

So what does the Bible say?

20 And God spake all these words, saying,

² I am the LORD thy God, which have brought thee out of the land of Egypt, out of the house of bondage.

³ Thou shalt have no other gods before me.

⁴ Thou shalt not make unto thee any graven image, or any likeness of any thing that is in heaven above, or that is in the earth beneath, or that is in the water under the earth.

⁵ Thou shalt not bow down thyself to them, nor serve them: for I the LORD thy God am a jealous God, visiting the iniquity of the fathers upon the children unto the third and fourth generation of them that hate me;

Exodus 20:1-5

²⁸ And one of the scribes came, and having heard them reasoning together, and perceiving that he had answered them well, asked him, Which is the first commandment of all?

²⁹ And Jesus answered him, The first of all the commandments is, Hear, O Israel; The Lord our God is one Lord:

³⁰ And thou shalt love the Lord thy God with all thy heart, and with all thy soul, and with all thy mind, and with all thy strength: this is the first commandment.

³¹ And the second is like, namely this, Thou shalt love thy neighbour as thyself. There is none other commandment greater than these.

Mark 12:28-31

Now the question is why didn't I see all this as nonsense before? Because of the deception and poor Bible knowledge, I thought I knew the True God, but my True God didn't forsake me, He saved me out of this new age stuff, now I am definitely reading the Bible and got saved out of all of this. If I knew my Bible the following would have happened,

[16] All scripture is given by inspiration of God, and is profitable for doctrine, for reproof, for correction, for instruction in righteousness:
[17] That the man of God may be perfect, thoroughly furnished unto all good works.

2 Timothy 3:16-17

[12] For the word of God is quick, and powerful, and sharper than any twoedged sword, piercing even to the dividing asunder of soul and spirit, and of the joints and marrow, and is a discerner of the thoughts and intents of the heart.

Hebrews 4:12

[3] For though we walk in the flesh, we do not war after the flesh:
[4] (For the weapons of our warfare are not carnal, but mighty through God to the pulling down of strong holds;)
[5] Casting down imaginations, and every high thing that exalteth itself against the knowledge of God, and bringing into captivity every thought to the obedience of Christ;
[6] And having in a readiness to revenge all disobedience, when your obedience is fulfilled.

2 Corinthians 10:3-6

So I would have known the truth and the truth would have set me free.

New Age theology is actually the combining of different religions and false doctrines and to give this to the New World. New Age theology wants to cut off the Jesus part from the Bible, why? Because it is the Jesus part and His salvation that will save you from hell.
He died on the cross for the forgiveness of your sins and total salvation.

Hélèné Fulton

For me deception was the lie I believed on the websites of new age theology. Ok but if it was a lie why didn't I see it. This is where the deception kicks in, when you read websites that are demon inspired, demons or familiar spirits will start to monitor you in the spiritual realm. They know you inside out from child birth untill now and if your knowledge of the Bible is lacking like mine at that time, demons will come in.

So these demons masquerading as light fills your mind and the feeling you get out of this feels like you are anointed with knowledge and you the person felt elevated above everyone else (DECEPTION). You will not know you are in the wrong, until someone helps you to get out of it or until it is too late. And all the people who are doing channelling are under this false anointing and there is no feeling that you are WRONG because you mind is clouded by demons and you cannot see the real truth because it is HIDDEN from you.

My next testimony is, during this whole scenario while I was giving this decrees and prayers I wanted to do more, why? Because the ascended masters whole doctrine runs around doing good for humanity (deception). So, I decided to become, a Reiki Master. Doing reiki is actually giving healing energy to sick people physically or over a distance, now this is where the fun started (deception). My reiki attunements was done by someone also a reiki master and she was in USA and I was in South Africa but we were not in touch with each other. So how does it work? Attunement means you are attuned to some sort of ENERGY whether it will be healing like reiki or you can attune yourself to (hold on to your chair again) gold energy, silver energy, god and goddess energy, plant energy, herbal energy, Ascended Master energy, sacred locations, pyramid energy and all the Archangels, everything that has energy you want to use for you daily life. Reiki attunements are much like the same when you stand in front of a person you lay your hands on them, much like if you want to bless someone. But we did it over distance, my reiki master will create an energy chi ball with her mind, send in the spiritual realm and I will call it down to me, does it work? Yes it does, all the time. What I am telling you now is an abomination to the Lord and it is WRONG! It is not biblical to do these things; it is the works of the devil.

So what does this all mean, in true Christianity? You are saved because of your faith in Jesus Christ and what Jesus did on the cross at Calvary 2000 years ago. In all the above Satan wants to remove Jesus out of the picture and put the focus on you, you can save yourself according to him (deception).

What does the Bible teach?

[6] Jesus saith unto him, I am the way, the truth, and the life: no man cometh unto the Father, but by me.

John 14:6

[8] He that committeth sin is of the devil; for the devil sinneth from the beginning. For this purpose the Son of God was manifested, that he might destroy the works of the devil.

1 John 3:8

Where did all this started? With Adam and Eve, what did the Devil told them? You can eat of the fruit of the forbidden tree because you will not die and be like GOD.

What does the Bible teach?

3 Now the serpent was more subtil than any beast of the field which the Lord God had made. And he said unto the woman, Yea, hath God said, Ye shall not eat of every tree of the garden?
² And the woman said unto the serpent, We may eat of the fruit of the trees of the garden:
³ But of the fruit of the tree which is in the midst of the garden, God hath said, Ye shall not eat of it, neither shall ye touch it, lest ye die.
⁴ And the serpent said unto the woman, Ye shall not surely die:
⁵ For God doth know that in the day ye eat thereof, then your eyes shall be opened, and ye shall be as gods, knowing good and evil.

Genesis 3:1-5

This is the deception and in it the lie. Why was Lucifer kicked out of Heaven? He wanted to have the same credentials as GOD and want to be seen as a GOD so let's read the Bible.

¹² How art thou fallen from heaven, O Lucifer, son of the morning! how art thou cut down to the ground, which didst weaken the nations!
¹³ For thou hast said in thine heart, I will ascend into heaven, I will exalt my throne above the stars of God: I will sit also upon the mount of the congregation, in the sides of the north:
¹⁴ I will ascend above the heights of the clouds; I will be like the most High.

Isaiah 14:12-14

What happened to Satan?

[7] And there was war in heaven: Michael and his angels fought against the dragon; and the dragon fought and his angels,
[8] And prevailed not; neither was their place found any more in heaven.
[9] And the great dragon was cast out, that old serpent, called the Devil, and Satan, which deceiveth the whole world: he was cast out into the earth, and his angels were cast out with him.

Revelations 12:7-9

What does the Bible say about him now?

[10] The thief cometh not, but for to steal, and to kill, and to destroy: I am come that they might have life, and that they might have it more abundantly.

John 10:10

[8] But the fearful, and unbelieving, and the abominable, and murderers, and whoremongers, and sorcerers, and idolaters, and all liars, shall have their part in the lake which burneth with fire and brimstone: which is the second death.

Revelation 21:8

[20] And the beast was taken, and with him the false prophet that wrought miracles before him, with which he deceived them that had received the mark of the beast, and them that worshipped his image. These both were cast alive into a lake of fire burning with brimstone.

Revelation 19:20

[10] And the devil that deceived them was cast into the lake of fire and brimstone, where the beast and the false prophet are, and shall be tormented day and night for ever and ever.

Revelation 20:10

My conclusion is that what the devil wanted to achieve when in Heaven failed woefully. God placed humans

in the garden of Eden and what the devil could not accomplished in Heaven he (Satan) tried to convince Adam and Eve that they can become Gods if they eat of the forbidden tree. My testimony is proof that New Age theology and false religions want to shift the focus from GOD and the works of Jesus Christ to YOU. All these false religions and new age stuff is to give you false power to make you feel that you are in control of your life without the saving grace of God the Father and Creator. The rest is up to you. Just now that if you follow New Age and false religion you will end up like the devil, kicked out of Heaven just like He was a long time ago and destined for hell.

The right thing to do is turn you're focus back to the Holy Trinity it is THEY that doeth the works behind the scenes, not you, Jesus did HIS works on the cross,

[16] For God so loved the world, that he gave his only begotten Son, that whosoever believeth in him should not perish, but have everlasting life.

John 3:16 "

What you have to do is believe in the works that Jesus did for you on the cross. Accept Jesus as Lord and Saviour of your life.

[9] That if thou shalt confess with thy mouth the Lord Jesus, and shalt believe in thine heart that God hath raised him from the dead, thou shalt be saved.

Romans 10:9

[32] Whosoever therefore shall confess me before men, him will I confess also before my Father which is in heaven.

Hélèné Fulton

³³ But whosoever shall deny me before men, him will I also deny before my Father which is in heaven.

Matthew 10:32-33

Thank you for reading my testimony I hope you have a better understanding of New Age and false religions and the deception that goes along with it. God bless.

Chapter 10: Wicca

Written By: Remona Gericke

Beliefs

Let's start this off with the meaning of the word Wicca.

Wic is an old English word which means to bend or to manipulate, while the word Wicca refers to a male and Wicce to a female. Wiccan is the plural form referring to both males and females as a group. Today modern English dictionaries refer to the word as witch or witches. It does not mean "wise one" as thought by many.

Gardnerian, Alexandrian, Blue Moon, Celtic, Druidic, Welsh Traditions, Georgian, Dianic, Church of Wicca etc are all part of the same pudding but each with a different sauce. They all worship nature or nature deity and practice some degree of witchcraft. The size or amount is irrelevant due to the fact that it will always be seen by God as an abomination.

He feels so strongly about the matter that he even gave the Israelites instruction to kill any witch among them.

"Thou salt not suffer a witch to live."
Exodus 22:18 (KJV)

As harsh as it may sound it shows us His intense disapproval with the cult. A lot has changed since the time Moses presented the law of God to the Israelites.

Hélèné Fulton

Today witchcraft is seen almost everywhere and unfortunately has become part of our daily lives. Without realizing we invited it into our homes. We are bombarded with books, slogans, products and TV shows like Charmed, Harry Potter, Lord of the Rings, Wizards of Waverly Place, Sabrina the teenage witch, Aladdin, Hercules, the Power Puff girls, Gummy Bears, Medium, Dragon Ball Z, Pokémon and just so Raven just to name a few. To make matters worse Satan makes it look so appealing and harmless. I mean what could possibly be wrong with watching a cartoon? Talk about hiding something in plain sight.

If God feels so strongly regarding the matter then why is it being treated so lightly? You might say to me that nothing can be done about the situation and to some extent you will be right because God said that we can expect so, however don't we at least have to try and turn away from things that can influence us badly? Shouldn't we at least try to teach our children that witchcraft is wrong in the eyes of our Lord and Saviour instead of thinking our kids are so cute when they mimic these characters and cute chants?

"Bring forth therefore fruits meet for repentance:"
Matthew 3:8 (KJV)

Ask yourself this... How would you feel if suddenly God Almighty Himself would appear with all His glory and majesty while you are watching the next episode of – whatever you watch – because you are so hooked you just can't miss it? Guess what? God is omnipresent which means that He is standing next to you while you enjoy being entertained by Satan instead of reading your Bible and praying.

"The LORD looked down from heaven upon the children of men, to see if there were any that did understand, *and* seek God."
Psalms 14:2 (KJV)

"God looked down from heaven upon the children of men, to see if there were *any* that did understand, that did seek God."
Psalms 53:2 (KJV)

"For he hath looked down from the height of his sanctuary; from heaven did the LORD behold the earth;"
Psalms 102:19 (KJV)

Yes, God loves all sinners but He hates their sin. Why then do we as Christians want to be associated with anything that God hates so clearly? I am not trying to make you run from God, despite what you might think. He is not a distant and angry God, but He is the complete expression of love. He would much rather choose to forgive a repentant heart than to judge.

"If we confess our sins, he is faithful and just to forgive us *our* sins, and to cleanse us from all unrighteousness."
1 John 1:9 (KJV)

"For thou, Lord, *art* good, and ready to forgive; and plenteous in mercy unto all them that call upon thee."
Psalms 86:5 (KJV)

My intent is to rather make you realize that we need to re-look our priorities and moral values. We wouldn't dare to wear a T-shirt of a rival rugby team, but we care so little about our spiritual team. Remember you are either on God's side or Satan's. There is no grey area.

"No man can serve two masters: for either he will hate the one, and love the other; or else he will hold to the one, and despise the other. Ye cannot serve God and mammon."

Matthew 6:24 (KJV)

Wicca is categorized into the Pagan/Neo-Wiccan faith growing in numbers all over the world but it seems that the majority resides mostly in die European countries and British Isles. They see themselves as very spiritual people that live harmoniously with nature believing to blend in with nature rather than to stand out having authority over it. It is interesting to know that Wiccans share a great concern for the environment.

The issue I have with the abovementioned is that there is only one true God. He is the Creator of heaven and earth. The great I Am. Nature is just part of the creation that the Creator made and should not be worshiped. To put it in more understandable terms – Graham Bell invented the telephone and instead of people acknowledging and honoring him for the creation, they would rather honor the phone that would have never existed if the inventor hadn't invented it? How would this make sense?

"And God said, Let us make man in our image, after our likeness: and let them have dominion over the fish of the sea, and over the fowl of the air, and over the cattle, and over all the earth, and over every creeping thing that creepeth upon the earth."

Genesis 1:26 (KJV)

"Hast thou not known? hast thou not heard, *that* the everlasting God, the LORD, the Creator of the ends of the earth, fainteth not, neither is weary? *there is* no searching of his understanding."

Isaiah 40:28 (KJV)

"I *am* the LORD, your Holy One, the Creator of Israel, your King."
Isaiah 43:15 (KJV)

"Who changed the truth of God into a lie, and worshipped and served the creature more than the Creator, who is blessed for ever. Amen. [26]For this cause God gave them up unto vile affections: for even their women did change the natural use into that which is against nature: [27]And likewise also the men, leaving the natural use of the woman, burned in their lust one toward another; men with men working that which is unseemly, and receiving in themselves that recompence of their error which was meet."
Romans 1:25-27 (KJV)

"Because they exchanged the truth of God for a lie and worshiped and served the creature rather than the Creator, Who is blessed forever! Amen (so be it). [26]For this reason God gave them over and abandoned them to vile affections and degrading passions. For their women exchanged their natural function for an unnatural and abnormal one, [27]And the men also turned from natural relations with women and were set ablaze (burning out, consumed) with lust for one another - men committing shameful acts with men and suffering in their own bodies and personalities the inevitable consequences and penalty of their wrong-doing and going astray, which was [their] fitting retribution."
Romans 1:25-27 (The Amplified Bible)

Wiccan members believe primarily in the dual gods – the "Goddess" also called the "Great Mother or Lady" that represents the females and the reproduction of all living things and her spouse the "God" also called "the Horned One" representing the males. They place more emphasis on the goddess rather than on the god. This is a direct quote from someone who was in the practice "I walked the earth and felt her a living breathing thing and I worshiped her as Holy Mother Earth, she was with me from the beginning and was attained at the end of desire" Notice that the person is speaking in the Past Tense? This is because he gave his heart to Christ and he is now sharing his experience with as many as possible.

Even though they worship these two gods, the worshiping of other gods especially the old European gods/deities like Pan, Diana, Cernunnos are allowed because of their view that all gods form part of one being.

The second issue being that there is only ONE God. Yes we know Him as God the Father, God the Son, and God the Holy Spirit – but they are ONE and the same. This shouldn't be hard to understand because we exist out of a body, soul and spirit.

"Hear, O Israel: The LORD our God *is* one LORD:"
Deuteronomy 6:4 (KJV)

"And Jesus answered him, The first of all the commandments *is,* Hear, O Israel; The Lord our God is one Lord:"
Mark 12:29 (KJV)

"And the scribe said unto him, Well, Master, thou hast said the truth: for there is one God; and there is none other but He:"
Mark 12:32 (KJV)

"Seeing *it is* one God, which shall justify the circumcision by faith, and uncircumcision through faith."
Romans 3:30 (KJV)

"As concerning therefore the eating of those things that are offered in sacrifice unto idols, we know that an idol *is* nothing in the world, and that *there is* none other God but one."

1 Corinthians 8:4 (KJV)

"One God and Father of all, who *is* above all, and through all, and in you all."

Ephesians 4:6 (KJV)

"Thou believest that there is one God; thou doest well: the devils also believe, and tremble."

James 2:19 (KJV)

The Wiccan groups dedicate their time in trying to understand the deities, ancestors as well as the rhythms and tides of nature and believe that nature objects have a life and a soul. This kind of reminds me of that popular children movie, Pocahontas. Some Wiccan members will have a pet (mainly cat) that they will call their familiar. Dead people can never come back to earth and for that reason it is impossible to communicate with relatives, ancestors of years back. They are demons in disguise and you should not listen to them. When King Saul went to see a witch and asked to bring back the spirit of Samuel he became insane afterwards. He lost everything!

"And the king said unto her, Be not afraid: for what sawest thou? And the woman said unto Saul, I saw gods ascending out of the earth. [14] And he said unto her, What form *is* he of? And she said, An old man cometh up; and he *is* covered with a mantle. And Saul perceived that it *was* Samuel, and he stooped with *his* face to the ground, and bowed himself."

1 Samuel 28:13 (KJV)

The word "perceived" clearly gives us the understanding that it was not a given fact, it was Saul's assumption.

Magic also plays a big role in the Wiccan believes. At first most of them refuse to use magick but sooner or later they cave. They use it to get to their goals by casting spells either from their list of traditional spells or those they do experimentally whereby in some cases it does cause "unintentional side effects". These spells are written in a book they call the "Book of Shadows". In case you were wondering the difference between magick and magic is this. Magick has to do with spells, healing and physic forces etc, while magic refers to illusions and tricks performed by people for entertainment.

Any type of spell, curse, incantation etc. requires a demon to be called to influence circumstances so it may take place accordingly.

"But I say unto you, That every idle word that men shall speak, they shall give account thereof in the day of judgment. For by thy words thou shalt be justified, and by thy words thou shalt be condemned."

Matthew 12:36-37 (KJV)

Now let us see what was God's clear instructions regarding witchcraft.

"Ye shall not eat *any thing* with the blood: neither shall ye use enchantment, nor observe times."

Leviticus 19:26 (KJV)

> "You shall not eat anything with the blood; neither shall you use magic, omens, or witchcraft [or predict events by horoscope or signs and lucky days]."
>
> **Leviticus 19:26 (The Amplified Bible)**

Why does anyone need spells to get to their goals or obtain money and so forth? Did God not say that if we first seek the kingdom of God and His righteousness that He will provide us with the rest of the stuff we need?

> "Therefore take no thought, saying, What shall we eat? or, What shall we drink? or, Wherewithal shall we be clothed? ^{32} (For after all these things do the Gentiles seek:) for your heavenly Father knoweth that ye have need of all these things. ^{33} But seek ye first the kingdom of God, and his righteousness; and all these things shall be added unto you. "
>
> **Matthew 6:31-33 (KJV)**

There are five basic believes of Wicca. The Wiccan Rede, the law of attraction, harmony and serenity, power through knowledge and reincarnation.

Some other core believes of the Wiccan tradition include the following.

Satan is a myth created by Christians. Satan is real whether you believe it or not. So many people would testify to that, so I am not going to try and argue about it.

> "For many deceivers are entered into the world, who confess not that Jesus Christ is come in the flesh. This is a deceiver and an antichrist."
>
> **2 John 1:7 (KJV)**

Hélèné Fulton

Mr Bill Schnoebelen's book "Wicca: Satan's little white lie" give some insight into the web of confusion, lies, fables, myths and deceit found in Wicca. He was an "initiate into the Alexandrian Wicca on Imbolc, February 2, 1973 and made a High Priest and Magus in September of that same year. That summer his lady and he were also promoted to the High Priestly rank in the Druidic Craft of the wise. They also helped establish a Church of All Worlds "nest" in Milwaukee and studied under Gavin and Yvonne Frost and their Church and School of Wicca. They presided over one of the oldest and largest networks of covens in the Midwest." Bill eventually went on to Satanism.

Yes, for a while he was also one who thought that Wicca was a harmless nature-worshipping religion. It was only when he got inside and going from one high position to another that he discovered that Wicca is one of Satan's cleverest ideas to lead as many as possible people astray and actually worship Satan. His story is a personal testimony of what he experienced and how Jesus Christ saved him.

Due to the fact that they do not believe in Satan they also believe that there is a huge difference between Paganism and Satanism. People must remember that no difference could be too big or too small when one's soul is on the line.

"And I saw the dead, small and great, stand before God; and the books were opened: and another book was opened, which is *the book* of life: and the dead were judged out of those things which were written in the books, according to their works."

Revelation 20:12 (KJV)

Just to clear things up a little more Lucifer is the Devil/Satan/Old Serpent/the Dragon. Satan and Lucifer are one and the same and are not two different entities as believed.

It is clear that even the Bible warns us that we all will be judge for what we have done. A little white lie is still a lie. The Bible is clear that if you lie, Satan is your father.

"Ye are of *your* father the devil, and the lusts of your father ye will do. He was a murderer from the beginning, and abode not in the truth, because there is no truth in him. When he speaketh a lie, he speaketh of his own: for he is a liar, and the father of it."
John 8:44 (KJV)

Manipulating is still witchcraft and any other form of witchcraft as well - no matter how different it is from other witchcraft groups. Rebellion is also seen as witchcraft in God's eyes.

"For rebellion *is as* the sin of witchcraft, and stubbornness *is as* iniquity and idolatry. Because thou hast rejected the word of the LORD, he hath also rejected thee from *being* king."
1 Samuel 15:23 (KJV)

They believe that Wicca is much older than Christianity (not a Biblical word) and that their roots are of more pure faith. There is no proof what so ever that the religion is even older than the 20th Century. The truth is that witchcraft is not older than the worship of the true God. It started with Adam and continues even on this very day. Wicca as a group is not old. Mr Schnoebelen explains this more clearly in his book "Wicca: Satan's little white lie". I quote the following.

"Although much of the extant literature written by witches (and Dr. Margaret Murray's work) would lead one to believe that Wicca is a survival of the ancient pagan fertility cults, especially of Northern Europe and the British Isles; there is not a shred of real historical proof for any connection between Bronze Age cults and modern witchcraft."

"…it seemed that Wicca is, in fact, a manufactured religion not much older than this century. There did not seem to be evidence for any Book of Shadows (a combined "bible" and ritual book for Wiccans) much older than the 1910's! (the Book of Shadows was probably the result of a collaboration between Gerald Gardner and the notorious Satanist Aleister Crowley,p22)".

The concept of Wicca might not be very new but the focus behind it is not. Another quote from Wicca: Satan's little white lie explains…

"Gardner claimed there were covens of witches in Britain practicing not an anti-Christian religion, but a "pre-Christian" religion. This he claimed was called Wicca…

This he asserted was the "Old Religion", an animistic worship of the principals of nature and reproduction; rather like a warmed-over rehash of Fraser's anthropological chestnut, THE GOLDEN BOUGH. The gods of this Old Religion were a supreme Mother Goddess who ruled the earth, the moon, the sea, and things agricultural. Her secret name (in this coven anyway) was Arayda. There was also a Horned God who ruled the sun and hunting, which was variously called Herne, Cernunnos or Pan.

Thus, Wicca was not an attack on Christianity, but was supposedly a much older religion whose gods were old when Yahweh of the Bible was in knee pants. According to Gardner, witches worshipped naked (or "skyclad" as he preferred to call it" and were matriarchal…"

Many higher level witches would know that Wicca is a compilation of myths while the lower level will believe anything they are taught. The book further explains…

"It is now a matter of common knowledge that much of Gardner's story is fiction. Yet, most witches aren't bothered by that. Since the seventies, many witches wanted to be totally creative and make up their religion out of their heads – without trying to make any pretentious claims about having "unbroken lines of power" back to the medieval "kings" of the witches. Most Neo-pagan groups fall into this category. They are based on myths, fantasy or even science-fiction stories."

On the other hand the Bible was written about God over such massive time lapse makes it even more indescribable because they all delivered the same message. The writers were not even in the same location nor did the writers get their information from any secondary source, and neither was all the writers born Jews. Yes, there are evidence of the Old and New Testament dating years back.

Wiccan members believe in Karma "what goes around comes around" and also in the afterlife including reincarnation.

"And as it is appointed unto men once to die, but after this the judgment:"
Hebrews 9:27 (KJV)

The Wiccan Rede states "and it harm none – do what ye will" which bears a very close resemblance to the Satanism creed – "Do what you wilt shall be the whole law". The statement is kind of contradicting because it suggests freedom, but yet bound by a law. A better statement would have been – Do what you wilt as there is no law – and this is not the only almost similarity between the two groups. Both worship the pagan god Pan, the goddess' spouse.

They do not see anything wrong with what they are doing and they are convinced they do everything for the benefit of humans and the earth; they consider it as being good and not evil. According to the Bible there is no such thing as a good witch. They shouldn't be considered good or harmless just because they believe in fairy stories and legends of the Grail. They shouldn't be considered good or harmless just because they worship mother earth and care about the environment.

With the above said we can understand that they do not believe in sin, and if there is no sin, there is no need for a god.

"For all have sinned, and come short of the glory of God;"
Romans 3:23 (KJV)

"Neither is there salvation in any other: for there is none other name under heaven given among men, whereby we must be saved."

Acts 4:12 (KJV)

No heaven and no hell, but strangely they do believe in a Summerland or a land of eternal youth. Wiccan high priest Sharhawk says: "We can now open new eyes and see there is nothing to be saved from, no struggle of live against the universe, no God outside the world to be feared and obeyed."

Some food for thought, if they don't believe in good and evil, right and wrong then what is the purpose of the Wiccan Rede? How will it be possible to harm someone if there is no line between good and bad? They must believe in some way that there are good and bad, which also means that they are contradicting themselves.

Let me give you some more food for thought. If Wiccan's are right about heaven and hell, then we as Christians loose nothing, but on the contrary if we are right about heaven and hell, then some will have a problem. Sadly we also learn that people would rather choose evil above good.

"The heart *is* deceitful above all *things,* and desperately wicked: who can know it? I the LORD search the heart, *I* try the reins, even to give every man according to his ways, *and* according to the fruit of his doings."

Jeremiah 17:9-10 (KJV)

Look at the Bible prophesies that have been fulfilled, which other religion can say the same? How can it be a co-incidence if there are so many and to the last bit of detail? We are bluffing ourselves with a false peace if we think otherwise.

Wiccan groups believe that their ancestors are watching them and therefore they always have to speak respectfully of them.

You will find no governing body in charge of the Wiccan groups and also no set of laws to be followed. The high priest and priestess are there to assist with any group conflicts. This also allows them to choose what they want to believe and how to go about those rites. For instance some chose to do it in the nude and others prefer robes. Some choose to perform alone and others in groups.

They don't dress anything different than anyone else and therefore it will not be possible to identify them as easily. Although there might be a rule to the exception most are militantly feminists. Some Christians like to wear a cross necklace or bracelet to show publically that they are Christians so Wiccan members also like to wear the pentagram on them in order to recognize each other in the public where traditional witches will not wear anything to help them from being detected.

It is easy to see why people fall into Satan's trap. Everyone needs love so Satan confuses people by thinking true love and sex is the same thing. He plays on their emotional scars caused by rejection, also leading to so many trying to prove that they are good enough and competing with the next door neighbor. Satan has the world blinded to the true meaning of creation. We were all created by God and for God.

"And to make all *men* see what *is* the fellowship of the mystery, which from the beginning of the world hath been hid in God, who created all things by Jesus Christ:"

Ephesians 3:9 (KJV)

Human sexuality is valued and they regard it as a gift of the goddess and god, to be engaged in with joy and responsibility and without manipulation or coercion. They believe that there are three the normal, natural and unchosen sexual orientations: heterosexuality (male and female), homosexuality (female and female or male and male) and then bisexuality (both woman and men alike).

When it Started

Here is a list of the most popular Wiccan groups and a brief overview of their history.

Gardnerian Wicca: Founded by Gerald Gardner (1884-1964) just after the Second World War. Gardner said that the roots of his coven were from the old "New Forest Coven" who also initiated him. It is a widely accepted fact that Gardnerian Wicca is one of the earliest Wicca traditions and it is also the basis for most other traditions such as Alexandrian Wicca, Georgian tradition, Green witchcraft, Hedge witchery, Kitchen witchcraft, Maiden hill Wicca, and Northern Way tradition, Nova Wicca, Order of the Golden Dawn, Picti-Wica, and the Sacred Wheel etc.

Gardnerian members divide themselves into groups of about 13 people and each group is led by a high priest and high priestess. The coven was made public after England changed their witchcraft law. They work on a degree system which is oath bound and initiatory. The

Book of Shadows was said to being invented by Gardner and the book contains spells and rituals usually performed. Each new initiate copied the book by hand and may add to it as he or she sees fit. When they (the initiates) would step into a higher rank they would give the copy of their book to the new initiates who then copy the book by hand and so the process continues.

They worship the "Lady and the Lord". Wicca is not an ancient religion, but Gardner did incorporate some old exotic knowledge into his original tradition, including Eastern mysticism, Qaballah and British legends.

Georgian Wicca: Founded by George Patterson, Zanoni Silverknife and Tanith during the 1970's in the home of Patterson in Bakerfield, CA. Patterson applied for legal status as an incorporated church in 1971. He obtained a charter and ministerial credentials for himself and Zanoni. Most of the Georgian covens reside in British Columbia, California, Florida, Oregon, Colorado, Maryland, Michigan, Washington and Oklahoma. The tools they use are very similar to those of the Alexandrian group.

Green witchcraft: Founded by Ann Moura and uses names of the pagan deities as she strongly believes that her family's witchcraft tradition was pagan. There is no certainty of her mother's and grandmother's practices and everything Moura learned from them was only what they told her verbally. There are no documents or books to make sure that the information doesn't get lost when passed on to the following generation.

Hedge witchery: This coven highly focuses on communicating with the spirits of the "other world". These witches travel to the spiritual world to get information from spirits and ancestors with regards to chants, herbs believed to bring healing, brews and potions. Their practices are fundamental of European witchcraft, shamanism and herbalism.

They do not follow the Wiccan Rede as other pagan groups do. Each witch creates their own set of rules and moral values and therefore most of them work alone. Many years ago these witches lived close to a forest to be closer to nature and also because they believed that there was a lot of spiritual activity in forests. The coven is most popular in Europe and the east and west coast of the US.

Kitchen witchcraft is a form of witchcraft and as the world implies uses tools in and around the kitchen. They like to cook and bake while chanting and casting spells. The magic practices are combined with other form of spirituality. They find everything they do in the house and garden as meaningful.

They worship the goddess and believe they honor her by turning everyday house chores into a sacred and joyful experience. They love arts and crafts such as traditional and dying crafts. The practices and rituals are self-taught and self-initiated, while some was passed down from previous generations. Most of the food they cook and eat where planted by themselves.

Maidenhill Wicca is a group inspired by Blue Star Wicca and worships the goddess and her spouse, the horned one, whilst not limited to the worshiping of the particular cultural ethnic "tradition". The coven started in England round about 1979, and is linked to the coven of Rhiannon from Manchester, England. They teach their students based on the foundations of Gardnerian Wicca but after "graduating" the students may choose to take their own path that fits with their own believe. This is one of the least popular Wiccan groups in North America.

Northern Way is a non-initiatory tradition and works robed. The group focuses the re-making and re-creating of the Old Norse tradition, however not hereditary which means that any person can't join regardless of their family or ethnic group. The god-names used are Old Norse and not Teutonic.

Nova Wicca forms part of the Eclectic group. They work roped as Esbats and Sabbaths and nude at initiations. The same deities are worshiped as those of the Gardnerian group, but some groups may use others. They use a degree system which is detailed-orientated and students receive in-depth training, while newcomers may attend select classes. Grand Sabbaths are also open to anyone who might by interested, at the coven's discretion.

Order of the Golden Dawn is a coven founded by free masons William Robert Woodman, William Wynn Westcott and Samuel Liddlell MacGregor Mathers whom was also members of SRIA (Societas Rosicruciana in Anglia). Main focuses include the study and practice of the occult, metaphysics and paranormal activities, and the coven is based in Great Britain.

The golden dawn was the first of three orders. The first order taught esoteric philosophy bases on the Hermetic Qaballah and personal development through study and awareness of the elements including basics of astrology, tarot divination and geomancy. The second order - the Ruby Rose and cross of gold taught proper magic including scrying, astral travel and alchemy. The third order – the secret chiefs are highly skilled and directed the activities of the lower two orders by spirit communication with the chiefs of the second order.

Picti-Wita is a Scottish solitary tradition. Aiden Breac teaches students in his home at Castle Carnacae, Scotland. The tradition is tuned into the solar and lunar changes worshiping the god and goddess. Meditation and divination plays a big role and they teach on several variations on the solitary working of magick.

Sacred Wheel founded by Jim Welch and Ivo Dominquez Jr. In September of 1983 they posted a flyer at their store Hen's teeth in Wilmington, DE to form a study group. The store was a bookstore with a large occult section. Ivo studied in 1974 and got connected with pagan communities in 1978.

The coven had a lot of influences but majorities of it are those of Gardnerian and Alexandrian Wicca, KAM style, Sabian Society, Sun Bear's teachings, Patricia Hayes' teachings, masonry, the Golden Dawn and the Western Magical Tradition as a whole. They also focus on astrology, Qaballah, hermeticism.

Eclectic Wicca is the most popular within the American region. They practice in solitude and rarely come together in groups. There is no specific definition of what these groups do. They use a blend of different believes and practices with foundations of Gardnerian and Alexandrian Wicca but with many changes and modifications. Each person can create his/her own tradition, believes and practices, which means that they don't necessarily use oath bound, initiatory material.

Feary Wicca sometimes referred to as the Feri Tradition forms part of the eclectic group. This tradition is all about sex – the experience, awareness, sexual mysticism – which is not limited to heterosexual expression. The tradition shares some basics of Huna, Vodou, Faery lore, Qaballah, Hoodoo, Tantra and Gnosticism. They believe in the reality that can't be seen. They value the wisdom of nature bardic and mantic creativity. They have a love for beautiful things. The three souls of black heart of innocence form their core believes. Their ritual structures and tools are similar to those of Wiccan practices.

Frost Wicca is another offspring of the eclectic tradition, and based on Welsh. In the early 1970's Gavin and Yvonne Frost gave birth to this tradition. The learning material is send to the students either by mail or post just like the Church and School of Wicca does it. The course is the same as the material presented in their book. The witches' bible at first did not mention the goddess at all and there were variously sexual aspects which dismayed many who were otherwise drawn to the tradition. The last mentioned situation has been modified and there is now mention of the goddess.

Dianic Wicca was founded by Morgan McFarland and Mark Robberts. Most of the members reside in Texas and in Western Europe. Dianic Wicca is divided into two groups. There are those who worship the goddess and horned god and those that only worship the goddess. They are usually called feminists and are mainly a woman only tradition. Most members are lesbian, however woman who aren't lesbian are also accepted into the group. Leadership is rather given to a woman and a priestess must always open a circle.

Discordianism is a religion/philosophy based on the worship of Eris, the Greco-Roman goddess of chaos, or archetypes or ideals associated with her. They believe that order and disorder are both illusions imposed on the universe by the human nervous system, and that neither one of these illusions is any more accurate or objectively true than the other. Discordians use subversive humor to spread the belief and to prevent the belief from coming dogmatic.

Celtic Wicca founded by Gavin and Yvonne Frost. They focused on a male deity but recently added a goddess. They call themselves Baptist Wicca. The religion is a combination of high magick, eclectic Wicca and Celtic Wicca. The use of three circles is very common and made out of salt, sulpher and herbs and includes a white handled athame. This group shares some elements of Celtic mythology and share the same theology, rituals and beliefs as most other form of Wicca. Celtic Wicca is also a combination of Druid and Gardnerian Wicca. They believe in the healing power of plants, stones, flowers, trees, elemental spirits, little people, gnomes and fairies.

Church of Y Tylwyth Teg's main focus is to search out the values of all people. Human dignity, human side of our daily activities, service to fellow humans, happiness is all part of their main focuses.

Church of the Crescent Moon is a cohesive, small group of people. Each priestess and priest maintains service of the goddess or god that he or she serves. They believe in many paths to the ultimate oneness with the absolute. They don't call themselves Wiccans and their purposes include perpetuating "the uncorrupted religion of the ancient Ireland" and providing "information and instruction about the goddesses and gods in general, Irish culture, and many occult subjects".

Circle Wicca born in 1974. The founders are Selina Fox and Jim Alan. The headquarters are at Circle Sanctuary, a 200 acre nature preserve and organic hat farm in the rolling hills of south western Wisconsin.

Coven of the Gorest: Far and Forever. This is a newer denomination and therefore not found as widely spread as some of the others listed. It was formed by a priest and priestess with collective experiences in Dianic, hereditary Spanish, Egyptian and Gardnerian Wicca and Qaballah. The equally important goddess and god are living representatives of more fundamental, living forces which manifest on a variety of levels. They want to be a vessel for them, by invoking them to balance and develop their own natures and grow closer to the universe. They worship in the nude, without drugs. With each moon Esbats are held and it is important to them that the book of shadows is personally handwritten.

Covenant of the Goddess began in 1975 when Wiccan elders of various traditions wanted to form an organization for Wiccan members. The reason is to increase co-operation among witches and to give legal protection by members of other religions.

Deboran witchdom is part of the eclectic group. They make little ritual use of nudity. They work with balance and polarities. They wanted to reconstruct the craft as it would have been if the burning times had never happened. They open Sabbaths to guests but close them for Esbats. They view the craft as priesthood with a ministry and their principle job, as witches, is to help others find pathways to religious experience and to their own power. The Deboran tradition was founded by Claudia Haldene.

Seax Wica was founded by Raymond Buckland in 1973. A new denomination but has a Saxon basis. They accept coven or solitary practice as well as self-initiation. Covens are led by a priest and/or priestess and work either skyclad or robed. Raymond Buckland was a high priest of Gardnerian Wicca. They worship Germanic deities such as Woden and Freya – believing to be representations of the Wiccan horned god and the mother goddess.

Slavic witchcraft is more of a horror movie in real life. Everything they do is to remind coming generations of the times before the Dark Ages. Slavic culture likes to brag about their tales, ghost stories, and legends about witches. Their believed that Baba Yaga is a supernatural being that's deformed or ferocious looking, flying around in a mortal, wields a pestle, and dwells deep in the forest in a hut usually described as standing on chicken legs.

They believe that Baba Yaga may help or hinder those that encounter or seek her out and may play a maternal role and has associations with forest wildlife. Slavic nations have been under severe suppression by Satanists and some Christians; however some witches and sorcerers still live in the Slavic lands, hidden by peasants in rural communities.

Solitary witchcraft is exactly what the word implies; these persons choose to practice in private. They do not partake in group activities but may make an appearance in some communal activities such as the Sabbaths. They are Neo-pagans and have a mixture of beliefs and traditions.

Stregheria is mostly popular with Italians, rooted in the Etruscan tradition; the belief was born in the US during the 1980's time period. Stregheria is a mixture of Gardnerian Wicca and Italian witchcraft and lore. Some worship the Roman Diana her twin brother Apollo and their daughter Aradia, while others worship Lucifer/Hesperus whom they believe is not connected with Satan.

Teutonic witchcraft is a craft with few members and has been recognized as a group of people who speak the Germanic group of languages. They find inspiration in traditional myths and legends and worship the goddess and god where these languages began. Some activities include the raising of storms, the selling of pieces of knotted rope, divination and prophecy (secondary sight) and acquiring invisibility. The sea is the chief element of the witch of the northern Teutons.

Alexandrian Wicca founded by Alex Sanders. The tradition has its roots in Gardnerian Wicca. They worship the lady and the lord. Sanders were known for doing his own thing and loving the attention he got from the media after he made his coven known to the world. He worked together with his wife Maxine (a Roman Catholic). They were later called the "king and queen" of Wicca. Sanders liked to experiment with magick and taught his discoveries to his followers. Among some of the other things he experimented with include homosexuality.

"If a man also lie with mankind, as he lieth with a woman, both of them have committed an abomination: they shall surely be put to death; their blood *shall be* upon them."
Leviticus 20:13 (KJV)

They work in three levels and initiation is done cross gendered. The newcomers called priest and priestess, the second level called high priest and high priestess and finally a coven elder. A lot of new traditions sprouted out of the Alexandrian Wicca, such as American Wicca, Australian Wicca and Blue Moon Wicca. They share the same foundational beliefs but with a few tweaks here and there. A second grade Alexandrian will have an inverted pentagram drawn somewhere on their body.

"Ye shall not make any cuttings in your flesh for the dead, nor print any marks upon you: I *am* the LORD."

The symbolism behind it refers to the seven sephirot of the Qabalistic tree of life. It also symbolizes the satanic goat of Mendez. The name Alexandrian has its existence from one of two possibilities. The first and most common is that it got its name from Alex Sanders. His followers were referred to as Alexandrians to separate them completely from other wiccans due to the disagreement between the two groups of witches (the ones valuing the secrecy of the practice and those that don't – like the Alexandrians) and the second that it was named after the ancient occult Library of Alexandria. The library does not exist anymore as it has been burnt down by in the early 1900's. Alex Sanders passed away on the 30th of April 1988 after losing his battle with lung cancer.

American Wicca started in the late 1960's, early 1970's. The founder was Jessica Bell (Lady Sheba). The practices and rituals are rooted in Gardnerian Wicca. They are not the solitary type and do ceremonial magick preferably robed.

Australian Wicca started in the beginning of 1984 and as the name suggest originated in Australia. The coven is based on Alexandrian Wicca.

Blue Moon Wicca became an autonomous tradition in July 2001 after ex-blue star Wiccan Forest Jones and Joe Brutera broke away to start their own thing.

Tradition

As mentioned before, the Wicca tradition's primary believes is centered on the idea of gender polarity – the worshipping of a goddess and god. These two gods are seen as lovers and equals who created the universe. They are complete opposites that intertwine with each other building on the concept of the yin and yang. In the beginning of the huge explosion in the Wiccan movement the lineage was only passed down by means of initiation. Today that's no longer the case. More groups started their own thing and some of them were not initiated before starting the group. It leaves many solitary practitioners choosing not to associate themselves with any specific tradition, but instead chooses their influences and practices eclectically.

Even though there isn't a specific leader or authority there is however a few rules they choose to submit to.

A list of the rules include:

- By no means should you intentionally hurt someone else – the extent of the rule depends on the different coven opinions. Some would say that this includes not eating meat; joining the military while others believe that the rule will not apply to self-defense.
- One must take responsibility for your own actions. You decide your behavior and you carry the consequences and you live by your own standards. This also should not be forced on someone else.

Most traditions are still oath bound and mostly secretive to some extent, making it very difficult to obtain the details on how they work. Only those that have been through the initiation process are allowed to experience what they do.

Rituals

Let's start off explaining a bit about the pentagram being used in most of the rituals. It symbolizes the eternal cycle of life and its ultimate perfection, a symbolic model of the universe. They use the pentagram believing to generate spiritual power. There are eight different ways to draw the pentagram and each represents a different type of invoked power.

Rituals are done mostly outdoors where possible. The members of the coven come together and form a circle with an altar in the middle or at the northern candle. Enough space is provided for the sphere, or cylinder to confine healing power until it is released. The circle is then purified and the candles are lit. Majority of the meeting is dedicated to the full moon, new moon, a Sabbat or a ceremony depending on the reason for the meeting.

"And they left all the commandments of the LORD their God, and made them molten images, *even* two calves, and made a grove, and worshipped all the host of heaven, and served Baal."
2 Kings 17:16

"And lest thou lift up thine eyes unto heaven, and when thou seest the sun, and the moon, and the stars, *even* all the host of heaven, shouldest be driven to worship them, and serve them, which the LORD thy God hath divided unto all nations under the whole heaven."

Deuteronomy 4:19 (KJV)

"The word of the LORD which came unto Zephaniah the son of Cushi, the son of Gedaliah, the son of Amariah, the son of Hizkiah, in the days of Josiah the son of Amon, king of Judah. I will utterly consume all *things* from off the land, saith the LORD. I will consume man and beast; I will consume the fowls of the heaven, and the fishes of the sea, and the stumblingblocks with the wicked; and I will cut off man from off the land, saith the LORD.

I will also stretch out mine hand upon Judah, and upon all the inhabitants of Jerusalem; and I will cut off the remnant of Baal from this place, *and* the name of the Chemarims with the priests; And them that worship the host of heaven upon the housetops; and them that worship *and* that swear by the LORD, and that swear by Malcham;"

Zephaniah 1:1-5 (KJV)

The rituals can include healing, divinations, teaching, consecration of tools, discussion, or other nature based activities. It starts off with a ritual bath of purification and sometimes fasting the day before the ritual. This should include grounding and centering to balance oneself before the ritual. After casting of the circle the "guardians" are then invoked.

The members wearing the five pointed pentagram will stands before the elements and the presiding spirit. The gathering then concludes with the eating of food and thereafter the circle is banished.

Some of the tools being used include common household items. Although some groups may choose differently from the majority – the most popular tools used are the following:

- Athame which is a double sided knife with a black handle. The knife is used for many purposes but never to cut something.
- Altars are also very important and can be any share and made from any material.
- A wand or sword used for the casting of the circle.
- A circle with a diameter of about 9 feet. The material used for the circle can be formed from rope or small rocks.
- Four candles outside the circle pointing towards the four basic directions.

The rites of passage are a special occasion and include the following

- Dedication – when a person shows interest in the practice.
- Initiation – when a person symbolically dies and is reborn as a Wiccan.
- Handfasting – almost like a wedding ceremony traditionally valid for one year but nowadays the couples may choose to stay together.
- Parting of the Ways – the practice is done to symbolize the end of a marriage.
- Wiccaning – is the celebration of a newborn baby.
- Funeral Ceremony – formal gathering for a Wiccan that died.

You may have also heard of the Great Rite being one of the most popular celebrated rites within the Wiccan culture. It symbolizes the sexual union of the goddess and god who created all life forms and who renews it every spring season. This rite is performed symbolically when most of the main work has been completed and just before they get together for food and drinks.

A male holds the athame and a female holds the chalice filled with wine. The athame is then held high above the chalice, blade downward, and a chant is spoken.

There are Wiccan couples that use this opportunity to commit to a relationship that will include having sex during the Great Rite. This is done privately and will only involve the two Wiccans.

Here follows a list of rituals commonly practiced

Lesser Banishing and Invoking Ritual of the Pentagram is a ritual that they usually start and end of with. A pentagram also seen as a symbol of energy, war, strife and conquest the hand or womb of the goddess filled with creative fire - the feminine power. Traditionally both hands are used – might I just add that further examination of the ancient Egyptian ritual gestures and dances will show that the way the hands are held has far more meaning than simply a common prayer gesture adopted by Christians.

Cabalistic Cross – being one of the first rituals Wicca members learn – involves connecting with your inner-self. It is said to clear your mind and to make you aware of your surroundings. It is also said to teach you to control your mind and to remember that everything created comes from the power of thinking. The cross is used to map down position (north, south, east and west). Have you ever heard the words "being the centre of your own universe"? This is its origin.

Middle Pillar ritual is all about drawing energy from the body for the purpose of spiritual practices. It is said that it will bring down the light of the Golden Dawn which will in turn leave the body and bring healing.

"But if thine eye be evil, thy whole body shall be full of darkness. If therefore the light that is in thee be darkness, how great *is* that darkness!"
Matthew 6:23 (KJV)

"Then spake Jesus again unto them, saying, I am the light of the world: he that followeth me shall not walk in darkness, but shall have the light of life."
John 8:12 (KJV)

Superior Pentagram Ritual starts off with the Qabbalistic Cross ritual. Thereafter the invoking pentagram is drawn with the sigil element is drawn in the middle; the chants are said in the correct order and finishes of with the Lesser Ritual of the Pentagram.

Rose Cross Ritual acts like a protective layer against "outside" interruptions and also draws attention to you from the deities. If there is too much destruction some may use the pentagrams to banish and the rose cross ritual to maintain peace. Its objective is to log into another part of your consciousness and disconnected with the physical. They say that beginners do this rite in their imagination whilst lying down and still feel the sensation of walking around outside of your body. This can also be done to another person by building an astral image of that person in the centre of the room. The light will then be called upon that person after he/she is surrounded by the six crosses. When done with the ceremony the astral shape is send back to the person.

On the full moon purging ritual they write words on a piece of paper that they would want to get rid of for example bad habits, bad relationships or addictions and then each takes turn throwing the pieces of paper into a fire whiles standing in a circle.

Holidays

The majority of wiccans celebrate the full moons and holidays they call Sabbaths as this is the time that the earth's energies are at peak.

Their holidays include the celebration of the eight Sabbaths of the wheel of the year.

Important dates include:

December 21 – Yule (meaning wheel) takes place in the winter and represents the death and rebirth of the sun god. The European countries mainly fall in the Northern Hemisphere and therefore experience winter during the December month. They also celebrate the defeat of the Holly King (hence the use of the holly plant during Christmas). The Goddess (queen of the cold darkness) is believed to give birth to the "child of promise" who will re-fertilize her and is said to bring back warmth and light to her kingdom.

While we are on the subject of Christmas let's have a look at the pagan symbolism found in this age old celebration. The Holly King that we mentioned earlier represents Santa Claus. The sleigh represents the solar chariot. The eight reindeers represent the eight Sabbaths while their horns represent the "Horned One". The North Pole represents the Land of the Shadows. Have you ever wondered why specifically the North Pole and how it really looks like during Christmas?

During the period October to March the North Pole experiences its darkest time of the year with no sunlight or even twilight since mid October. Scientists also say that by 21 December the North Pole experiences its darkest time being in the middle of the winter. Makes one wonder why only poor Santa Clause gets send to the coldest, darkest place on earth while the rest of the earth are having a "joyful time", yet Santa still delivers gift to the whole world.

The gifts are used to welcome the Oak King as the sun reborn and to greet the Holly King for his departure. They honor the Maiden as the Bride on this day. Corn Dollies are made and placed in baskets with white flower bedding. Young girls will then carry the corn dollies from door to door and then gifts are bestowed upon the image from each household. Later at the traditional feast the older women made acorn wands for the dollies. The next morning they will check of the magic wands left marks as an indication of a good omen.

A besom is placed by the front door as an indicator that the old is being swept out and the new getting in. Candles are then lit in each room to honor the re-birth of the Sun.

Other coincidences to consider include. We read in the Bible that the angels bow down and worship God day and night using the following words "Holy, Holy, Holy."

"And one cried unto another, and said, Holy, holy, holy, *is* the LORD of hosts: the whole earth *is* full of his glory."
Isaiah 6:3 (KJV)

"And the four beasts had each of them six wings about *him*; and *they were* full of eyes within: and they rest not day and night, saying, Holy, holy, holy, Lord God Almighty, which was, and is, and is to come."
Revelation 4:8 (KJV)

Santa's laugh goes like this... ho, ho, ho! Why only three times – why couldn't it have been four or five?

The Bible tells us about Jesus wearing a red robe and having snow white hair.

"And in the midst of the seven candlesticks *one* like unto the Son of man, clothed with a garment down to the foot, and girt about the paps with a golden girdle. [14] His head and *his* hairs *were* white like wool, as white as snow; and his eyes *were* as a flame of fire;"
Revelation 1:13 (KJV)

"The sceptre shall not depart from Judah, nor a lawgiver from between his feet, until Shiloh come; and unto him *shall* the gathering of the people *be*. [11] Binding his foal unto the vine, and his ass's colt unto the choice vine; he washed his garments in wine, and his clothes in the blood of grapes:"
Genesis 49:10 (KJV)

February 2 – Imbolc. This celebration has a lot to do with the preparation of soil for the planting of crops. Children dressed up in costume go from door to door dragging a decorated plough with them asking for food, drink or money. If the household refuses to give them something the front garden gets ploughed up.

March 21 – Ostara comes from the name Eostre the name of the European moon Goddess whose power peaks at this time of year. Ostara takes place in the beginning of spring also named Lady Day. Day and night is of equal length and has a lot of meaning in the spiritual world. Christians will know this time as Easter. The maiden goddess is unattached and free from any bindings with either man or child regardless if she had sex with the god or not.

The child god is still growing at this stage as well as his power. He is in charge of the wild spirit of youth and nature. Some of the pagan symbolism used during Easter includes the decorating, hiding and the search for eggs - specifically rabbit eggs because Eostre was connected to rabbits. This is where the term "Easter Bunny" comes from.

No rabbit was ever connected to the crucifixion of Jesus or the His rising from the dead three days later, but still the "Easter Bunny" and "Easter Eggs" are found and associated with the time of Easter in the Christian homes. Colors associated with Ostara are pastel colors like blue, yellow, pink and green and that is why Easter is so colorful.

April 30 – Beltane meaning fire of Belinos is a celebration in honor of the sun god's coronation. April is the month when most of the northern hemisphere marks the start of spring. This festival celebrates fertility of both nature and man and it involves shamelessly having sex with multitudes of people. Young people would go into the woods and spend the night A-Maying while older married couples are allowed to take off their wedding rings for this one night and do whatever as if they were not married. Early next morning they would go out to collect flowers and branches to decorate their home. Girls would braid flowers into their hair and both men and woman would decorate their bodies.

June 21 – Midsummer being the longest day and shortest night of the year in the Northern Hemisphere. This time of year is celebrated by doing traditional rituals and casting of spells.

August 1 – Lughnasadh (also known as Lammas) is a holiday rarely celebrated in today's day and age. It marks the start of harvest time where everyone gather together to help collect the harvest in the fields and celebrate the first fruits for the season.

September 21 – Mabon is a pagan thanksgiving festival. Pagans will volunteer helping in soup kitchens or donate animals for rituals. They honor the dead during this time. The gain that was harvest serves as a symbol of the dying god who will be reborn in spring.

October 31 – Samhain better known as Halloween. Winter would begin and animals that didn't look strong or fat enough to survive winter used to be slaughtered. Today they don't have as much opportunity to do that and instead bread is baked in the shape of animals. These animals are then charged with life energy and slaughtered according to the normal ritual. Most pagan religions during this time celebrate life and death.

Wedding Ceremony

We call it wedding, they call it hand fasting. Hand fasting refers to a ceremony where two people commit to each other. Most of the traditions are the same as those that we know. They choose the guest list (if they want guests). The venue and themes are also chosen by the couple. Hand fasting also requires the couple to tie a bow around their clutched hands. Do the words "tie the knot" ring a bell?

Afterwards some couples may choose to jump over a broom or small fire. They have vows but the vow says one thing other than what we say… "As long as love shall last". The difference is that they stay committed to each other until they no longer love each other and as soon as that happen the couple is allowed to separate.

Other

The following is a direct quote from someone involved in paganism. "Horned One, Lover, Son, leaper in the corn — He is our role model, our mentor, our guide, our brother, and in many (not all) Traditions, He is a father figure as well; but He is not a judge or an executioner. No matter that some insist that "Sam Hain" is a devilish Lord of the Dead, the Sabbath's name and significance to modern Wiccans is consistent with our world view. This Sabbath marks the end of summer and the beginning of winter, and so we begin our look at the Winter Sabbaths with Samhain".

> ➢ I literally sat a whole while trying to rap my thoughts around this statement. All that I can think of is the verse in the Bible saying that Satan will appear as being an angel of light, and the second thing I thought of is that Satan desperately tries to be like God. He even gives himself some of the characteristics of our Heavenly Father.
> ➢ Referring to the specific line in which is stated "and in many (not all) Traditions, He is a father figure as well; but He is not a judge or an executioner" shows me the fear that Satan has because he knows that his day of judgment is drawing near and in order to draw as many people possible to him, he makes it sound like he is loving and caring and will not harm a fly. He misleads people and makes it sound like God the Father is angry and trying to squash all people and that God the Father's heart is to destroy. How ironic is it that it is just the exact opposite. He send His only beloved Son to die for our sins, that is how much He loves us but instead people (including Christians) believe that he is angry and distant.
> ➢ God created hell for Satan and his followers – it was never meant to be created for us.
> ➢ Some interesting facts that I have discovered while doing my research is that a Wiccan will call himself a Wiccan when asked by someone while Traditional Witches will call themselves

Wiccan(s) when asked by someone. Should Traditional Witches not feel comfortable disclosing who they are some would actually say that they are Catholics.

They refer to witchcraft as "dark witchcraft" which is weird because witchcraft is witchcraft. There is no such thing as good or bad magic - both is regarded as an abomination before God.

Wiccan members have an altar in their homes and like to decorate their homes with the start of each new season.

They follow no moral doctrine and many of them are atheist (does not believe in God or a god) which also does not make sense because everything they do is somehow linked to the "Lady of the moon" and the "Horned one" whom they call gods.

Something also made me stop for a moment when I read the words of a Wiccan saying that there are a bit of witchcraft in Christianity although the Christians like to refer to that as "something else". Was he right in his statement?

I also found a very interesting quote from Ross Douthat, a columnist for the New York Times. He explains that the movie Avatar by James Cameron has brought some of the most popular Pagan and Pantheistic beliefs to the screen. This is what he said: "Avatar is Cameron's long apologia for pantheism – a faith that equates god with nature, and calls humanity into religious communion with the natural world. The Na'Vi (race) is saved by the movie's hero, a turncoat

Marine, but they're also saved by their faith in [21]Eywa, the "All Mother", described variously as a network of energy and the sum total of every living thing."

"If this narrative arc sounds familiar, that's because pantheism has been Hollywood's religion of choice for a generation now. It's the truth that Kevin Costner discovered when he went dancing with wolves. It's the metaphysic woven through Disney cartoons like "The Lion King" and "Pocahontas" and it's the dogma of George Lucas's Jedi, whose mystical Force "surrounds us, penetrates us, and binds the galaxy together."

He also says that: "Hollywood keeps returning to these themes because millions of Americans respond favorably to them. From Deepak Chopra to Eckhart Tolle, the "religion and inspiration" section in your local bookstore is crowded with titles pushing a pantheistic message"

"At the same time, pantheism opens a path to numinous experience for people uncomfortable with the literal-mindedness of the monotheistic religions – with their miracle-working deities and holy books, their virgin births and resurrected bodies. As the Polish

---

[21] In the movie Avatar - Eywa is also mentioned as their mother. See the following quote from the website

> "***Who's Eywa? Only their deity! Their goddess, made up of all living things. Everything they know! You'd know this if you had any training whatsoever.***"
> - Norm explaining Eywa to Jake.

Eywa is the guiding force and deity of Pandora and the Na'vi. The Na'vi believe that Eywa acts to keep the ecosystem of Pandora in perfect equilibrium.

philosopher Leszek Kolakowski noted, attributing divinity to the natural world helps "bring god closer to human experience while depriving him of recognizable personal traits'."

It is no surprise that this is happening. God reveals it to us in the book of Timothy.

> For the time will come when they will not endure sound doctrine; but after their own lusts shall they heap to themselves teachers, having itching ears; And they shall turn away *their* ears from the truth, and shall be turned unto fables.
>
> **2 Timothy 4:3-4 (KJV)**

There are testimonies that most Alexandrian Wiccans suffer some kind of trauma due to what they see during the rituals. He tells about a surge of energy rushing through your body at a very high voltage and if at some point the energy cannot be controlled someone would get hurt.

He also asked a really good question worth thinking about. Even though Wicca is greatly focused on fertility, most of them do not have children of their own. Those that eventually have children find themselves or their children in life threatening situations putting a damp on the practices.

After Alex Sanders of the Alexandrian Wicca Tradition admitted to his mother that he is a witch see soon had a nervous breakdown afterwards and was treated for it. He was previously married to Doreen Stretton at the age of 22. They had two children together, but that was not enough for Alex. He wanted more children but Doreen refused, she also rejected things to do with the supernatural. The marriage came to a breaking point when Alex turned 26. Doreen left with the two children. According to Maxine (his second wife) Alex was very upset and then cursed Doreen with fertility. After Doreen remarried she has three sets of twins.

The time between his first and second marriage was disastrous. He went from one low rank job to the other and had sex with both men and woman. He admitted that he later used black magic to gain more wealth and more sex. He met a very wealthy middle-aged couple while walking down the Manchester streets. The couple stopped him and told him that he reminded them of their son. He became part of their family and was later granted a house of his own. He held expensive parties, bought expensive clothes. They gave him everything that he wished for.

With all the success that he was now getting he soon realized that it came with a price. Alex had one specific mistress which he liked very much. The mistress for some reason committed suicide. Thereafter Alex learned that his sister was hurt in an accidental shooting and soon after she was diagnosed with terminal cancer. He decided to stop using black magic and rather teach it to others. Ok, so he is not going to practice it because it destroys, but it is ok to teach it to others?

Did you know that Gerald Gardner was a Freemason?

Today we are grateful to God for loving us so dearly that He sends his only Son, Jesus, to die on the cross so that even the worst sinner can be forgiven.

Hélèné Fulton

"For God so loved the world that he gave his only begotten Son, that whosoever believeth in him should not perish, but have everlasting life. For God sent not his Son into the world to condemn the world; but that the world through him might be saved."

John 3:16-17 (KJV)

Hélèné Fulton

Chapter 11: [22]South African Orthodox churches

The **Nederduitsch Hervormde Kerk van Afrika** (**Ned. Herv. Kerk** or **NHK**) is a Reformed Christian denomination in Southern Africa. Along with the Nederduitse Gereformeerde Kerk (NGK) and the Gereformeerde Kerke (GK) it forms part of the Dutch Reformed group of churches[23].

History

The Dutch Reformed Church was introduced to South Africa by the Dutch East India Company's settlement at the Cape in 1652. The first formal congregation was established in 1665 under the jurisdiction of the Amsterdam *classis* (presbytery). Despite the permanent British takeover of the Cape Colony in 1806, the church remained semi-established, with congregations supported from government funds. In 1824 an autonomous synod was established at the Cape, removing the church from control from the Netherlands. The unwillingness of Dutch ministers to serve in a British-controlled colony meant that Scottish Presbyterian ministers with British sympathies were introduced to the church.[24]

In the Great Trek of the 1830s and 1840s, Boers left the Cape Colony and established republics in the interior of South Africa. The Dutch Reformed Church

---

[22] http://en.wikipedia.org/wiki/Nederduitsch_Hervormde_Kerk_van_Afrika
[23] http://en.wikipedia.org/wiki/Reformed_Christian
[24] Prozesky, Martin; de Gruchy, John Wesley, eds. (1995). Living Faiths in South Africa. Cape Town: David Philip. pp. 30–31. ISBN 9780864862532.

of the Cape, with its connections to the colonial government, did not minister to them. The South African Republic (ZAR) was established in 1852, and in 1853 Dirk van der Hoff arrived from the Netherlands as the first minister of the newly established Nederduitsch Hervormde Kerk, which became the state church of the ZAR in 1860. In 1858, meanwhile, some members known as "Doppers" broke away from the NHK over the question of hymn-singing and formed the Gereformeerde Kerk (GK). The Cape church, by now known as the Nederduitse Gereformeerde Kerk (NGK) also subsequently established congregations within the Transvaal. In 1885 the NGK and the NHK were united into a single church, but some NHK members and congregations rejected the union; it is from these members that the current NHK descends.

Doctrine

The church recognises the Apostles Creed, Athanasian Creed, Nicene Creed, Heidelberg Catechism, Canons of Dort and the Belgic Confession.

[25]Apostles Creed

The Apostles' Creed (Latin: Symbolum Apostolorum or Symbolum Apostolicum), sometimes titled Symbol of the Apostles, is an early statement of Christian belief, a creed or "symbol". It is widely used by a number of Christian denominations for both liturgical and catechetical purposes, most visibly by liturgical Churches of Western tradition, including the Roman Catholic Church, Lutheranism, Anglicanism, and

---

[25] http://en.wikipedia.org/wiki/Apostles_Creed

Western Orthodoxy. It is also used by Presbyterians, Methodists, and Congregationalists.

The Apostles' Creed was based on Christian theological understanding of the Canonical gospels, the letters of the New Testament and to a lesser extent the Old Testament. Its basis appears to be the old Roman Creed. Because of the early origin of its original form, it does not address some Christological issues defined in the Nicene and other Christian Creeds. It thus says nothing explicitly about the divinity of either Jesus or of the Holy Spirit. This makes it acceptable to many Arians and Unitarians. Nor does it address many other theological questions that became objects of dispute centuries later.

The first mention of the expression "Apostles' Creed" occurs in a letter of 390 from a synod in Milan and may have been associated with the belief, widely accepted in the 4th century, that, under the inspiration of the Holy Spirit, each of the Twelve Apostles contributed an article of a creed.

Text in Latin
Credo in Deum Patrem omnipotentem, Creatorem caeli et terrae,
et in Iesum Christum, Filium Eius unicum, Dominum nostrum,
qui conceptus est de Spiritu Sancto, natus ex Maria Virgine,
passus sub Pontio Pilato, crucifixus, mortuus, et sepultus,
descendit ad inferos, tertia die resurrexit a mortuis,
ascendit ad caelos, sedet ad dexteram Patris omnipotentis,

inde venturus est iudicare vivos et mortuos.
Credo in Spiritum Sanctum,
sanctam Ecclesiam catholicam, sanctorum communionem,
remissionem peccatorum,
carnis resurrectionem,
vitam aeternam.
Amen.

[26]English translation

If you visit the webpage you will notice that many of the religions mentioned in this book and also in Part 1 and 2 use this in their doctrine.

I believe in God,
the Father almighty,
Creator of heaven and earth,
and in Jesus Christ, his only Son, our Lord,
who was conceived by the Holy Spirit,
born of the Virgin Mary,
suffered under Pontius Pilate,
was crucified, died and was buried;
he descended into hell;
on the third day he rose again from the dead;
he ascended into heaven,
and is seated at the right hand of God the Father almighty;
from there he will come to judge the living and the dead.
I believe in the Holy Spirit,
the holy catholic Church, *(In Part 2 of this book, I explain why the Catholic church is a false religion.)*
the communion of saints,

---

[26] http://en.wikipedia.org/wiki/Apostles_Creed

the forgiveness of sins,
the resurrection of the body,
and life everlasting. Amen.

[27]Athanasian Creed

The **Athanasian Creed**, or *Quicunque Vult* (also *Quicumque Vult*), is a Christian statement of belief focused on Trinitarian doctrine and Christology. The Latin name of the creed, *Quicumque vult*, is taken from the opening words, "Whosoever wishes". The creed has been used by Christian churches since the sixth century. It is the first creed in which the equality of the three persons of the Trinity is explicitly stated. It differs from the Nicene-Constantinopolitan and Apostles' Creeds in the inclusion of anathemas, or condemnations of those who disagree with the creed (like the original Nicene Creed).
Widely accepted among Western Christians, including the Roman Catholic Church, the Anglican Communion, the Lutheran Churches and ancient, liturgical churches generally, the Athanasian Creed has been used in public worship less and less frequently, but part of it can be found as an "Authorized Affirmation of Faith" in the recent (2000) Common Worship liturgy of the Church of England [Main Volume page 145]. The creed has never gained much acceptance in liturgy among Eastern Christians.

English Translation

Whosoever will be saved, before all things it is necessary that he hold the [28]catholic faith. Which

---

[27] http://en.wikipedia.org/wiki/Athanasian_Creed
[28] *(In Part 2 of this book, I explain why the Catholic church is a false*

faith except every one do keep whole and undefiled; without doubt he shall perish everlastingly. And the catholic faith is this: That we worship one God in Trinity, and Trinity in Unity; Neither confounding the Persons; nor dividing the Essence. For there is one Person of the Father; another of the Son; and another of the Holy Ghost. But the Godhead of the Father, of the Son, and of the Holy Ghost, is all one; the Glory equal, the Majesty coeternal. Such as the Father is; such is the Son; and such is the Holy Ghost. The Father uncreated; the Son uncreated; and the Holy Ghost uncreated. The Father unlimited; the Son unlimited; and the Holy Ghost unlimited. The Father eternal; the Son eternal; and the Holy Ghost eternal. And yet they are not three eternals; but one eternal. As also there are not three uncreated; nor three infinites, but one uncreated; and one infinite. So likewise the Father is Almighty; the Son Almighty; and the Holy Ghost Almighty. And yet they are not three Almighties; but one Almighty. So the Father is God; the Son is God; and the Holy Ghost is God. And yet they are not three Gods; but one God. So likewise the Father is Lord; the Son Lord; and the Holy Ghost Lord. And yet not three Lords; but one Lord. For like as we are compelled by the Christian verity; to acknowledge every Person by himself to be God and Lord; So are we forbidden by the catholic religion; to say, There are three Gods, or three Lords. The Father is made of none; neither created, nor begotten. The Son is of the Father alone; not made, nor created; but begotten. The Holy Ghost is of the Father and of the Son; neither made, nor created, nor begotten; but proceeding. So there is one Father, not three Fathers; one Son, not three Sons; one Holy Ghost, not three

religion.)

Holy Ghosts. And in this Trinity none is before, or after another; none is greater, or less than another. But the whole three Persons are coeternal, and coequal. So that in all things, as aforesaid; the Unity in Trinity, and the Trinity in Unity, is to be worshipped. He therefore that will be saved, let him thus think of the Trinity. Furthermore it is necessary to everlasting salvation; that he also believe faithfully the Incarnation of our Lord Jesus Christ. For the right Faith is, that we believe and confess; that our Lord Jesus Christ, the Son of God, is God and Man; God, of the Essence of the Father; begotten before the worlds; and Man, of the Essence of his Mother, born in the world. Perfect God; and perfect Man, of a reasonable soul and human flesh subsisting. Equal to the Father, as touching his Godhead; and inferior to the Father as touching his Manhood. Who although he is God and Man; yet he is not two, but one Christ. One; not by conversion of the Godhead into flesh; but by assumption of the Manhood by God. One altogether; not by confusion of Essence; but by unity of Person. For as the reasonable soul and flesh is one man; so God and Man is one Christ; Who suffered for our salvation; descended into hell; rose again the third day from the dead. He ascended into heaven, he sitteth on the right hand of the God the Father Almighty, from whence he will come to judge the living and the dead. At whose coming all men will rise again with their bodies; And shall give account for their own works. And they that have done good shall go into life everlasting; and they that have done evil, into everlasting fire. This is the catholic faith; which except a man believe truly and firmly, he cannot be saved.

Nicene Creed

The **Nicene Creed** (Greek: Σύμβολον τῆς Νίκαιας, Latin: Symbolum Nicaenum) is the profession of faith or creed that is most widely used in Christian liturgy. It forms the mainstream definition of Christianity for most Christians.

It is called Nicene /ˈnaɪsiːn/ because, in its original form, it was adopted in the city of Nicaea (present day Iznik in Turkey) by the first ecumenical council, which met there in the year 325.

The Nicene Creed has been normative for the Catholic Church, the Eastern Orthodox Church, the Church of the East, the Oriental Orthodox churches, the Anglican Communion, and Protestant denominations. It forms the mainstream definition of Christianity itself in Nicene Christianity.

English translation of the Armenian version

We believe in one God, the Father Almighty, the maker of heaven and earth, of things visible and invisible.

And in one Lord Jesus Christ, the Son of God, the begotten of God the Father, the Only-begotten, that is of the essence of the Father.

God of God, Light of Light, true God of true God, begotten and not made; of the very same nature of the Father, by Whom all things came into being, in heaven and on earth, visible and invisible.

Who for us humanity and for our salvation came down from heaven, was incarnate, was made human, was born perfectly of the holy virgin Mary by the Holy Spirit.

---

[29] http://en.wikipedia.org/wiki/Nicene_Creed

By whom He took body, soul, and mind, and everything that is in man, truly and not in semblance. He suffered, was crucified, was buried, rose again on the third day, ascended into heaven with the same body, [and] sat at the right hand of the Father.

He is to come with the same body and with the glory of the Father, to judge the living and the dead; of His kingdom there is no end.

We believe in the Holy Spirit, in the uncreated and the perfect; Who spoke through the Law, prophets, and Gospels; Who came down upon the Jordan, preached through the apostles, and lived in the saints.

We believe also in only One, Universal, Apostolic, and [Holy] Church; in one baptism in repentance, for the remission, and forgiveness of sins; and in the resurrection of the dead, in the everlasting judgement of souls and bodies, and the Kingdom of Heaven and in the everlasting life.

[30]Heidelberg Catechism

The **Heidelberg Catechism**, one of the Three Forms of Unity, is a Protestant confessional document taking the form of a series of questions and answers, for use in teaching Reformed Christian doctrine. It has been translated into many languages and is regarded as one of the most influential of the Reformed catechisms.

This consist of questions and answers which you can read on (http://www.reformed.org/documents/index.html?mainframe=http://www.reformed.org/documents/heidelberg.html)

---

[30] http://en.wikipedia.org/wiki/Heidelberg_Catechism

[31]Canons of Dort

The **Canons of Dort**, or **Canons of Dordrecht**, formally titled **The Decision of the Synod of Dort on the Five Main Points of Doctrine in Dispute in the Netherlands**, is the judgment of the National Synod held in the Dutch city of Dordrecht in 1618–19. At the time, Dordrecht was often referred to in English as *Dort*.

Today the Canons of Dort form part of the Three Forms of Unity, one of the confessional standards of many of the Reformed churches around the world, including the Netherlands, South Africa, Australia, and North America. Their continued use as a standard still forms an unbridgable problem preventing close cooperation between the followers of Jacob Arminius, the Remonstrants, and Dutch Reformed Churches. These canons are in actuality a judicial decision on the doctrinal points in dispute from the Arminian controversy of that day. Following the death of Arminius (1560–1609), his followers set forth a Remonstrance (published in 1610) in five articles formulating their points of departure from the stricter Calvinism of the Belgic Confession. The Canons are the judgment of the Synod against this Remonstrance. Regardless, Arminian theology later received official acceptance by the State and has since continued in various forms within Protestantism.

[32]Belgic Confession

---

[31] http://en.wikipedia.org/wiki/Canons_of_Dort
[32] http://en.wikipedia.org/wiki/Belgic_Confession

Hélèné Fulton

The **Confession of Faith**, popularly known as the **Belgic Confession**, is a doctrinal standard document to which many of the Reformed churches subscribe. The Confession forms part of the Three Forms of Unity of the Reformed Church, which are still the official subordinate standards of the Dutch Reformed Church. The confession's chief author was Guido de Brès, a preacher of the Reformed churches of the Netherlands, who died a martyr to the faith in 1567.

I have one question for the churches that follows these creeds. Why do you find it necessary to confess your faith to man out loud when all you need to do is **love God and keep His commandments** like the Bible teach us.

[16] Ye shall know them by their fruits. Do men gather grapes of thorns, or figs of thistles?

Matthew 7:16

This group of churches also believes in baptizing babies. Again one question for you. If this was the correct baptism, why was Jesus not baptized as a baby? After all He is our perfect example.

The do not believe in being born again. They do not believe in casting out demons. They also do not believe in the Power of the Blood of Jesus Christ or that you can use the name of Jesus Christ to cast out demons or stop satan in his tracts.

In fact a few years back the Leaders in Pretoria Head Office of these churches said that it is every member of there church own responsibility to decide whether there is a devil or not. This was after one of their

Hélèné Fulton

ministers started casting out demons and praying for people to be healed. They "fired" this minister because of this.

Chapter 12: Atheism & Agnostics

Written By: Nyasha Muzvidzwa

Atheism is the rejection (or absence) of the belief that God, or any other deities, exists.
An Atheist is someone who believes that God does not exist (Cambridge dictionary).
Theism is belief in the existence of a god or gods (Cambridge dictionary).
Although the term "atheism" originated in the sixteenth century – based on Ancient Greek to mean - "godless, denying the gods, ungodly" (An Introduction to Atheism, 1997).

Belief

Atheism is characterized by an absence of belief in the existence of gods. This absence of belief generally comes about either through deliberate choice, or from an inherent inability to believe religious teachings which seem literally incredible. It is not a lack of belief born out of simple ignorance of religious teachings (An Introduction to Atheism, 1997).

Some atheists go beyond a mere absence of belief in gods: they actively believe that particular gods, or all gods, do not exist. Just lacking belief in Gods is often referred to as the "weak atheist" position; whereas believing that gods do not (or cannot) exist is known as "strong atheism." (An Introduction to Atheism, 1997).

Thus saith the LORD the maker thereof, the LORD that formed it, to establish it; the LORD is his name;

Hélèné Fulton

Call unto me, and I will answer thee, and shew thee great and mighty things, which thou knowest not.

Jeremiah 33: 2-3

The above verses clearly state that God is responsible for creating heaven and earth, so if we call unto him about anything, He will answer us, which shows that God exists.

It is important, however, to note the difference between the strong and weak atheist positions. "Weak atheism" is simple scepticism; disbelief in the existence of God. "Strong atheism" is an explicitly held belief that God does not exist. Please do not fall into the trap of assuming that all atheists are "strong atheists." There is a qualitative difference in the "strong" and "weak" positions; it's not just a matter of degree. Some atheists believe in the non-existence of all Gods; others limit their atheism to specific Gods, such as the Christian God, rather than making flat-out denials (An Introduction to Atheism, 1997).

Disbelief in a proposition means that one does not believe it to be true. Not believing that something is true is not equivalent to believing that it is false; one may simply have no idea whether it is true or not. Which brings us to agnosticism (An Introduction to Atheism, 1997).

What is agnosticism then?

The term "agnosticism" was coined by Professor T.H. Huxley at a meeting of the Metaphysical Society in 1876. He defined an "agnostic" as someone who disclaimed both ("strong") atheism and theism, and who believed that the question of whether a higher power existed was unsolved and insoluble. Another way of putting it is that an agnostic is someone who believes that we do not know for sure whether God exists. Some agnostics believe that we can never know (An Introduction to Atheism, 1997).

In recent years, however, the term agnostic has also been used to describe those who simply believe that the evidence for or against God is inconclusive, and therefore are undecided about the issue.

Faith is also used to refer to belief without supporting evidence or proof. According to the bible:

Now faith is being sure of what we hope for and certain of what we do not see.
Hebrews 11:1

By faith Abraham, even though he was past-age and Sarah herself was barren- was enabled to become a father because he considered him faithful who made the promise.
Hebrews 11:11

Most atheists take a "live and let live" attitude. Unless questioned, they will not usually mention their atheism, except perhaps to close friends. Of course, this may be in part because atheism is not "socially acceptable" in many countries. I had the opportunity to speak to one of my colleagues who regards himself to be an Atheist.

The following is what he said in his own words:

"What atheism means to me is the rejection/disbelief in a deity, which is also known as supernatural being which can be considered sacred or holy. To take on atheism I follow is that I have no inclination to believe in any form of deity/deities from any religion or belief system. Sometimes atheism is confused with theism".

"There are two main reasons for my becoming an atheist. It is due to my mind-set and influence from a very staunch catholic school for 5 years. During my high school career, I went to a strong Catholic school where I was forced into religion on a daily basis. This involved having to attend morning services daily, daily religious education classes and monthly masses. From my knowledge of religion, it should not be forced upon anyone and they should be able to make their own choice. As a teenager, I was already sceptical about religion as a whole as it was conflicting with my mild views of evolution and science as a more plausible form of creation" (Glenn Perry).

He was baptized as an Anglican and went to a Catholic school for high school but even though he is officially still baptized an Anglican, he does not believe in it at all.
Also, unless he has some sort of religious encounter or experience, he highly doubts that he will be converting or changing over to another religion (Glenn Perry).

"What about the term "free-thinker"? What does that mean?"

A free-thinker is one who thinks freely - one who is prepared to consider any possibility, and who determines which ideas are right or wrong by bringing reason to bear, according to a consistent set of rules such as the scientific method (An Introduction to Atheism, 1997).

When it started

The Soviet Union was originally dedicated to separation of church and state, just like the USA. Soviet citizens were legally free to worship as they wished. The institution of "state atheism" came about when Stalin took control of the Soviet Union and tried to destroy the churches in order to gain complete power over the population (An Introduction to Atheism, 1997).

Traditions

Atheists sometimes also argue that theists should question their beliefs because of the very real harm they can cause - not just to the believers, but to everyone else.

Some writers say that Atheism is not just bus ads, and it does have a long tradition. Where its tradition has been stifled and its history untold this has been because of the power and reach of authoritarian religious dominance. That atheism has been suppressed is not a sign of the inferior imagination or talents of atheists. Many of their greatest scientists, inventors, philosophers, artists are atheists–but they don't call their work "atheism", they call it just figuring out actual stuff or just creating actual things and implicitly it's "atheistic" for not needing gods to do it– and for being possible only by ignoring gods and religious authorities' meddling. Rather, atheists' apparent absences are a sign of religious intolerance and not something that a cosmopolitan, ecumenically minded religious believer and political progressive should be proud of or use to bully atheists.

"What sort of harm?"

Religion represents a huge financial and work burden on mankind. It's not just a matter of religious believers wasting their money on church buildings; think of all the time and effort spent building churches, praying, and so on. Imagine how that effort could be better spent.

Many theists believe in miracle healing. There have been plenty of instances of ill people being "healed" by a priest, ceasing to take the medicines prescribed to them by doctors, and dying as a result. Some theists have died because they have refused blood transfusions on religious grounds.

It is arguable that the Catholic Church's opposition to birth control - and condoms in particular - is increasing the problem of overpopulation in many third-world countries and contributing to the spread of AIDS worldwide.

Religious believers have been known to murder their children rather than allow their children to become atheists or marry someone of a different religion. Religious leaders have been known to justify murder on the grounds of blasphemy.

There have been many religious wars. Even if we accept the argument that religion was not the true cause of those wars, it was still used as an effective justification for them (An Introduction to Atheism, 1997).

Rituals

Rituals and celebrations, as long as they are not empty of personal meaning, can be worth preserving. Rituals are not inherently irrational, as some may allege, but they can be irrational if they are simply followed for the sake of tradition, or because that is what is expected of you, etc. For rituals to be rational, they must be consciously chosen as a means to achieve some goal, such as those suggested above.

Rituals can be important because they are often important means of social communication. We cannot, after all, observe relationships - what we observe is people's behavior towards one another. Very often, that behavior takes place in the context of "ritual" acts - behaviors which may not have obvious functional utility but which do nevertheless reinforce the ways people relate to one another.

Thus, it is often accurate to say that ritual is a type of behavior which "says things" rather than "does things." Sometimes what is said can be negative, for example rituals which serve to reinforce a person's status as someone subordinate when they should really be equal. Often, however, what is said can be quite positive because it lets others know that you continue to care about them (An Introduction to Atheism, 1997).

My colleague mentioned that he doesn't take part in any rituals in connection to being an Atheist.

Hélèné Fulton

Holidays

Holidays can serve to form a connection to your own past by evoking memories of past celebration. Holidays can form and reinforce connections with the friends and family with whom you celebrate. Holiday events can also create connections across an entire society as people develop parallel experiences which forge subtle bonds.

So yes, holiday celebrations and ritual events can have importance and value quite independent of whatever religious significance they may also carry for others. The question which then faces the atheist who rejects such religious significance is: do I participate in any fashion in any of these events? And if so, how? Why?

In the end, a person's answer to religious holidays must be wholly individual and personal - and it will often depend upon the holiday in question. No one answer can exist for all atheists and no one answer can fit all events (An Introduction to Atheism, 1997).

Atheist emphasis:

Along with the development of atheist pride, it is natural that we also develop our own celebrations. The Winter Solstice is probably the most widely recognized day in the atheist community. It allows atheists to retain cultural traditions we enjoy but to put them in a strictly secular context. Perhaps because of the importance of the Winter Solstice, many atheists also note the Summer Solstice. On a personal basis, I note the times and locations of the sunrise and sunset on the Winter Solstice, but do little else. The Summer Solstice is more important to me, as it is a great day for camping and celebrating the longest period of daylight in the year (Born Atheist, 2014).

Other celebrations developing a following in the atheist community include:

Atheist Pride/Freedom from Religion Day, February 12 (Darwin's birthday);

Everybody Draw Mohammed Day, May 20 (protesting Muslim violence toward artists, who draw Mohammed, National Day of Reason, the first Thursday in May (on the same day as, and in response to, the National Day of Prayer);

LGBT Pride Day, June 28, (in recognition of the shared struggle of LGBT people and atheists for equal right [see Chapter 26, Learning from the Gay Rights Movement]).

Religion has had enormous influence on the Western calendar, from making the number of the year a recognition of Jesus' alleged birth, to making the "lord's day" the first day of the week and religious holidays the most important of the year. As atheists build our identity and pride, it is natural that we will refuse to honor the destructive religious myths that form the basis for religious holidays. Atheists will instead focus on celebrations that have meaning to us (Born Atheist, 2014).

Wedding

Marriage is an ancient tradition which has changed, as most things tend to do, as societies have merged and as people's understanding and values have changed. Ancient Sumerian and Babylonian laws describe the earliest marriage traditions on record, establishing a contract-based system where marriages were typically arranged by the parents. In most cases, the father of the groom would provide the "bride price," or dower, to the father of the bride, who would often hand this payment over to the bride, along with her dowry after the wedding, thus returning the bride-price to the groom. In other cases, brides were simply purchased in exchange for land or livestock (Matt Dillahunty, 2008).

While their contract system was very detailed and almost modern in its coverage of rights and responsibilities, women had no say in their future and there was no requirement that either consent to marriage (Matt Dillahunty, 2008).

The changes in marriage are the result of the ongoing struggle for true freedom. In the United States, 40 States had laws that prohibited interracial marriage, and the social prejudice which labelled these unions as "unnatural" or "immoral" ensured that it was uncommon in those states without these laws. After a number of legal battles, the United States Supreme Court eliminated these laws, nation-wide by declaring that:

- all Americans enjoy the freedom to marry,
- marriage is one of our vital personal rights, and
- the right to marry is essential to the orderly pursuit of happiness by a free people.

This dramatic change occurred in 1967 and many people in this room are old enough to remember it (Matt Dillahunty, 2008).

A wedding takes place between two people with an exchange of vows, an exchange of rings, and the lighting of a candle (Matt Dillahunty, 2008).

Below is an example of some vows from a wedding that took place. As you're reading through these, just keep in mind that there are so many ways to show your love for your partner and a god doesn't have to be included in the mix for those words (and the whole ceremony, for that matter) to be special for everyone in the audience.

Diana and her husband Gabriel used traditional, but godless, vows (PDF), found via Internet sources and friends' suggestions:

Let your love be stronger than your anger.

Learn the wisdom of compromise, for it is better to bend than to break.

Look for the best in your beloved rather than the worst.

Confide in your partner and ask for help when you need it.

Remember that true friendship is the basis for any lasting relationship.

Give your spouse the same courtesies and kindnesses you bestow on your friends.

Say "I love you" every day (Atheist wedding vows).

Ceremonies

Perhaps the biggest loss in not attending religious ceremonies at a church and not participating in religion-themed rituals is the loss of joint family activities and the diminishing of a family tradition.

Other

Atheists may listen to heavy metal - backwards, even - or they may prefer a Verdi Requiem, even if they know the words. They may wear Hawaiian shirts, they may dress all in black, they may even wear orange robes. (Many Buddhists lack a belief in any sort of God.) Some atheists even carry a copy of the Bible around - for arguing against, of course (An Introduction to Atheism, 1997).

A survey conducted by the Roper Organization found that behavior deteriorated after "born again" experiences. While only 4% of respondents said they had driven intoxicated before being "born again," 12% had done so after conversion. Similarly, 5% had used illegal drugs before conversion, 9% after. Two percent admitted to engaging in illicit sex before salvation; 5% after. [Free-thought Today, September 1991, p. 12.] (An Introduction to Atheism, 1997).

So it seems that at best, religion does not have a monopoly on moral behavior.

Of course, a great many people are converted to (and from) Christianity during adolescence and their early twenties. This is also the time at which people begin to drink and become sexually active. It could be that the above figures merely indicate that Christianity has no effect on moral behavior, or insufficient effect to result in an overall fall in immoral behavior (An Introduction to Atheism, 1997).

"So how do atheists find comfort in time of danger?"

There are many ways of obtaining comfort:

- Your family and friends
- Pets
- Food and drink
- Music, television, literature, arts and entertainment
- Sports or exercise
- Meditation
- Psychotherapy
- Drugs
- Work

The bible clearly states that God can offer peace and joy as long as you seek him.

Many are asking, "Who can show us and good?" Let the light of your face shine upon us, O Lord.
You have filled my heart with greater joy than when their grain and new wine abound.

Psalms 4: 6-7

Be joyful always, pray continually; give thanks in all circumstances, for this is God's will for you in Christ Jesus.

Hélèné Fulton

1 Thessalonians 5:16-18

(A Psalm of David.) The LORD is my shepherd; I shall not want.

Psalm 23:1

Chapter 13: Methodist

Written By: Sanet Gericke

Introduction

"He (the Pope) is in an emphatical sense, the Man of Sin, as he increases all manner of sin above measure. And he is, too, properly styled the Son of Perdition, as he has caused the death of numberless multitudes, both of his opposers and followers... He it is...that exalteth himself above all that is called God, or that is worshipped...claiming the highest power, and highest honour...claiming the prerogatives which belong to God alone."
(John Wesley, Antichrist and His Ten Kingdoms, page 110)

That was written by John Wesley, co-founder of the Methodist Church in the 18th Century. Today, it is not uncommon for Methodist churches to visit Roman Catholic churches to hold services there,

History Of The Methodist Church

The Methodist Church began in the late 18th century as a movement within the Church of England. A small group of students formed a group on the Oxford University campus. The group included brothers John and Charles Wesley and focused on Bible study, methodical study of scripture and living a holy life. Other students mocked the group by calling it the Holy Club. They also called them the Methodists. The Methodist started individual societies for members of the Church of England who wanted to live a more sacred life. Methodist preachers gave long sermons in open air fields to all people. The Church today is primarily Wesleyan in tradition. John Wesley was influenced by the Arminian theology that believed people could only be redeemed by grace. Methodist began sending missionaries to America in the 1760's. The missionaries were not ordained ministers. The societies that they formed received the sacraments from ordained members of the Church of England. Most of that clergy fled America when the Revolutionary War began. Due to the lack of clergy natives ordained their own. John Wesley sent Rev. Dr. Thomas Coke to start the American Methodist Church in 1784. Francis Asbury, stayed in United States despite the crisis, was set to be ordained as joint superintendent of the church. He only accepted the appointment after the assembled conference agreed to it. Asbury and Coke were named bishops of the American Methodist Church but John Wesley did not like the title. Early Methodist clergy were known as Circuit Riders. They travelled throughout a area ministering to congregations and delivers sermons. Francis Asbury travelled 270,000 miles and preached 16,000 sermons. In 1792 several factions split off from the American Methodist Episcopal Church, they did not agree with the church's use of Episcopal power. Methodism believe in free will and not predestination. Their liturgy is not considered church but varies from congregation to congregation. Methodist affirms the Trinity and the Apostles Creed. British Methodism don't have Bishops. American Methodist bishops are elected by the church members . In 1968 the American United Methodist Church was formed, when the Evangelical United Brethen and the Methodist

Church formed one body. Evangelical United Brethen was formed by German speaking Methodist churches. The symbol of the United Methodist Church is a cross and flame which symbolizes the Holy Spirit and God through Christ.

Believe

One of the fundamental tenants of the Methodist church is that all can be saved.

No person is beyond the love of God and everyone can find salvation. This includes people that has not invited Jesus Christ to be their Lord and Savior.

As we navigate this world that sometimes seems unjust, unfair and sinful is it comforting to know that salvation awaits us all.

As Christians, the Methodist church believes that Jesus preached to us the gospel of the Kingdom of God. Through His death and resurrection all may be saved and forgiven.

By opening ourselves to the Holy Spirit, God can help us fully live life.

Methodists believe in what John Wesley –the church's founder - calls "social holiness" or the need for us to meet and grow with other Christians wherever we may be. This is why the Methodist church is active in ministry outreach all over the globe.

Methodist Doctrine

God is all-knowing, possesses infinite love and goodness, is all-powerful, and the creator of all things.

God has always existed and will always continue to exist.

God is **three persons in one**, the Father, the Son (Jesus Christ), and the Holy Spirit.

God is the master of all creation and humans are meant to live in a holy covenant with him. Humans have broken this covenant by their sins, and can only be forgiven if they truly have faith in the love and saving grace of Jesus Christ.

Jesus was God on Earth (conceived of a virgin), in the form of a man who was crucified for the sins of all people, and who was physically resurrected to bring them the hope of eternal life.

The **grace** of God is seen by people through the work of the **Holy Spirit** in their lives and in their world.

Close adherence to the teachings of Scripture is essential to the faith because Scripture is the Word of God.

Christians are part of a universal church and must work with all Christians to spread the love of God.

Baptism is a sacrament or ceremony in which a person is anointed with water to symbolize being brought into the community of faith. They believe in baptizing babies.

Hélèné Fulton

Communion is a sacrament in which participants eat bread and drink juice to show that they continue to take part in Christ's redeeming resurrection by symbolically taking part in His body (the bread) and blood (the juice).
Wesley taught his followers that Baptism and Communion are not only sacraments, but also sacrifices to God.

People can only be saved through faith in Jesus Christ, not by any other acts of **redemption** such as good deeds.

When researching the Methodist Church they found that there are three main parties. Most of them came together to form the United Methodist Church Denomination. However, outside of the United Methodist Church, you find the Wesleyan Methodist Church and the Methodist Church. The one thing they all have in common is this: The United Methodist Church shares a common history and heritage with other Methodist and Wesleyan bodies. The lives and ministries of John Wesley and of his brother, Charles, mark the origin of their common roots. The fact that the Methodist Church, and all of their factions, started with men makes this religion absolutely false!
The Wesley Brother's Church Rather Than The Church of Christ

Jesus Christ promised He would establish His church.

[13] When Jesus came into the coasts of Caesarea Philippi, he asked his disciples, saying, Whom do men say that I the Son of man am?

[4] And they said, Some say that thou art John the Baptist: some, Elias; and others, Jeremias, or one of the prophets.
[15] He saith unto them, But whom say ye that I am?
[16] And Simon Peter answered and said, Thou art the Christ, the Son of the living God.
[17] And Jesus answered and said unto him, Blessed art thou, Simon Barjona: for flesh and blood hath not revealed it unto thee, but my Father which is in heaven.
[18] And I say also unto thee, That thou art Peter, and upon this rock I will build my church; and the gates of hell shall not prevail against it.

Matthew 16:13-18[1]

The first converts to Christ, after His death, were added to His [33]church.

Praising God, and having favour with all the people. And the Lord added to the church daily such as should be saved.

Acts 2:47

The church existed then, in the first century. Jesus's church is known as the church of Christ.

Salute one another with an holy kiss. The churches of Christ salute you.

Romans 16:16

The church is the body of Christ

[22] And hath put all things under his feet, and gave him to be the head over all things to the church,[23] Which is his body, the fulness of him that filleth all in all.

---

[33] Please refer to the beginning of this book on the explanation on who is the church according to the Bible

Hélèné Fulton

Ephesians 1:22-23

He is the head of His body, the church.

For the husband is the head of the wife, even as Christ is the head of the church: and he is the saviour of the body.
Ephesians 5:23

Just as there is one Father, one faith, one baptism, etc., there is only one body/church.

[4] There is one body, and one Spirit, even as ye are called in one hope of your calling;
[5] One Lord, one faith, one baptism,
[6] One God and Father of all, who is above all, and through all, and in you all.

Ephesians 4:4-6

Therefore, by the very fact that man started every form of Methodist Churches, we have proven the Methodist Church is not pleasing to God!

[21] Not every one that saith unto me, Lord, Lord, shall enter into the kingdom of heaven; but he that doeth the will of my Father which is in heaven.
[22] Many will say to me in that day, Lord, Lord, have we not prophesied in thy name? and in thy name have cast out devils? and in thy name done many wonderful works?
[23] And then will I profess unto them, I never knew you: depart from me, ye that work iniquity.

Matthew 7:21-23

Like all denominations, their foundation is not the only thing that exists without God's involvement.

Hélèné Fulton

The Methodist Church Is Guided By The Doctrines Of Men

"Who makes decisions for The United Methodist Church if there is no one person in charge? Good question. The only body that can set official policy and speak for the denomination is the General Conference. If you search the New Testament for the "General Conference" you will not find any such thing. The closest thing you will find to a "General Conference" in the New Testament is when the rulers of the Jews, elders, scribes, and the high priest came together in Jerusalem to forbid the preaching of the Gospel of Jesus Christ

5 And it came to pass on the morrow, that their rulers, and elders, and scribes,
6 And Annas the high priest, and Caiaphas, and John, and Alexander, and as many as were of the kindred of the high priest, were gathered together at Jerusalem.
7 And when they had set them in the midst, they asked, By what power, or by what name, have ye done this?
8 Then Peter, filled with the Holy Ghost, said unto them, Ye rulers of the people, and elders of Israel,
9 If we this day be examined of the good deed done to the impotent man, by what means he is made whole;
10 Be it known unto you all, and to all the people of Israel, that by the name of Jesus Christ of Nazareth, whom ye crucified, whom God raised from the dead, even by him doth this man stand here before you whole.
11 This is the stone which was set at nought of you builders, which is become the head of the corner.
12 Neither is there salvation in any other: for there is none other name under heaven given among men, whereby we must be saved.

¹³ Now when they saw the boldness of Peter and John, and perceived that they were unlearned and ignorant men, they marvelled; and they took knowledge of them, that they had been with Jesus.

¹⁴ And beholding the man which was healed standing with them, they could say nothing against it.

¹⁵ But when they had commanded them to go aside out of the council, they conferred among themselves,

¹⁶ Saying, What shall we do to these men? for that indeed a notable miracle hath been done by them is manifest to all them that dwell in Jerusalem; and we cannot deny it.

¹⁷ But that it spread no further among the people, let us straitly threaten them, that they speak henceforth to no man in this name.

¹⁸ And they called them, and commanded them not to speak at all nor teach in the name of Jesus.

¹⁹ But Peter and John answered and said unto them, Whether it be right in the sight of God to hearken unto you more than unto God, judge ye.

²⁰ For we cannot but speak the things which we have seen and heard.

²¹ So when they had further threatened them, they let them go, finding nothing how they might punish them, because of the people: for all men glorified God for that which was done.

Acts 4:5-22

Just like then, when man forms conferences to make decisions those decisions are ALWAYS contrary to the will of God. How can a person make such a statement? Well, just the fact that men come together and think beyond God's word is enough to condemn such an idea.

⁵ Every word of God is pure: he is a shield unto them that put their trust in him.

⁶ Add thou not unto his words, lest he reprove thee, and thou be found a liar.

Proverbs 30:5-6

The judgment of man is flawed. We simply need to see what God says and do it as He said.

Man's goings are of the LORD; how can a man then understand his own way?

Proverbs 20:24

¹⁸ And Jesus came and spake unto them, saying, All power is given unto me in heaven and in earth.
¹⁹ Go ye therefore, and teach all nations, baptizing them in the name of the Father, and of the Son, and of the Holy Ghost:
²⁰ Teaching them to observe all things whatsoever I have commanded you: and, lo, I am with you always, even unto the end of the world. Amen.

Matthew 28:18-20

The doctrines of men are not just found in the "General Conference" of the Methodist Church. Methodist Churches are also admittedly guided by human traditions: "Between the New Testament age and our own era stand countless witnesses on whom we rely in our theological journey. Through their words in creed, hymn, discourse, and prayer, through their music and art, through their courageous deeds, we discover Christian insight by which our study of the Bible is illuminated. This living tradition comes from many ages and many cultures. Even today Christians living in far different circumstances from our own—in Africa, in Latin America, in Asia—are helping us discover fresh understanding of the Gospel's power". You cannot follow the traditions of man and please

God at the same time. Their human traditions extend to their doctrines on baptism.

Then came to Jesus scribes and Pharisees, which were of Jerusalem, saying,
² Why do thy disciples transgress the tradition of the elders? for they wash not their hands when they eat bread.
³ But he answered and said unto them, Why do ye also transgress the commandment of God by your tradition?
⁴ For God commanded, saying, Honour thy father and mother: and, He that curseth father or mother, let him die the death.
⁵ But ye say, Whosoever shall say to his father or his mother, It is a gift, by whatsoever thou mightest be profited by me;
⁶ And honour not his father or his mother, he shall be free. Thus have ye made the commandment of God of none effect by your tradition.
⁷ Ye hypocrites, well did Esaias prophesy of you, saying,
⁸ This people draweth nigh unto me with their mouth, and honoureth me with their lips; but their heart is far from me.
⁹ But in vain they do worship me, teaching for doctrines the commandments of men.

Matthew 15:1-9

Beware lest any man spoil you through philosophy and vain deceit, after the tradition of men, after the rudiments of the world, and not after Christ.

Colossians 2:8

The Methodists Believe Error On Water Baptism

Notice the Methodist doctrines on baptism: "Persons of any age can be baptized, *this includes infants*. They baptize by sprinkling or pouring". In the Scriptures you can see that one has to be able to hear the truth, believe it, repent of our sins, confess Christ, prior to baptism. Please read our teaching in the beginning of this book on Baptism. One has to be able to understand the Lord's will to obey Him. Immersion is the only method of baptism in the Scriptures.

Then Peter said unto them, Repent, and be baptized every one of you in the name of Jesus Christ for the remission of sins, and ye shall receive the gift of the Holy Ghost.

Acts 2:38

^{36} And as they went on their way, they came unto a certain water: and the eunuch said, See, here is water; what doth hinder me to be baptized?
^{37} And Philip said, If thou believest with all thine heart, thou mayest. And he answered and said, I believe that Jesus Christ is the Son of God.
^{38} And he commanded the chariot to stand still: and they went down both into the water, both Philip and the eunuch; and he baptized him.

Acts 8:36-38

Wherefore be ye not unwise, but understanding what the will of the Lord is.

Ephesians 5:17

^{3} Know ye not, that so many of us as were baptized into Jesus Christ were baptized into his death?
^{4} Therefore we are buried with him by baptism into death: that like as Christ was raised up from the dead by the glory of the Father, even so we also should walk in newness of life.
^{5} For if we have been planted together in the likeness of his death, we shall be also in the likeness of his resurrection:
^{6} Knowing this, that our old man is crucified with him, that the body of sin might be destroyed, that henceforth we should not serve sin.

Hélèné Fulton

Romans 6:3-6

¹⁵ And he said unto them, Go ye into all the world, and preach the gospel to every creature.
¹⁶ He that believeth and is baptized shall be saved; but he that believeth not shall be damned.

Mark 16:15-16

And now why tarriest thou? arise, and be baptized, and wash away thy sins, calling on the name of the Lord.

Acts 22:16

²⁰ Which sometime were disobedient, when once the longsuffering of God waited in the days of Noah, while the ark was a preparing, wherein few, that is, eight souls were saved by water.
²¹ The like figure whereunto even baptism doth also now save us (not the putting away of the filth of the flesh, but the answer of a good conscience toward God,) by the resurrection of Jesus Christ:

1 Peter 3:20-21

The Methodists Are A Unity In Diversity Denomination

The United Methodist Church in El Paso wants to open doors in their fellowship by offering a wide variety of false works. Notice this quote: "We believe our church is a safe place where everyone is welcome - We believe in offering a wide variety of ministries providing many doors of entrance into our fellowship". You, the Methodists, I, or anyone else are not permitted to write our own terms of godly fellowship. Those in fellowship with God are those who meet the biblical terms of who is indeed in fellowship with the Lord. There is only one way into that fellowship and this is through Christ. No one can open any doors into the fellowship of the Lord. The draft behind their statement is unity in diversity, which is a false doctrine.

Whosoever transgresseth, and abideth not in the doctrine of Christ, hath not God. He that abideth in the doctrine of Christ, he hath both the Father and the Son.

2 John 9:11

[14] But I have a few things against thee, because thou hast there them that hold the doctrine of Balaam, who taught Balac to cast a stumblingblock before the children of Israel, to eat things sacrificed unto idols, and to commit fornication.
[15] So hast thou also them that hold the doctrine of the Nicolaitanes, which thing I hate.

Revelation 2:14-15

[3] That which we have seen and heard declare we unto you, that ye also may have fellowship with us: and truly our fellowship is with the Father, and with his Son Jesus Christ.
[4] And these things write we unto you, that your joy may be full.
[5] This then is the message which we have heard of him, and declare unto you, that God is light, and in him is no darkness at all.
[6] If we say that we have fellowship with him, and walk in darkness, we lie, and do not the truth:
[7] But if we walk in the light, as he is in the light, we have fellowship one with another, and the blood of Jesus Christ his Son cleanseth us from all sin.

1 John 1:3-7

According to Rev Alan Storey's book on Foundations for Disciples, the Methodists does not believe that there is a physical hell. They believe that it will be a mental torment because you will be removed from God.

"In flaming fire taking vengeance on them that know not God, and that obey not the gospel of our Lord Jesus Christ: Who shall be punished with everlasting destruction..."
2 Thessalonians 1:8-9

So many people today don't believe in a literal place called Hell that burns with fire and brimstone (Revelation 21:8), where all who die in their sins without Jesus Christ go to be punished for all eternity. Sadly, there are countless people who twist the Scriptures in an attempt to teach that Hell is not what the Bible says it is... a place of flaming torment.

The Bible contains an overwhelming amount of irrefutable evidence teaching that Hell is indeed a literal place of torment, where those who die in their sins without Jesus Christ are punished in flaming fire and vengeance by God (2nd Thessalonians 1:8,9).

Here are many Scriptures to consider...

"And the earth opened her mouth, and swallowed them up together with Korah, when that company died, what time the fire devoured two hundred and fifty men: and they became a sign."
Numbers 26:10

Korah and the men who rebelled with him against Moses were swallowed into Hell beneath.

"The wicked shall be turned into hell, and all the nations that forget God."

Psalm 9:17

Carefully notice that "hell" here cannot merely mean "the grave" as some foolishly teach. For if "hell" only means the grave, then where do the righteous go? The Bible plainly teaches that the righteous and the wicked do NOT go to the same place. The wicked are turned into Hell; but the righteous unto life eternal.

"If I ascend up into heaven, thou art there: if I make my bed in hell, behold, thou art there."

Psalm 139:8

The contrast here is between Heaven and Hell; not between Heaven and the grave. Also notice the interesting phrase... "If I make my bed in hell." Everyone who goes to Hell chooses to go there by rejecting Jesus as their Christ. It is sinful men who make their own bed in Hell. No sinner must go to Hell. The gift of eternal life is freely offered to all mankind through faith in Christ Jesus (John 14:6; Acts 10:43; Revelation 22:17).

"Therefore hell hath enlarged herself, and opened her mouth without measure: and their glory, and their multitude, and their pomp, and he that rejoiceth, shall descend into it."

Isaiah 5:14

It wouldn't make any sense if "hell" merely meant the grave. What point would there be in condemning the wicked to hell if that's the same place where the righteous go? Clearly, Hell is a place only for the wicked who die in their sins. The righteous go to heaven to be with the Lord (2 Corinthians 5:8).

"I made the nations to shake at the sound of his fall, when I cast him down to hell with them that descend into the pit..."

Ezekiel 31:16

Clearly, this Scripture defines "hell" as being more than the grave. The Bible speaks about "descending into the pit." The Bible also speaks of being "cast into Hell," which clearly implies judgment from a holy God. If "hell" merely meant grave as Mormons, Jehovah's Witness and other false prophets teach, then God would have said that the righteous shall be cast into hell too; but the Bible NEVER says that anywhere!!! Only the wicked shall be cast into Hell, a bottomless pit, where Satan is called "the angel of the bottomless pit" (Revelation 9:11).

"But I say unto you, That whosoever looketh on a woman to lust after her hath committed adultery with her already in his heart. And if thy right eye offend thee, pluck it out, and cast it from thee: for it is profitable for thee that one of thy members should perish, and not that thy whole body should be cast into hell."
Matthew 5:28-29

The Bible plainly teaches that all sinners are condemned to Hell. If "hell" simply means grave or torment in the mind, then what harm or worry is there in fornicating, getting drunk, raping, murdering, partying with illegal drugs and committing all sorts of other sins? There would be none. If there is NO place of punishment in eternity, then there is NO justice for all the victims of crimes committed in this earthly life. So then what advantage is there to being righteous? If one believes that the Bible is God's Word, then you absolutely must believe that Hell is a literal place of torment and anguish, that burns with searing flames of fire and brimstone, where sinners are punished for their sins against a holy God.

Hélèné Fulton

Chapter 14: ??????

Written By: Nyasha Muzvidzwa

Atheism is the rejection (or absence) of the belief that

Hélèné Fulton

Pagan Traditions

Chapter 15: ?????

Written By: Nyasha Muzvidzwa

Atheism is the rejection (or absence) of the belief that

Appendix 1
Religions: The Occult Connection - 1

What if I were to tell you my friend, that most of the religious people in this world were being misled? What if I were to tell you, that there is a vast Satanic conspiracy to deceive the masses of every society on earth? What if I were to tell you that the top leaders of the world's religions were in league with the Devil? Would you think I'm crazy? I would! Yet, the truth is stranger than fiction!

You have been lied to my friend.

Few people in the world today are aware of just how much Satan has infiltrated organized religion. The Word of God warns us in 2 Corinthians 11:13-14 that Satan and his false teachers, always come to us in sheep's clothing to deceive us …

[13] For such are false apostles, deceitful workers, transforming themselves into the apostles of Christ.
[14] And no marvel; for Satan himself is transformed into an angel of light.

2 Corinthians 11:13-14

Our only defence is the incorruptible Word of God. The Bible also warns us in 2 Timothy 4:3, that in the last days, people will no longer listen to the truth …

---

[34] For this Appendix we used the King James Version

[3] For the time will come when they will not endure sound doctrine; but after their own lusts shall they heap to themselves teachers, having itching ears;

2 Timothy 4:3

All we see on TV are televangelists begging for more money, telling people what they want to hear—promises of health, wealth, and prosperity; BUT, they never preach against sin, and never tell people that trusting in good works for salvation is a road straight to Hell. Well, I'm going to share with you the truth of God's Word because I care about you.

Let me state right from the start, that salvation is not found in <u>ANY</u> religion; BUT, only in a Person—The Lord Jesus Christ. No amount of good works can take a person to Heaven. Only through the precious blood of Jesus Christ can a person have their sins forgiven, and be saved eternally.

[18] Forasmuch as ye know that ye were not redeemed with corruptible things, as silver and gold, from your vain conversation received by tradition from your fathers;
[19] But with the precious blood of Christ, as of a lamb without blemish and without spot:

1 Peter 1:18-19

Satan is so subtle. One of the biggest Satanic deceptions today are false prophets who preach the Gospel (I.e., the death, burial, and resurrection of Jesus Christ); BUT, then ADD works to it. Such false prophets are Catholics, Mormons, Jehovah's Witnesses, etc. They all teach works salvation. The Word of God clearly states in…

⁵ But to him that worketh not, but believeth on him that justifieth the ungodly, his faith is counted for righteousness.

Romans 4:5

The Biblical Gospel excludes ALL self-righteousness!

The Occult connection

We see the occult everywhere nowadays. The most common symbols are the illuminati pyramid and the all-seeing eye of Horus. You see friend, 2 Corinthians 4:4 reveals that Satan is the god of this world's wickedness.

⁴ In whom the god of this world hath blinded the minds of them which believe not, lest the light of the glorious gospel of Christ, who is the image of God, should shine unto them.

2 Corinthians 4:4

Satan controls the world through occult (secret) organizations, whose members are devout followers of Satan. "Illuminati" is a term used to refer to the occult-inspired leaders of this world. Hitler was infatuated with the occult, as were many of histories top leaders. George W. Bush and John Kerry are BOTH members of the occult group, Skull and Bones (represented by the official symbol in the photo above to the right). What's even more disturbing is that we see the exact **same** Satanic emblem displayed on the Catholic cross in our next picture…

Above : A Catholic priest holds an occult cross, carefully notice the Skull and Bones emblem.

One of the biggest occult groups is Freemasonry, who's false god is Baphomet, pictured to the left. Few people know that Charles Taze Russell (founder of the Jehovah's Witnesses), and Joseph Smith (founder of Mormonism) were BOTH 33rd degree Freemasons. I was watching EWTN (the Catholic's *Eternal Word Television Network*) the other day. It was their morning mass between 8 to 9A.M. daily and behold, the priest was walking around with a golden monstrance (shaped like an illuminati pyramid) for everyone to see. This is no coincidence. The photo to the left is the official symbol of the Masonic lodge. Notice the illuminati pyramid at the top, and the occult handshake beneath. Also, notice the eye of Horus within the pyramid. This is pure Satanism folks!

Keep reading, you may lose some sleep tonight. Take a look at the occult illuminati eye in the photo below.

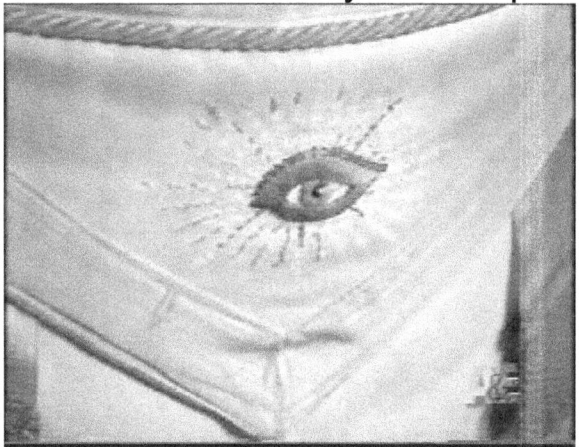

Above: A Mormon apron as seen on A&E TV, inside the Salt Lake City Temple.

This apron is located in the Mormon temple in Salt Lake City. Below is the front entrance to the same Mormon temple. Notice the same Masonic handshake (as seen above) within the all-seeing eye.

Above: Another entrance to the Salt Lake City, Utah, Mormon Temple. Mormon founder, Joseph Smith, was a 33rd degree Freemason.

Hélèné Fulton

You see, the Devil requires allegiance from those who would become successful in this world. This allegiance has infested the music industry and the corporate world as well. Satan is working relentlessly to corrupt the masses. The image below is sister Faustina's *Image of Divine Mercy*, worshipped around the world by Catholics...

Notice the illuminati pyramid! This is no joke friends, you have been deceived by the Devil, the father of all liars. Most people in the world today have churchianity without Christianity, and religion without truth. I'm not trying to be unkind; but to warn you about Satan's works of darkness. Whether it is Mormonism, Catholicism, or the Jehovah's Witnesses - they're all in league with Satan! God never started a religion -

Hélèné Fulton

Jesus simply came to save sinners, asking us to believe upon Him alone to forgive our sins.

¹⁶ For God so loved the world, that he gave his only begotten Son, that whosoever believeth in him should not perish, but have everlasting life.
¹⁷ For God sent not his Son into the world to condemn the world; but that the world through him might be saved.
¹⁸ He that believeth on him is not condemned: but he that believeth not is condemned already, because he hath not believed in the name of the only begotten Son of God.

John 3:16-18

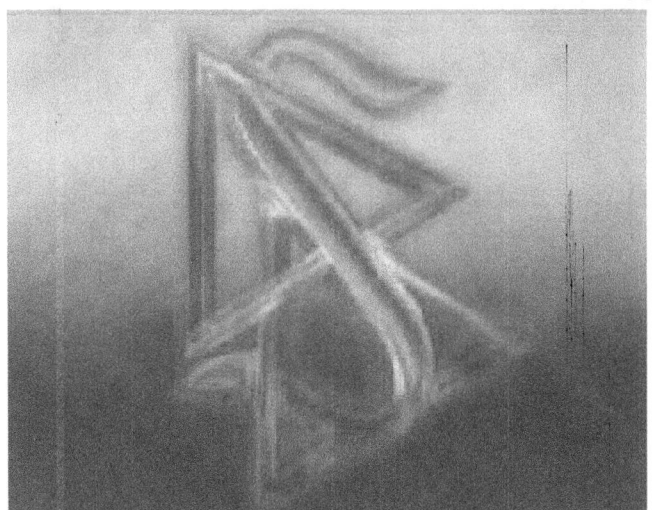

**Above is the logo for the *Church of Scientology* cult.
Notice the two illuminati Pyramids!**

Below is a photo of where Jehovah's Witness' founder, Charles T. Russell, is buried in the *Greater Pittsburgh Masonic Center* Cemetery. As you can see, Satan is behind ALL false religion. Notice the creepy illuminati pyramid ...

Hélèné Fulton

Above: This is the inscription on the same pyramid above, where Jehovah's Witness' founder, and occult Mason, Charles T. Russell, is buried. Freaky huh?

Above: a close-up of the inscription on the pyramid
**Freemasons Donate Illuminati Pyramid as
Gift for Grave of Mary Baker Eddy**

Christian Science is another **False Masonic Religion**

Hélèné Fulton

Mary Baker Eddy is the founder of the **CHRISTIAN SCIENTIST** religion. They have reading rooms all across the United States where you can go in, sit down, and be indoctrinated into their religious false cult. It is more than mere coincidence that the demonic Jehovah's Witnesses gave an Masonic pyramid to place on Eddy's grave, just as Charles Russell (founder of the Jehovah's Witnesses) has a giant illuminati pyramid parked on his grave (as seen in pictures on precious page).

Freemasons are the visible organization, the work horse to carry out Satan's sinister plot for a Godless Global Totalitarian Communism Police State, aka, a New World Order. Russell even named his perversion of the Bible, the **New World Translation**. That's about as blatant as you can get.

When I witness to a Jehovah's Witnessed, I show them a photo of Russell's grave and the occult connection between the religions. Most Jehovah's Witnesses are victims of the organization, they've been lied to and deceived. We as believers need to expose all these Masonic religions for what they are. Freemasonry is a diabolic, Satanic, religious cult; they operate in dual fashion, literally operating as two separate entities, an organization within an organization.

What is it with all the pyramids and all-seeing eyes? The explanation is simple. Satan uses images, just as "The Great Oz" in the movie, *The Wizard of Oz*. Satan is the little peon behind the curtain.

[16] They that see thee shall narrowly look upon thee, and consider thee, saying, Is this the man that made the earth to tremble, that did shake kingdoms

Isaiah 14:16

The purpose of the *IMAGE* is to magnify a person, or thing, to give a bigger than life IMAGE. This is why king Nebuchadnezzar had a 90-foot tall, 9-foot wide, statue made of gold for the people to bow and worship, on his behalf.

[35]**1921** - On the 100th anniversary of Mary Baker Eddy's birth, an exact replica of the Great Pyramid, made from a single piece of granite and weighing over 100 tons and 11 feet on each side, was carved and placed near the house where Eddy had been born, in New Hampshire. It was a gift from Freemasons. In the "Mary Baker Eddy Letter," December 25, 1997, **we learn** that when "the Board of Directors noted that too many Christian Scientists were visiting the grand granite marker at Bow ... that marked Mary Baker Eddy's birthplace, they had it destroyed, dynamited to bits!"

Eddy's first husband, George Washington Glover, was a Mason, **and "thereafter** membership in the Masonic Order was the one single 'outside' affiliation that was allowed to church members by Mrs. Eddy."

35

http://www.conspiracyarchive.com/Commentary/Oprah_The_Secret.htm

Christian Science and Freemasonry have maintained a symbiotic relationship. Many of the first churches established around the United States had gathered in Masonic Temples. To this day one can find the headquarters for many Christian Science associations having an address corresponding to the local Masonic lodge.
SOURCE: Oprah Winfrey, New Thought, "The Secret" and the "New Alchemy"

What you see on the tombstone

Who Are *Contemporary Christian Music* (CCM) Fans Really Worshipping?

I preach a lot against CCM singers, because they are deceivers. No one wonders what Marilyn Manson is about. We all know that he rips up Bibles, hates God and is a fool. However, sinister ecumenical ministers and apostate so- 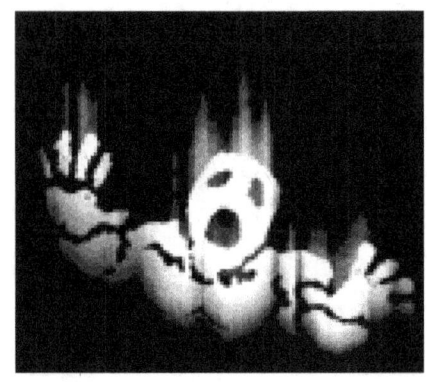 called *Christian* singers claim to love God and want to reach people with A MESSAGE of love and unity; BUT the sad truth is that they are leading churchgoers into apostasy, a false Catholic Gospel, and unbiblical unity with unbelievers. **ChristianityToday** even labels God as a Drama Queen (it is apostasy)! They ought to be honest and call themselves apostates!

We all know where Elton John stands; but TobyMac deceives people, and it is sinful to do so. TobyMac claims to be helping his fans through his music; but he is leading them astray, pushing them toward the Catholic religion. Pope Benedict XVI says people can be saved without any Biblical faith. Pope Benedict XVI is a fool. ALL CCM singers accept the Catholic Church and never say a negative word, because many of their fans are Catholic... cha-ching, money, money, money! At least Pink Floyd sings about money and doesn't try to hide anything. God hates a proud look and a lying tongue.

¹⁶ These six things doth the Lord hate: yea, seven are an abomination unto him:
¹⁷ A proud look, a lying tongue, and hands that shed innocent blood,
¹⁸ An heart that deviseth wicked imaginations, feet that be swift in running to mischief,
¹⁹ A false witness that speaketh lies, and he that soweth discord among brethren.

Proverb 6:16-19

The Old Testament tells us that wicked king Nebuchadnezzar set up a golden *IMAGE* and demanded that everyone worship the *IMAGE* or be killed...

⁵ That at what time ye hear the sound of the cornet, flute, harp, sackbut, psaltery, dulcimer, and all kinds of musick, ye fall down and worship the golden image that Nebuchadnezzar the king hath set up:
⁶ And whoso falleth not down and **worshippeth shall the same hour be cast into the midst of a burning fiery furnace**.
⁷ Therefore at that time, when all the people heard the sound of the cornet, flute, harp, sackbut, psaltery, and all kinds of musick, all the people, the nations, and the languages, fell down and worshipped the golden image that Nebuchadnezzar the king had set up.

Daniel 3:5-7

Carefully notice that Revelation 13:15 tells us that the same thing will happen when the Antichrist comes, i.e., he will demand worship of the *IMAGE* (just as Nebuchadnezzar did), or else the masses of people will be killed...

¹⁵ And he had power to give life unto the **image of the beast**, that the **image of the beast** should both speak, and cause that as many **as would not worship the image of the beast should be killed**.

Revelation 13:15

It is very interesting that king Nebuchadnezzar didn't ask the people to worship him directly; but instead, worship an *IMAGE*. Nebuchadnezzar wanted to be worshipped, but he knew that he was just a man; so he needed an image 90-feet tall of pure gold to magnify himself through the image. The Antichrist will just be a man; but he will magnify himself through an *IMAGE* that the Bible says will speak and come to life (Revelation 13:15).

Those who refuse to worship the Beast's *IMAGE* will be killed, just as Nebuchadnezzar proclaimed death to anyone who didn't bow to worship his *IMAGE*. This is important to understand, showing us **why** Satan is using the Masonic pyramid and All-seeing Eye to recruit followers to the New World Order. It is for the same purpose as Nebuchadnezzar's *IMAGE*.

So where does *Contemporary Christian Music* (CCM) come into play? It's for the same purpose as all worldly music today.

> [5] That at what time ye hear the sound of the cornet, flute, harp, sackbut, psaltery, dulcimer, and all kinds of musick, ye fall down and worship the golden image that Nebuchadnezzar the king hath set up:
>
> **Daniel 3:5**

Everyone was instructed to worship Nebuchadnezzar's image when they heard the music, all kinds of music. The Bible lists all sorts of musical instruments. It wasn't about singing or lyrics, but THE MUSIC.

Likewise, in these Last Days Satan is conditioning the masses of this world to worship the Beast, and the *IMAGE* of the Beast, through music. The similarities between Nebuchadnezzar's *IMAGE* and the Antichrist's *IMAGE* are more than mere coincidental. Satan's methods haven't changed in thousands of years.

Let's go further...

George Harrison of *The Beatles* sang his hit song, ***MY SWEET LORD***. Christian youth all across the world and America were singing along... *My Sweet Lord*. But then AT THE END of the song, Harrison deceitfully changed the lyrics to, MY SWEET LORD, HARE KRISHNA!!! Harrison's 1971 song *MY SWEET LORD*, is a song of praise to the Hindu god, Krishna. **In fact, Harrison admits that he did that to trick people**.

In his 1982 interview with the Hare Krishna organization George Harrison stated...

"I wanted to show that Hallelujah and Hare Krishna are quite the same thing. I did the voices singing 'Hallelujah' and then the change to 'Hare Krishna'

so that people would be chanting the maha-mantra-before they knew what was going on! I had been chanting Hare Krishna for a long time, and this song was a simple idea of how to do a Western pop equivalent of a mantra which repeats over and over again the holy names. I don't feel guilty or bad about it; in fact it saved many a heroin addict's life."
(emphasis added)
SOURCE: George Harrison Interview: Hare Krishna Mantra - There's Nothing Higher (1982)

People who would normally be offended by someone praising "Hare Krishna my sweet Lord," were caught off guard by the way the song was arranged. The listener would follow along with the words "Hallelujah, my sweet Lord" several times before it subtly changed to "Hare Krishna, my sweet Lord."

By that time the listener had already been mesmerized by the music and the song. George Harrison was an imposter who rejected Jesus Christ, and is burning in the fires of Hell forever because he died in his sins without Jesus Christ. I say this with sadness. 2 Peter 3:9 declares that "God is not willing for any to perish" in their sins.

[9] The Lord is not slack concerning his promise, as some men count slackness; but is longsuffering to us-ward, not willing that any should perish, but that all should come to repentance.
2 Peter 3:9

CCM is leading the religious world into the New World Order. This is plainly evidenced by all the occult imagery on their album covers, and the Ecumenical Movement (i.e., let's unite by error, rather than divide over truth). CCM's true colors will come out **IN THE**

END, when the Antichrist appears; just as George Harrison's song MY SWEET LORD, deceived millions of people to worship Hare Krishna of the Hindu religion. You are being deceived my friend.
Yes, **Contemporary Christian Music** is beautiful. ***Third Day***, ***Mercy Me*** and ***Tree63*** sing some really pretty music, uplifting one's spirit. I love all kinds of music, naturally. But as a Christian I have to side with THE TRUTH, and God's Word. I don't like being the bearer of bad news; but if the bad news is THE TRUTH, then so be it.

The Gospel is two-thirds bad news... Jesus died and was buried. Those were very sad occasions to the Lord's friends, even though they knew it was necessary for redemption. So even though the Gospel is two-thirds bad news, we call it the "Gospel" (i.e., the good news) because it was all a good thing that the Lord was doing to redeem us. Amen!

I've researched the CCM crowd and their music, and they're all rubbing shoulders with the sinful world.

They're all using corrupt Bibles. They're all doctrinally compromised, prioritizing love and unity over truth and righteousness. They all sell their music for profit and the CCM industry rakes in billions-of-dollars annually. The lyrics are extremely vague and none of their websites tell anyone how to be saved to enter Heaven.

It is self-evident that music will be a big part of Satan's New World Order. Just as millions of fans idolize their favorite Rock stars these days, so will the masses of society idolize and worship the Antichrist when he comes; who may very well be a Rock star, such as Bono from U2 (who is a member of the CFR and has worldwide influence). If 11,000,000 Americans will buy Marilyn Manson's garbage, then they'll certainly follow the Antichrist when he comes.

Thus, you now know why Satan is using **IMAGES**. The purpose is the exact same reason that the *Wizard of Oz* constructed a giant fire-breathing Oz, bellowing out, "***I AM THE GREAT OZ***," to intimidate people. Here is what the Bible teaches about Lucifer, the Devil...

16 They that see thee shall narrowly look upon thee, and consider thee, saying, Is this the man that made the earth to tremble, that did shake kingdoms;

Isaiah 14:16

The all-seeing eye is bigger than life, and all the occult symbols around us; behind shoved in our faces, and down our throats... saying, ***We are the great architects of the New World Order, composed of Freemasons and other occult organizations, Luciferian worshippers, and you are our slaves!!!***

The All-Seeing Eye, Occult Images are Everywhere!

Just as wicked king Nebuchadnezzar made an IMAGE for the people to bow to, so will the Devil make an IMAGE when the Antichrist comes, and kill those who refuse to bow (Revelation 13:15); just as Nebuchadnezzar ordered death to anyone who didn't bow to his golden IMAGE (Daniel 3:5-7).

Hélèné Fulton

The New World Order will adhere to a Luciferian religion.

Clearly, there is an occult connection between many false religions and Satan. You don't have to believe it if you don't want to, but the evidence is solid.

As I mentioned earlier, Satan requires an allegiance. The photo to the right shows the *CBS'* logo—the all-seeing eye. To the left, an  illuminati eye is seen in a *Starbuck's* window.

Society is so infested with Satanism that few people even realize what is happening nowadays. Below is an image from *Nickelodeon*....

Devil Companies

These are symbols of the coming beast system of the antichrist.

This is why the apostate Israelites in the Wilderness demanded a golden calf, an **IMAGE**, to bow and worship. They needed an object of worship, something bigger than themselves.

This is why the wicked men at Babel rose against God to build a Tower, a place, something bigger than themselves to unite them as one, but without God. The Antichrist will create an **IMAGE**, and demand that everyone worship it or die (Revelation 13:15).

Why do world leaders and the who's who of top corporations and newsmedia meet at Bohemia Grove every July in California to worship a 40-foot owl? Again, we see an **IMAGE**. Images and symbols are critically important to occult and Luciferian Devil worship. Since it is not befitting for men to outright admit to worshipping Satan, then disguise their worship with **IMAGES** instead. The Illuminati have created a bigger-than-life feeling around the world with their Masonic pyramid and all-seeing eye.

We see this in the "HOLLYWOOD" sign in West Hollywood. That sign generates a bigger-than-life feeling and atmosphere; just seeing the sign, because it appears in so many movies, and it has become a part of everyday life in the United States. Likewise, we are seeing the Masonic pyramid and all-seeing eye everywhere these days; they have become a part of our daily lives, embedded in our brains, and I sincerely believe that the Antichrist's **IMAGE** (Revelation 13:15) may be the all-seeing eye and ***The Great Pyramid*** (it is very interesting that *The Great Pyramid*, thought to have been built around 2,600 B.C., never had the capstone put into place). The Masonic pyramid on the back of every dollar has the capstone separated from the base. The capstone are the Illuminati, the architects of the New World Order, the occult elite.

The fact that *The Great Pyramid* was built without a capstone indicates that the New World Order has been in the planning for millenniums. God segregated men at Babel, scattering people across the world, to safeguard humanity from corruption.

[26] And hath made of one blood all nations of men for to dwell on all the face of the earth, and hath determined the times before appointed, and the bounds of their habitation;
[27] That they should seek the Lord, if haply they might feel after him, and find him, though he be not far from every one of us:
Acts 17:26-27

Satan has been trying to undo what God did, and unite men against God ever since. Today, in God's permissive and sovereign will, Satan is uniting the world; breaking down language, cultural and denominational barriers, to unite men once again against God in a Luciferian worship (New Age).

This is why apostate *Contemporary Christian Music* (CCM) singers, sinister ecumenical ministers, and the entire secular world, are all promoting unity in every form. This is why so many movies, like **JUNGLE FEVER**, featuring interracial marriage, have been used to corrupt America, breaking down cultural barriers. This is why the U.S. borders remain wide open, because without a border there is no country. The evil elite powers controlling everything from behind the scenes.

"No one will enter the New World Order unless he or she will make a pledge to worship Lucifer. No one will

enter the New Age unless he will take a Luciferian Initiation." - David Spangler, Director of Planetary Initiative, United Nations

What does this all mean?

Few people realize just how connected false religions are with the occult, and Satan. Freemasonry is of the Devil, forbidding any of its members from praying "in Jesus' name" in any of their lodges! Freemasonry teaches the New Age lie that there are many paths to the light; BUT, the Word of God declares in John 14:6 there's ONLY one …

⁶ Jesus saith unto him, I am the way, the truth, and the life: no man cometh unto the Father, but by me.

John 14:6

It's Jesus or Hell. All the religion in the world never saved anyone. In fact, religion is the worst thing that ever happened to this sin-cursed world! Jesus came to set us free from sin, and to give us eternal life through His blood …

¹⁴ In whom we have redemption through his blood, even the forgiveness of sins:

Colossians 1:14

If you'd like to know for sure, that if you died today you would go to Heaven, then simply believe upon Jesus

Hélèné Fulton

Christ, who came to this earth as God Almighty in the flesh

[1] In the beginning was the Word, and the Word was with God, and the Word was God.

[14] And the Word was made flesh, and dwelt among us, (and we beheld his glory, the glory as of the only begotten of the Father,) full of grace and truth.

John 1:1&14

[9] For in him dwelleth all the fulness of the Godhead bodily.

Colossians 2:9

to die for your sins and mine. Simply ask Jesus to forgive your sins, and trust Him ALONE for your salvation. Adding anything to faith alone in Christ is NO faith at all.

[8] For by grace are ye saved through faith; and that not of yourselves: it is the gift of God:
[9] Not of works, lest any man should boast.

Ephesians 2:8-9

Won't you trust Jesus now as your personal Savior?

I understand that the truth often makes people angry, but the truth can be dealt with … a lie cannot. Who loves you more, the person who tells you the truth, even if it makes you mad? … or the liar who wants your money, and would never tell you what I just did? The Apostle Paul said, *"Am I therefore become your enemy, because I tell you the truth?"*

Appendix 2
Religions: The Occult Connection - 2

What you see on the tombstone of the founder of the Watchtower movement is the *Knights Templar* Symbol for the *York Rite* of Freemasonry (See below). This degree is equivalent to the 33rd Degree of Freemasonry and is the highest degree of the *York Rite* indicating that he knew whom he was serving. It was not Jesus Christ of Nazareth to be sure. Shown below are examples of how the Christian Science and Jehovah's Witnesses cults have used this symbol. This is where Charles Taze Russell (1852-1916), 33rd Degree Freemason and founder of the Jehovah's Witnesses cult is buried.

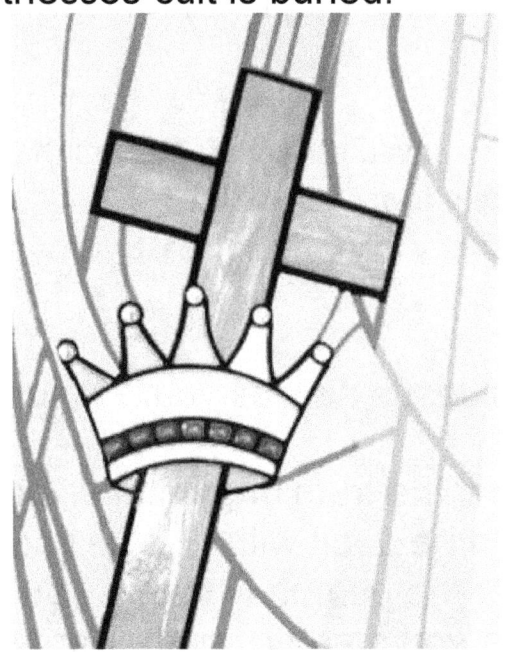

Christian Science symbol

---

[36] For this Appendix we used the King James Version
[37] http://www.christianscienceaspen.com/christianscience.html

Hélèné Fulton

Christian Science jewelry

(The main logo for the Christian Science faith, is also the Knights Templar symbol. (Christian Science Journal, Special Issue, December 1992). The symbolism dates back to 1100 A.D. and was developed by Templar Masons from the Knights Templar in Germany.)
SOURCE: http://www.antiquingonline.com/period-jewelry/html/christian-science-pin.ht

Founder of the Jehovah's Witnesses, Charles Taze Russell's Masonic grave

Masonic Knights Templar Symbol

Tim LaHaye's book, *The Power Of The Cross*, features an occult symbol on the cover

The above picture on the left is the cover of the recent book (1999) by Tim LaHaye called, *The Power of the Cross*. The one on the right is a centuries old Masonic symbol of the Knights Templar. Some might mistake it for a Christian symbol, but Masonic author Ray Denslow reveals its true sinister meaning:

"The Cross and Crown may be said to be confined almost exclusively to the historical degrees in Masonry as exemplified in the various orders of knighthood of York and Scottish rites. In Gaul we find the *cross to have been a solar symbol* when it had equal arms and angles; to the Phoenicians it was *an instrument of sacrifice* to their God, Baal; and to the Egyptians, the *crux ansata was his symbol of eternal life.*" (Ray V. Denslow, *Masonic Portraits,* Transactions of the Missouri Lodge of Research, vol. #29, p.7 — emphasis in the original)

Masonic authority Albert Pike also wrote of the meaning of the above symbol in his book *Morals and Dogma,* explaining that it has a **sexual connotation** to it as well. (Why is this symbol on a 'Christian' book cover). Was it also a coincidence that LaHaye and his associates set up their *Pretrib Research Center* in a place that's considered a vortex of occultic power in Washington D.C. They were located on L'Enfant Promenade, a street named after the Mason Pierre Charles L'Enfant who designed the city in Masonic and Occultic symbols. From there, coincidently, they moved their research center to the Dallas area, another city that is sacred to Freemasonry because of its proximity to the 33rd degree of latitude. Christians aren't supposed to believe in coincidences?

Hélèné Fulton

Above: Oral Roberts Medical Center. Notice the Illuminati pyramid. Oral Roberts was an occult 33rd degree Freemason. The Charismatic Movement teaches the lie of Lordship Salvation, a false Gospel.

Jack Chick caters to them in his tracts by requiring people to be willing to stop living in sin to be saved. It is not what you're doing that gets you to Heaven, **it's where you're looking. Look to Jesus!**

Washington Monument.

George Washington was a 33rd Degree Freemason.

Without prophetess Ellen G. White (November 26, 1827 — July 16, 1915) there would be no *Seventh-day Adventist* (SDA) *Church*; however, SDAs seek to avoid the issue because Ellen G. White's life was saturated with occultism, damnable heresies and bizarre experiences. SDAs revere White's writings as being equally inspired with the Bible.
Interestingly, Charles Taze Russell (founder of the Jehovah's Witnesses), Ron Hubbard (founder of Scientology), and Joseph Smith (founder of the Mormon religion) were all 33rd Degree Freemasons.
Mary Baker Eddy, the founder of *Christian Science*, was an associate of 33rd Degree Freemason Henry Steele Olcott who founded the Satan worshipping cult called the "Theosophical Society" with evil female Freemason, mother of the *New Age Movement* and Hitler's spiritual guide, Helena Petrovna Blavatsky.

Satan is the god of this sinful world (2 Corinthians 4:4) and operates through the occult to perform his works of darkness. 2 Corinthians 11:13-14 informs us that Satan transforms himself into an angel of light to deceive people, and his sinister ministers are transformed into ministers of righteousness.

[13] For such are false apostles, deceitful workers, transforming themselves into the apostles of Christ.
[14] And no marvel; for Satan himself is transformed into an angel of light.

2 Corinthians 11:13-14

Should it be surprising then that the Catholics, Mormons, Jehovah's Witnesses, Scientologists, Christian Scientists, Seventh-day Adventists, and other religions are all OF THE DEVIL.

There is a visible, obvious, verifiable occult connection between nearly all major religions today, especially with Freemasonry.

Just as Rick Warren, who is an Illuminati plant and CFR member, so is Max Lucado a part of the New World Order's Ecumenical Movement.
Ecumenicals are dangerous false prophets who profess to believe the fundamentals of the Bible in their statement of faith; but for filthy lucre's sake teach and promote something entirely different. Ecumenicals are very vague in their teachings, to avoid offending supporters or fans. Ecumenicals will say different things to different crowds, whatever it takes to make more money.

God is not the author of confusion; Satan is!

[33] For God is not the author of confusion, but of peace, as in all churches of the saints.

1 Corinthians 14:33

Some preachers just wants your money, and they have learned that people will give them their money if they makes them feel good. So many televangelists, preys upon people.

³ And through covetousness shall they with feigned words make merchandise of you: whose judgment now of a long time lingereth not, and their damnation slumbereth not.
2 Peter 2:3

Here are some general truthful observations about ecumenicalists:

- **Ecumenical ministries and Contemporary Christian Music (CCM) singers use occult symbols.**

- **Ecumenical preachers are part of the New World Order** (whether they realize it or not). And again, ecumenism is defined as: trying to unite religious people by error; rather than dividing over truth as God commands.

¹⁴ Be ye not unequally yoked together with unbelievers: for what fellowship hath righteousness with unrighteousness? and what communion hath light with darkness?
¹⁵ And what concord hath Christ with Belial? or what part hath he that believeth with an infidel?
¹⁶ And what agreement hath the temple of God with idols? for ye are the temple of the living God; as God hath said, I will dwell in them, and walk in them; and I will be their God, and they shall be my people.
¹⁷ Wherefore come out from among them, and be ye separate, saith the Lord, and touch not the unclean thing; and I will receive you.

Hélèné Fulton

2 Corinthians 6:14-17

Love and unity are sinful compromise if not based upon THE TRUTH

²⁴ God is a Spirit: and they that worship him must worship him in spirit and in truth.

John 4:24

➢ **Ecumenical preachers are greedy and have things to sell** (the love of money is truly the root of all evil)

➢ **Ecumenical preachers deceitfully claim to believe the fundamentals of the Bible** (Ninety-nine percent of everything they teach, publish, and do in public is apostate mumbo-jumbo, self-helps, how to become a success financially; virtually devoid of the fundamentals of the Bible, i.e., the Doctrine of Christ mentioned in 2nd John 1:9. Their statement of faith is a mere smokescreen to deceive their Bible-believing critics. Ecumenicalist are opportunists who will change like a chameleon lizard to whatever color necessary to make money and deceive their prey).

➢ **Ecumenicals almost always end up on the New York Times *Best Seller List* of books.** The Illuminati, i.e., the movers and shakers behind the evil New World Order, promote Ecumenicals because it helps achieve their goal; which is a one-world order, one-world religion, one-world economy, one-world government, one-world court, one-world everything!!! The Antichrist will be a dictator, who will bring order out of chaos to the world.

Ecumenicals want to unite all denominations in error; speaking the truth in one breath, while uniting with liars in the next. As mentioned, they post a statement of faith to look like genuine Christians; but all of their books and public teachings are completely devoid of THE TRUTH that matters. The Doctrine of Christ is ignored. Hell fire and damnation are not mentioned. The King James Bible is abandoned. Whatever true Biblical doctrine exists in ecumenism is buried behind worldly music, secular philosophies and unbiblical unity with apostates.

Satan knows if he can corrupt just a tiny bit, just get an inch in the door; he's home free! It only requires the tiniest amount of virus to infect the entire body. This is why it is very important that we as believers contend for the Biblical faith,

³ Beloved, when I gave all diligence to write unto you of the common salvation, it was needful for me to write unto you, and exhort you that ye should earnestly contend for the faith which was once delivered unto the saints.

Jude 1:3

earnestly fighting against those who pervert the simplicity that is in Christ,

³ But I fear, lest by any means, as the serpent beguiled Eve through his subtilty, so your minds should be corrupted from the simplicity that is in Christ.

2 Corinthians 11:3

identifying them who cause doctrinal riffs in the church

¹⁷ Now I beseech you, brethren, mark them which cause divisions and offences contrary to the doctrine which ye have learned; and avoid them.

Romans 16:17

rebuking with authority those who teach heresies

¹³ This witness is true. Wherefore rebuke them sharply, that they may be sound in the faith;

Titus 1:13

and refuting (exposing) all works of darkness

¹¹ And have no fellowship with the unfruitful works of darkness, but rather reprove them.

Ephesians 5:11

The Christian who is awake to righteousness and loves Jesus Christ has their hands full fighting the good fight of faith as a soldier.

³ Thou therefore endure hardness, as a good soldier of Jesus Christ.

2 Timothy 2:3

Satan is Subtle

When the Antichrist comes, that is, the Beast, he will seek for all men to worship him, including the churches and different denominational groups. The stage is now being set. False prophets like Joel Osteen, Max Lucado and Rick Warren are setting the stage for the Antichrist. As hard as it is to imagine, it's true. Lucado was named "America's Pastor" by apostate *Christianity Today* magazine and in 2005 was named by demonic *Reader's Digest* as "The Best Preacher in America." He has been featured on The Fox News Channel, NBC Nightly News, Larry King Live, USA Today, and a bunch of other worldly demonic shows.

[26] Woe unto you, when all men shall speak well of you! for so did their fathers to the false prophets.

Luke 6:26

There you have it! The Bible says it all! Jesus said that nearly everyone speaks well of false prophets!

In 2005, ChristianityToday voted Max Lucado as the

This is one more reason why I believe the Antichrist will come soon, which means that the Caught up (Rapture) of the saints is very near.

The Bible tells of a demon-possessed woman who followed the Apostles and told people to listen to them to be saved...

[16] And it came to pass, as we went to prayer, a certain damsel possessed with a spirit of divination met us, which brought her masters much gain by soothsaying:
[17] The same followed Paul and us, and cried, saying, These men are the servants of the most high God, which shew unto us the way of salvation.

Acts 16:16-17

Why would Satan influence this witch to tell people to listen to God's men? The answer is obviously that she was turning people away from the truth. She was causing a distraction, making people think she was crazy, as well as the Apostles. Satan is a dirty fiend and has so many dirty tactics that he employs to keep people from getting saved.

Did you ever stop to realize that every unsaved hellbound Catholic, Mormon, Church of Christ, Seventh-Day Adventist, Jehovah's Witness and Christian Science cult follower believes in the death, burial and resurrection of Jesus Christ? It's true! So what sets the true Gospel apart from what all these demonic cults teach and believe? I'll tell you.

The Bible speaks of the "simplicity that is in Christ" in

[3] But I fear, lest by any means, as the serpent beguiled Eve through his subtilty, so your minds should be corrupted from the simplicity that is in Christ.

2 Corinthians 11:3

The simple Gospel is that we are SINNERS and Jesus is the SAVIOR! Christ died, that's history; Christ died for me, that's salvation! The Biblical Gospel excludes all forms of **self-righteousness**; including water baptism, Holy Communion, Sabbath keeping, good works, church membership, speaking in tongues, amending one's ways, forsaking the world, et cetera. Eternal life is a free gift, paid for by Jesus' precious literal blood.

[18] Forasmuch as ye know that ye were not redeemed with corruptible things, as silver and gold, from your vain conversation received by tradition from your fathers;
[19] But with the precious blood of Christ, as of a lamb without blemish and without spot:

1 Peter 1:18-19

Héléné Fulton

Salvation is not something we do to get; it is a gift that we receive to have! We simply receive Jesus Christ as John 1:12 teaches, believing on the Son of God.

The Gospel is so delicate, so profoundly simple, that it is easily corrupted. By adding even the slightest alteration, the Gospel is corrupted into a lie of Satan. The serpent came to Eve in the Garden of Eden to deceive her, saying, **"Hath God said?"**

3 Now the serpent was more subtil than any beast of the field which the LORD God had made. And he said unto the woman, Yea, hath God said, Ye shall not eat of every tree of the garden?
Genesis 3:1

Satan called God a liar, tricking Eve. Similarly, there are many false religions and false prophets today who will tell you anything to get your money.

A business card from a Seventh-Day Adventist owned bookstore

I immediately recognized the all-seeing eye, which is a very popular occult symbol, showing one's allegiance to the New World Order. It seemed strange to me that a small advertised Christian bookstore would be a part of the New World Order, so I went back to the store to take a closer look. I figured that they must be a part of a bigger organization that is a part of the New World Order.

Hélèné Fulton

Sure enough, I found some works of darkness by Doug Bachelor, who is a popular Seventh-Day Adventist speaker in California. I went home and looked up the **GENERAL CONFERENCE OF SEVENTH DAY ADVENTISTS** website, and here is their official SDA logo . . .

Official Seventh-Day Adventist Logo, shaped as a Masonic pyramid

Notice the shape of the Masonic occult pyramid, which is also displayed on the back of every U.S. one-dollar bill to mock the stupidity of society, and to remind us that we are now slaves to the Masonic-controlled New

It is all creepy; but moreover, shows that Satan is in control of ALL organized religions.

As born-again Christians, Jesus taught that the Kingdom of God is within us.

²¹ Neither shall they say, Lo here! or, lo there! for, behold, the kingdom of God is within you.

Luke 17:2

Be warned my friend, Satan is behind all organized religions today, leading the masses to worship the coming Antichrist, the Beast. That's what the occult all-seeing eye and pyramid all represent, i.e., the completion of the New World Order, which will be led by the Beast.

Thank God for those few faithful New Testament churches still remaining today, who have not bowed their knee to Baal, who do not display Masonic occult symbols on their building and literature; and have a man or women of God as their pastor watching over their souls, contending for the doctrine of Christ, teaching personal soul-winning, and taking a Biblical stand against public wickedness.

Notes

Delete this instructional text below when formatting your book.

(Style = Notes)

The Notes for a book can be set as footnotes as the bottom of the page within the main body of the book or on a Notes page in the back matter. The Notes should come before the References or Bibliography (if included).

The font used in the Notes is generally set about 2 points smaller than the main body text. Notes are usually set in the same font as the body text, which is almost always a serif font such as Times or Garamond.

The first line of the note is usually set with a ¼-inch indent. If the main body text is left aligned then the notes should also be left aligned.

If your Notes require multiple pages, the final page should be on an even numbered page (left side of an open book). A section break is included below to automatically insert the required blank page if required.

If you are not including Notes, delete this page from the template.

References

**Delete this instructional text when formatting your book.
(Style = References Hanging Indent)**

The References section (or Bibliography) generally follows the Notes section if there is one. The references text can be set in the same font and size as the Notes.
The References are often set with a ragged right margin (i.e. not justified), especially if there are long website addresses that would make it difficult to justify the text without leaving big spaces between words. To make them easier to read, the References can be set with a small amount of extra space between entries, or with ¼-inch hanging indent, where the first line of text is flush left with the text margin and the following lines are indented.

If your list of References requires multiple pages, the final page should be on an even numbered page (left side of an open book). A section break is included below to automatically insert the required blank page if required.

If you are not including a list of References, delete this page from the template.

Glossary

Delete this instructional text when formatting your book. (Style = Glossary)

If the book has a glossary, it usually comes after the Notes and References sections if included. The Glossary text is usually set in the book's main body font and size, but it can be set smaller if page count is an issue.

The glossary terms are often set off in some way, using a bold or italic font. It is also common to set off the entries with a hanging indent and/or extra space between the terms.

If your Glossary requires multiple pages, the final page should be on an even numbered page (left side of an open book). A section break is included below to automatically insert the required blank page if required.

If you are not including a Glossary, delete this page from the template.

(Style = Normal Block)

IMPORTANT NOTE

The total number of pages (front matter, body, and back matter) in your book must be divisible by 4. If not, the printer will insert additional pages.

The final page (front and back) of your book must be left blank. If there is any print on the page, it will be rejected for distribution.

THEREFORE, DELETE THE TEXT FROM THIS PAGE BEFORE UPLOADING YOUR MANUSCRIPT!

www.ingramcontent.com/pod-product-compliance
Lightning Source LLC
Chambersburg PA
CBHW081413230426
43668CB00016B/2223